TRANSFERENCE AND COUNTERTRANSFERENCE

TRANSFERENCE AND COUNTERTRANSFERENCE

A Unifying Focus of Psychoanalysis

edited by

Jean Arundale and Debbie Bandler Bellman

Routledge
Taylor & Francis Group
LONDON AND NEW YORK

First published 2011 by Karnac Books Ltd.

Published 2018 by Routledge
2 Park Square, Milton Park, Abingdon, Oxon OX14 4RN
711 Third Avenue, New York, NY 10017, USA

Routledge is an imprint of the Taylor & Francis Group, an informa business

British Library Cataloguing in Publication Data

A C.I.P. for this book is available from the British Library

ISBN: 9781855757189 (pbk)

Edited, designed and produced by The Studio Publishing Services Ltd
www.publishingservicesuk.co.uk
e-mail: studio@publishingservicesuk.co.uk

CONTENTS

ACKNOWLEDGEMENTS

There are very many who have, directly and indirectly, facilitated the production of this book. We give heartfelt thanks to our contributors for their enthusiasm for writing chapters; for their willingness to work with us as their editors; for their patience in doing "just one more thing". Thanks are due to the British Psychoanalytic Association (BPA) for its support of this project, and to those members who have helped at various points. We are grateful to Karnac for the interest in publishing this volume, and especially to their production team.

Were it not for the existence of the BPA, we would not, of course, be publishing as members of this society. We would, thus, like to thank all those who were instrumental in its establishment. In particular, we are very grateful to the late Daniel Twomey, who, together with a small group of enthusiastic and determined colleagues, instigated the process that would form the BPA. We are indebted to Sharon Raeburn and Helen Alfille, who were part of this original group, and who continue to work tirelessly for the BPA. Many thanks go to the British Association of Psychotherapists (BAP), for grappling with the complicated issues involved in becoming an IPA society on home turf. We thank Helen Morgan, who, as Chair of the BAP while the BPA was being constituted, contributed many hours, much thought, and a great capacity for containment.

Our gratitude towards Dr Ludwig Haesler and Mme Jacqueline Godfrind-Haber, the members of the IPA Liaison Committee, is enormous. We are grateful to the IPA for supporting our application, and to members of the British Psychoanalytical Society who gave generously of their time and interest in all stages of our becoming a society.

To our psychoanalysts, supervisors, and teachers, we say thank you for playing an invaluable part in the continuum of our professional development. Many thanks are due to our patients, who give us the chance to practise the profession that we love. In order to protect the privacy of patients, all clinical illustrations have been disguised and any identifying details omitted.

Last, but importantly, we thank our friends and families. They have, for months, encouraged and put up with us, especially as the deadline for submission of the manuscript loomed: they even pretended they were as interested as we were in the finer points of not only psychoanalytic ideas but also of grammar and punctuation. Especial thanks go to Martin, Rachel, and Jessica; and to Scott and Lindsey.

ABOUT THE EDITORS AND CONTRIBUTORS

Jean Arundale is a founder member and training and supervising analyst of the British Psychoanalytic Association (BPA). She was a part of the formation of the BPA as a member of the Steering Group, and Executive, and is currently on the BPA Board as Chair of the Scientific Committee. She is a Senior Member and training and supervising analyst of the British Association of Psychotherapists. She works in private practice, has taught on training courses, is a part-time consultant psychotherapist in the NHS at Guy's Hospital, and is a past editor of the *British Journal of Psychotherapy*. She has published a number of psychoanalytic papers, and co-edited *Terrorism and War* (2002), published by Karnac.

Debbie Bandler Bellman is a Full Member of the British Psychoanalytic Association (BPA), and a member of the Board as Honorary Secretary of the Society. She is also a member of the BPA Scientific Committee. She is a Senior Member of the British Association of Psychotherapists, for which she has taught both clinical and theoretical seminars. Her first training was in child and adolescent psychotherapy, and she is a past editor of the *Journal of Child Psychotherapy*. Published topics include the suicidal adolescent, and transference and countertransference issues in an in-patient setting.

Ruth Berkowitz is a Full Member of the British Psychoanalytic Association, and teaches on its training in psychoanalysis. She is a Senior Member of the British Association of Psychotherapists, and involved in teaching on its psychotherapy trainings. She is also a training therapist for the Association of Child Psychotherapists. She is a consultant adult psychotherapist at the Portman Clinic, and works in private practice. Previous publications include papers on aspects of the transference and countertransference.

Sara Collins is a psychoanalyst in private practice. She is a Full Member of the British Psychoanalytic Association (BPA), is on the training committee, and teaches on the training in psychoanalysis. She is a Senior Member of the British Association of Psychotherapists and an Associate Fellow of the British Psychological Society. She has held a number of NHS posts, including at the Portman Clinic. She is engaged in supervision, and teaching both clinical and theoretical seminars. She has published papers exploring the parallels between psychoanalysis and literature, focusing on the telling of lives both in memoir and through reconstruction in psychoanalysis.

Irene Freeden is a psychoanalyst in private practice. She is a founder member and training and supervising analyst of the British Psychoanalytic Association. She is also a Senior Member and training and supervising analyst for the British Association of Psychotherapists, and a member of that association's training committee for the Wessex Psychoanalytic Psychotherapy Training. In addition, she has lectured within the UK and abroad, and has published clinical papers in the *British Journal of Psychotherapy* and the *Journal of the British Association of Psychotherapists.*

Michael Halton is a Full Member of the British Psychoanalytic Association (BPA), and is on the training committee of the BPA's training in psychoanalysis. He works in private practice, and is a part-time consultant clinical psychologist in psychotherapy. He is an Associate Fellow of the British Psychological Society, and a Senior Member of the British Association of Psychotherapists, and Tavistock Society of Psychotherapists. He is a training therapist and supervisor for a number of organizations, and lectures at the Tavistock Clinic. His publications include papers on Bion and Foulkes.

Jan Harvie-Clark is a founder member of the British Psychoanalytic Association (BPA), and was involved in the initial BPA Steering Group and Executive. She is a Full Member of the BPA, a training analyst and supervisor, and formerly a Board member in the capacity of Chair of the Training Analyst Committee. She is also a Senior Member of the British Association of Psychotherapists (BAP), and a training analyst and supervisor for the BAP, as well as for a number of other psychotherapy organizations. She works full-time in private practice.

Viqui Rosenberg is a founder member and training and supervising analyst of the British Psychoanalytic Association, and teaches on the training in psychoanalysis. She is a Senior Member and training analyst and supervisor for the British Association of Psychotherapists, and teaches on its psychoanalytic psychotherapy trainings. She works in private practice, and is also a part-time consultant psychotherapist within the Health Service. She has given lectures and workshops on a variety of subjects both within the UK and abroad. She has previously published on the topic of transference and countertransference, and is also a published novelist.

Philip Roys is a founder member of the BPA and a member of the BPA Board as Honorary Treasurer, and is on the Training Committee. He is a Senior Member of the British Association of Psychotherapists. He is also a member of the Wessex Psychoanalytic Psychotherapy Training Committee, where he teaches psychoanalytic theory. He is a training therapist for the Birmingham Training in Child Psychotherapy and has a private practice in psychoanalysis. A consultant adult psychotherapist in the NHS in Oxford, he has previously published on psychoanalytic theory.

Jessica Sacret Hering is a Full Member of the British Psychoanalytic Association, and a member of its Board as Chair of the Full Members Committee. She is a Senior Member of the British Association of Psychotherapists, has held a number of posts within the organization in connection to post-graduate development, and been involved in teaching. She works full-time in private practice. She has published papers on post-Kleinian theoretical issues and on trauma, and is a previous joint editor of the *Journal of the British Association of Psychotherapists*.

Introduction

Jean Arundale and Debbie Bandler Bellman

The aims of this book are twofold. The first is to contribute to the psychoanalytic literature on transference and countertransference. The second is to "introduce" the British Psychoanalytic Association.

This book is the first to publish a group of papers written by members of the British Psychoanalytic Association (BPA), a new society of the International Psychoanalytical Association, and the second society to be established in the UK. The BPA occupies a unique place in that it is a distinct society, with its own training, its own Constitution, Executive Board, officers, and committees, but one that resides within the well-established British Association of Psychotherapists in London. The analysts of the BPA are highly experienced practitioners: most worked for a number of years as psychoanalytic psychotherapists before gaining recognition as psychoanalysts from the IPA; a few are psychoanalysts, trained initially within an IPA Institute. In her "Prelude", Debbie Bandler Bellman explores various processes involved in becoming psychoanalysts of the BPA.

The book began with the editors' call for abstracts and papers from BPA members on subjects of interest to them. With very few exceptions, these pertained to aspects of work with transference and countertransference, with links frequently made between such work and psychic change. Thus, transference and countertransference became the theme of the book. The theoretical viewpoints illustrated and explored in the chapters are varied, and are reflective of Kleinian, Independent, and Contemporary Freudian theoretical orientations. As such, they represent the varied theoretical orientations of the members of the BPA.

Since Freud's discovery of transference, and the later development of countertransference, these vast and inexhaustible subjects have occupied psychoanalysts, who have written and argued about them from different theoretical perspectives. As editors from different theoretical orientations, jointly writing this Introduction, we have been particularly aware of the many facets and complexities of these topics, and of the impossibility of doing justice to them in a brief Introduction. Thus, without attempting to give a full historical account, or to concentrate on the various current trends of thought, we present an overview, highlighting main ways in which the field has developed, and leave it to the authors of the chapters to elaborate their views.

When psychoanalysis had its beginning with Freud and Breuer's treatment of hysterical patients, transference appeared initially as painful and puzzling experiences with patients; these experiences induced Freud, with ingenious insight, to give shape to meaningful and useful theories of mental functioning. At first, he thought transference interfered with treatment by standing in the way of the uncovering of unconscious traumatic experiences that lay at the root of symptoms. However, as Freud examined the phenomenon more closely, he grew to understand that the emotional quality of the patient's feelings towards the analyst had value as a means of understanding the patient's neurosis, and could be used as a tool. He began to see repetitions of past maladaptive relationships, inappropriately brought into the present, as fundamental to mental disturbance. In particular, his insights led to understanding the importance and centrality of the Oedipus complex.

In his paper "Remembering, repeating and working-through", Freud (1914g) wrote of the analytic setting as a playground for the repetition of past relationships and the development of the transference. He likened the setting to a wildlife preserve, an area set aside from reality and reason, where repressions could be lifted, drives and defences revealed, and where primitive emotions and fantasies could have their free expression, emphasizing that this process provided an invaluable opportunity for self-exploration, development, and change.

As Freud developed his ideas, he wrote of the "mild positive transference" as being the best climate in which the ongoing discovery of the unconscious could thrive. In this climate, the analytic work could take place *in the transference,* and it was unnecessary to interpret, or bring particular attention to, the transference, as such. When deviations from the "mild positive" occurred, bringing into the transference strong or primitive emotions, interpretations *of the transference* were required, particularly when the transference was used as a defence. Once the unconscious constellations were recognized and brought into the light of day, the process of *working through in the transference* was, and remains, central to analytic work and vital to a good conclusion.

Klein (1946) further developed the idea of transference as a re-enactment of psychic life and an expression of unconscious phantasy that, often disguised, required deciphering by the analyst. Laying emphasis on the emotional, she designated transference as "memory in feeling". For Klein, entering into the subjective world of the patient to bring out the *content* of unconscious anxieties was crucial. Recognizing that the analyst is often split into a good figure and a bad one, Klein was the first to put emphasis on the importance of analysing the negative transference, which serves to mitigate its influence.

Winnicott, meanwhile—circa 1940—had stated that, "There is no such thing as a baby", and later clarified that this meant that the infant does not exist on his own, but, rather, within a relationship, within the "nursing couple" (1952, p. 99). Similarly, the transference–countertransference was seen as a relationship between patient and analyst within which self and other could be experienced and explored. For Winnicott, not only the transference, but also the countertransference, played a central role in analytic work, as exemplified in his paper "Hate in the countertransference" (1947).

Regarding the countertransference, the analyst's specific and general feelings toward the patient, this was first dismissed by Freud as having to do with the analyst's own personal difficulties interfering with the treatment, signaling a deviation from the cool, "surgical" approach that he initially advocated. Since Freud's time, countertransference has been differently conceptualized. Heimann (1950), in a further move away from the "detached" analyst, described the emotions arising in the analyst as cues to understanding the mind and the personality of the patient. This led theorists such as Sandler (1976) to formulate his influential concept of "role responsiveness", where the analyst finds himself pulled into a role, or way of being, that he does not recognize as characteristic of him, which must then be analysed. Since countertransference has increasingly been explored, it has become seen as an indispensable part of the analytic interaction and an important implement for revealing the patient's state of mind and unconscious processes, particularly as analytic treatment generally has come more and more to be understood and described as a relationship.

The rise of the use of the countertransference coincided with Melanie Klein's (1946) concept of projective identification, both normal and pathological, an idea not developed by her, but by the many who followed her. The projection of early infantile states of mind, as well as states arising from subsequent stages of development, can be seen as clinically closely related to transference and countertransference, both in its communicative function and in what has been termed its evacuative function. Although many believe that, strictly speaking, the countertransference is unconscious, and it is projective identification that the analyst experiences and learns from, it is usual in psychoanalytic parlance to speak of the countertransference as whatever is felt by the analyst toward the patient that is stirred up within the analytic situation. Although Klein herself did not fully accept the importance of countertransference, believing there was danger in interpreting from the position of the analyst's subjectivity, eminent followers such as Bion (1952) placed emphasis on the concept, defining countertransference as the analyst being in the role of the patient's internal objects, while thinking about them and not acting them out.

In today's psychoanalytic world, Contemporary Freudians, Kleinians, and those of the Independent Tradition, all regard working with the transference and countertransference as seminal to their clinical work. Differences between viewpoints, and between individual practitioners, stem not from the recognition of transference and countertransference *per se*, but, rather, from how these phenomena are specifically conceptualized, the ways in which they are interpreted, the timing of interpretations, the weight that is given to transference interpretations in regard to psychic change in comparison with other types of interventions, and to which influences on the analytic process are regarded as transference and countertransference, and which might not be. To our minds, transference and countertransference, broadly conceptualized as manifestations of conscious and unconscious aspects of object relationships and psychic structures within the analytic process, ultimately transcend theoretical orientation. Thus, we feel they can be viewed as a unifying focus of psychoanalysis: hence the title of this book.

The richness and diversity of views concerning transference and countertransference are reflected in the various chapters. For example, although the reconstruction of the past is part of psychoanalysis, and we are all still influenced by Freud's notion of the recovery of repressed memories, the degree to which this in itself fosters psychic change is debatable. Sara Collins' chapter, "Why reconstruct? Perspectives on reconstruction within the transference", examines views on reconstruction from both historical and contemporary perspectives. Synthesizing past and current ideas, the author views reconstruction as an essential aspect of psychoanalytic work as long as it takes place "within the transference".

In Chapter Two, "Here and now interpretations", Jean Arundale focuses on transference interpretations given within the "here and now" of the analytic relationship as the instrument of psychic change. Her view is that to bring about structural change in unconscious patterns, these need to be brought into, and experienced in, the transference and countertransference, "lived through" in the analytic process, in what has been called the "transference neurosis".

Working with the sexual transference in the here and now is included in one of Arundale's clinical illustrations, and this is followed by two papers, by Viqui Rosenberg and Irene Freeden, respectively, that centre on the topic of sexuality and the sexual transference in the analytic relationship. Sexuality is a subject that, for the past few decades, has gone rather silent in the psychoanalytic literature, but has recently been the recipient of reawakened international interest (Fonagy, 2008; Stein, 2003).

A paper by Jan Harvie-Clark on love and hate in the analytic relationship follows, showing the intensity of feeling that the transference evokes and the significance of instinctual forces in the structuring of the mind. Using a "five-bar gate" as a metaphor for the structure of the mind, Harvie-Clark illustrates how the integration of love and hate leads to a greater capacity to experience life and its vicissitudes.

The following two chapters, "Terror, impasse, hope: fragmentation as resistance", by Jessica Sacret Hering, and "Phobic attachments: internal impediments to change", by Michael Halton, address theoretical and technical aspects of working with patients at the more disturbed end of the spectrum, where primitive anxieties and defences distort the personality and interfere with relationships. The group of patients Sacret Hering describes put up strong defences against the experience of disintegration that has been a consequence of their previous attempts at making relationships, including splitting, projective identification, and angry attacks. Halton's patients have a phobic response to maternal containment, a malignant maternal object, which is revived in the transference, a response in which intimacy presents a threat to psychic integrity. These papers describe and explore work with patients who present the analyst with various kinds of problems around relating in the transference, including the bid to be "at one" with the object, the threat of impasse, difficulties around separateness and intimacy, and the internalization of a good object.

The penultimate chapter, by Philip Roys, discusses issues around the patient's impulse to end analysis. Bringing up the question of ending can be used for various purposes, and Roys discusses the analyst's task of deciphering the meaning and purpose, whether it is a defensive manoeuvre to pressure the analyst, or to avoid entering into a deeper relationship, or whether it is a true wish to end and a sign of growth and development.

Ruth Berkowitz contributes the final chapter, "The elusive concept of analytic survival". Taking the view that "survival" of the analyst is fundamental to the analytic process, she examines the various meanings of this concept, in the theory and in her own clinical work. Interestingly, Berkowitz emphasizes that "survival", elusive as the concept may at times be, is, nevertheless, referred to and elaborated by authors of greatly varying theoretical viewpoints.

References

Bion, W. R. (1952). Group dynamics: a review. *International Journal of Psycho-Analysis, 33*: 235–247.

Fonagy, P. (2008). A genuinely developmental theory of sexual enjoyment and its implications for psychoanalytic technique. *Journal of the American Psychoanalytic Association, 56*: 11–36.

Freud, S. (1914g). Remembering, repeating and working through. *S.E., 12*: 147–156. London: Hogarth.

Heimann, P. (1950). On countertransference. *International Journal of Psycho-Analysis, 31*: 81–84.

Klein, M. (1946). Notes on some schizoid mechanisms. *International Journal of Psychoanalysis, 27*: 99–110 [republished in *The Writings of Melanie Klein, Vol. 3, Envy and Gratitude and Other Works*. London: Hogarth, 1975].

Sandler, J. (1976). Countertransference and role responsiveness. *International Review of Psycho-Analysis, 3*: 43–47.

Stein, R. (2003). Sexuality psychoanalytically conceived: the otherness of sexuality: loss, excitement, enigma. Paper presented to the Anna Freud Centre 25th Annual International Scientific Colloquium.

Winnicott, D. W. (1947). Hate in the countertransference. In: *Collected Papers: Through Paediatrics to Psycho-Analysis* (pp. 194–203). London: Tavistock, 1958.

Winnicott, D. W. (1952). Anxiety associated with insecurity. In: *Collected Papers:Through Paediatrics to Psycho-Analysis* (pp. 97–100). London: Tavistock, 1958.

PRELUDE

From psychotherapist to psychoanalyst: processes in the formation of an IPA society

Debbie Bandler Bellman

In so far as one aim of this book is to introduce the British Psychoanalytic Association (BPA), it feels fitting to begin with a section, a "Prelude", on the formation of our society and the processes involved in becoming psychoanalysts. Although a few in our society are long-standing members of the International Psychoanalytical Association (IPA), having undertaken an initial training in psychoanalysis, most have made the transition from psychoanalytic psychotherapist to psychoanalyst. Central to our story is, thus, a transition of professional identity, having as its core the development of clinical work, the development of our capacities to work with unconscious processes within the transference–countertransference. Questions of what it means to be a psychoanalyst have occupied us, both as individual practitioners and as an ever-increasing group, throughout the ten-year process of becoming a Component Society, a status awarded in January 2010.

In forming an IPA Society, we have had, on the one hand, to differentiate ourselves from our colleagues at the British Association of Psychotherapists (BAP), the organization the BPA is both distinct from and a part of, and, on the other, to begin to take our place beside the British Psychoanalytical Society (BPAS) as the second IPA Society within the UK. Becoming the second society has felt both historic and humbling. Many members of the BPAS were our trainers, both in our initial psychoanalytic psychotherapy training and in our becoming psychoanalysts according to IPA Equivalency Criteria (International Psychoanalytical Association, 1999). Alongside gratitude and admiration, there have been aspects of our relationship to the BPAS coloured by transference phenomena that we have had to work through in becoming psychoanalysts.

In the past twenty years especially, as psychoanalysis has frequently been deemed out of step with the Western trend for "fast-food treatment", much has been written about the identity of psychoanalysts and about the various models of training and structures of IPA Institutes and Societies. Parsons (2000), and Kennedy (2007), among others, have written eloquently about the former, and Kernberg (2006) about the latter. To my knowledge, less has been published about processes involved in the formation of IPA Societies. Kennedy (2007) wrote that "finding one's 'voice' as a psychoanalyst takes a considerable amount of time" (p. 1). This chapter, and indeed the book as a whole, could be deemed part of the process of finding our voice, a process that does not preclude also having something to say.

As to the "voice" here, I have been both a participant in and an observer of the processes under discussion. My voice is, thus, neither wholly subjective nor objective; although it reflects views within our society, it is not intended to be representative of it. Just as no two analysts would conduct identical analyses, someone else would have written differently on the subject.

The beginning

As a background to later sections, where the processes will be interwoven with the history, I will give a brief overview of the history of the BPA from 2000–2005. I am grateful to have been able to draw on the "Annual Report for the British Psychoanalytic Association" (2008) by Sharon Raeburn and Helen Alfille, current President and Vice President of the BPA, for factual details and the sequence of events.

As mentioned above, the BPA is both a part of and distinct from the BAP. The route towards differentiation without completely separating—splitting—from the BAP was complicated and, at times, treacherous. As an organization, the BAP is multi-faceted, with a core commitment to working with unconscious processes at a frequency of three times per week. The BPA developed from the Psychoanalytic Section of the BAP, where most members of the BPA trained in intensive psychoanalytic psychotherapy.

By 2000, there was a small group of BAP psychoanalytic psychotherapists interested in exploring the possibility of membership of the IPA, led by the late Daniel Twomey. Sharon Raeburn and Helen Alfille were the other members of this group, which became the Steering Group in 2001. (Upon Twomey's death in January 2005, Raeburn and Alfille became joint Chairs of the Steering Group. By that time, Jan Harvie-Clark, Ricardo Stramer, and Joscelyn Richards had not only joined the Group, but become long-serving members of it. Jean Arundale became a member of the Steering Group in February 2005. In 2006, the Steering Group, with the same Chairs and composition, became the BPA Executive.) Convened as a subcommittee of the Psychoanalytic Section, this Steering Group represented others within the Section who shared their preference and passion for the increased possibilities of in-depth work within the transference and countertransference attendant upon a greater frequency of sessions. Membership of the IPA would provide the opportunity for learning from and participating in an international community of psychoanalysts.

Between 2000 and 2003, there were many meetings within the BAP to discuss the implications of an application to the IPA, as well as parallel meetings between the Steering Group and several members of the BPAS. In 2003, a formal application was made to the IPA (informal approaches had already been made). A central question concerned whether or not the psychoanalytic psychotherapy training within the context of the BAP could be deemed equivalent to IPA standards. Extensive information about the BAP and its structures for governance, together with information about the training, as well as *curriculum vitae* from a number of members of the Psychoanalytic Section wishing to join the IPA, were forwarded to the IPA for an initial evaluation that would determine whether or not we could proceed further.

The response from the IPA was favourable; the theoretical curriculum of the psychoanalytic psychotherapy training was considered equivalent to IPA standards; the clinical components were praised, but were not in themselves sufficient for eligibility for membership of the IPA. In order to become eligible for membership according to the Equivalency Criteria, those who did not have sufficient clinical experience at a frequency of four-to-five times weekly would need to gain this. In July 2003, the IPA Board appointed an *ad hoc* Board Site Visit Committee to establish readiness for a group to form the basis of a Provisional Society, with Dr Ludwig Haesler of Germany and Mme Jacqueline Godfrind-Haber of Belgium appointed as the committee's members. For the coming years, until January 2010, Dr Haesler and Mme Godfrind-Haber became our assessors, mentors, and challengers, at times also our *agents provocateurs*.

Following two initial, rigorous site visits, and much work by the Steering Group and Site Visit Committee in between, in 2005, the Site Visit Committee recommended to the IPA that members of the Psychoanalytic Section with sufficient experience in four-to-five times weekly work be assessed for Direct Membership, in order to determine whether or not there was sufficient expertise to become an embryonic IPA Society. Six were assessed and recommended for IPA Training Analyst status (one was a long-standing member of the IPA), and seven for Direct Membership of the IPA. The IPA accepted the recommendations of the Site Visit Committee, and these thirteen analysts would become the founder members of our society. They were: Helen Alfille, Jean Arundale, Jan Harvie-Clark, Irene Freeden, Claudia Kramer, Sharon Raeburn, Joscelyn Richards, Viqui Rosenberg, Philip Roys, Stanley Ruszczynski, Ricardo Stramer, Mary Twyman (already a long-standing member of the IPA), and Anne Tyndale. Of these, Alfille, Arundale, Freeden, Kramer, Twyman, and Tyndale were the first BPA training analysts.

Questions of psychoanalytic identity

Over time, it had become apparent to the Steering Group that it would be difficult fully to establish an identity as an IPA Society within the BAP unless there was a distinct group comprised solely of those belonging to the IPA. The BAP agreed to the formation of such a group and, in January 2006, the IPA Board constituted the British Psychoanalytic Association, with its thirteen founder members, as an Interim Provisional Society.

Dr Haesler and Mme Godfrind-Haber agreed to continue to work with us as the Liaison Committee, with the specific mandate of exploring "the significant issue of psychoanalytic identity within the special context of being a group within a psychotherapeutic organization" (Raeburn & Alfille, 2008, p. 3). At the forefront of our application from the start, this complex issue of identity would continue to be a focal point in our development.

The process: becoming psychoanalysts and a Society

In his book, *The Dove that Returns, The Dove that Vanishes,* Parsons (2000) writes,

> Since the beginning of psychoanalysis there have been attempts to define its uniqueness, either in terms of its difference from psychotherapy, or by claiming some clinical or theoretical criterion, typically the transference neurosis, as specific to it. Neither approach has been very fruitful. Psychoanalytic psychotherapy has evolved over the years, becoming harder to differentiate from analysis. [p. 69]

Whatever conclusions we reached as to differences between psychotherapy and psychoanalysis, those of us wanting to become psychoanalysts by making the transition between the two professions attempted to differentiate between them. Equally, as a developing society mandated to explore the issue of psychoanalytic identity as a distinct group within a psychotherapy organization, we felt compelled to consider the question of differences.

In this section, I pose a number of questions, as I feel they surfaced in the process of becoming. We did not, however, become psychoanalysts or an IPA Society simply by asking questions; but questions can be a way of articulating and formulating issues and processes as they take conscious shape in the mind, a way of giving these processes a shape without precluding discussion, a way, to borrow from Shakespeare (*ca.* 1594), of "giving to airy nothing a local habitation and a name" (*A Midsummer-Night's Dream*, V.1:17, p. 137). Beyond this, those of us wanting to be part of an IPA Society within the BAP were asked questions.

From within and outside of the BAP, we were asked not only why we wanted to become psychoanalysts, but also why it was "not enough" to remain the psychoanalytic psychotherapists we had trained to be. By some, our wish to become psychoanalysts was equated with both denigration of our profession of psychotherapy and being greedy, viewpoints that I think missed the essential point. It was indeed "not enough" to remain psychotherapists: satisfying and enriching, yes, but not enough. Some way into the process of becoming an IPA Society, Vassilis Maoutsos wrote,

> The fact that a . . . proportion [of members trained in psychoanalytic psychotherapy at the BAP] would like to obtain IPA membership indicates to me that what they are (unconsciously) asking for is not simply to become IPA members, if this is feasible, but to become more specialized and more "deep" in their field of expertise. If I am right in saying that, then the initials "IPA" mean nothing else but the manifest content of a latent desire and legitimate ambition. [E-mail communication, 2005]

I think Maoutsos's comment beautifully captures the essence of our wish to become psychoanalysts.

Reaching the point where we felt it was a "legitimate ambition" to want to become psychoanalysts and develop a society took much work: within ourselves, within the BAP, and in relation to the BPAS, members of which, as noted earlier, had frequently played large roles in our psychoanalytic psychotherapy training as our analysts, our supervisors, and our seminar leaders.

Kernberg (2006) writes of the specific difficulties and dilemmas in resolving the transference to one's training analyst when one is becoming "like the analyst" professionally. In our case, although analysts were seminal to our training, we could not consider ourselves to be "like them". We were trained in three times weekly work, and ours was a qualification as a psychoanalytic psychotherapist. This situation engendered its own difficulties in transference resolution. While we identified with our analysts and supervisors in many ways, there was the spoken and unspoken, conscious and unconscious awareness that we were also "different". What exactly the differences were, however, usually was not spelled out. Alongside pleasure and pride in our training and profession, there existed less comfortable dynamics and also questions. Would our analysts and supervisors have analysed and supervised any differently had we been training in psychoanalysis? How similar and how different was what we did with our patients in the consulting room to psychoanalysis? Was our training substantially different from that offered at the British Society? Were we different, or "not as good as"?

On a deeper level, there seemed to be a prohibition, in that we "could not" be the same as our trainers. Was our wish to become psychoanalysts thus indicative of resolution of the Oedipal situation, whereby we realized it was legitimate to become "like the parents", or was it indicative of persistent Oedipal difficulties, whereby we were making an illegitimate challenge to enter the parental bedroom? This situation of being ostensibly both similar and different to analysts gave rise, as I see it, to a composite of complex feelings towards psychoanalysis and our trainers: not only admiration, but also idealization of psychoanalysis; not only gratitude towards, but also envy of, our trainers.

These questions and dynamics, which had existed within the Psychoanalytic Section of the BAP as an elusive undercurrent, surfaced in the initial stages of our approaches to the IPA, and were expressed and discussed in many different formats. The meetings we had about the pros and cons of seeking membership of the IPA provided the holding structures necessary to begin to work through our relationship to psychotherapy and psychoanalysis, or, to put it another way, to ourselves and to our trainers.

The aim of developing a society that would reside within the BAP was, to my mind, highly significant. I think it indicates that any idealization of psychoanalysis and our trainers had led neither towards a wish to separate from the BAP nor towards a denigration of psychoanalytic psychotherapy. Neither the Steering Group nor the Psychoanalytic Section as a whole wanted to initiate a process whereby members would leave the BAP; the goal was to explore and promote the possibility of a new development within it. In addition, I see the wish to remain within the BAP as an indication of the fate of the institutional envy towards the BPAS. We did not want to "be" our trainers, a situation that could have sprung from a denial of the envious aspects of our feelings. Nor did we turn away from our wish to become psychoanalysts because it contained a component of envy or resonated with any underlying Oedipal concerns. Rather, we wanted the opportunity to develop the increased depth in our work that our trainers already had, and had arrived at a point where we felt this to be a "legitimate ambition": legitimate to want to develop our own, different society.

The actual establishment of the BPA—with the need for differentiation from our psychotherapy colleagues—posed its own challenges, including the need to contain institutional tendencies towards splitting processes. Although wanted, the BPA was, none the less, a group to which only a few members of the BAP initially belonged. Questions of the differences between the qualifications of those solely in the Psychoanalytic Section and those also in the BPA, as well as the issue of whether or not those who were members of the BPA were "better qualified", emerged. In other words, not surprisingly, dynamics similar to those that had existed in relation to the BPAS now stemmed from within the BAP. In addition, there was, within the BPA, the potential for self-idealization. Working through these dynamics has included not only discussion, but also, and crucially, the development of new structures within the BAP and the structuring of the BPA.

Within the BPA, there was the question of admitting additional members, devising structures for governance that would be in accord with both the IPA and BAP, designing the training in psychoanalysis, beginning to organize our scientific life, as well as working out the details of the structure of the society. As Dr Ludwig Haesler (2009) stressed, there was, in societies, the need for "a clear frame", for "structures that enabled psychoanalysis to unfold" (p. 1). In the first instance, this frame enabled us as individuals to become psychoanalysts, and, as an ever-increasing group, truly to become a society of psychoanalysts.

A number of members of the Psychoanalytic Section wanted to belong to the BPA. In response, the "Window of Opportunity" was opened. Devised by the BPA Executive (formerly the Steering Group) in conjunction with the Liaison Committee and in consonance with the IPA document on Equivalency Criteria (1999), this "window" gave members of the Psychoanalytic Section a chance to become eligible for IPA/BPA Membership until such time as we would become a Component Society. Although this mitigated concerns about the BPA's exclusivity, there were, none the less, criteria to be met, and, ultimately, an interview and assessment. Individuals needed to consult themselves as to what were their professional aspirations and to struggle internally with issues of professional identity, both of which led to less confusion in the wider organization between personal and organizational issues.

The wish to become a BPA member was, for many, not without conflict. Some felt they would be "abandoning" their three-times weekly training and professional identity, as well as being disloyal to colleagues not applying to the BPA. There was also anxiety that if we became psychoanalysts we could be "transformed" into idealized or envied colleagues. Becoming a psychoanalyst meant acknowledging differences . . . or did it? Was the title wanted for its own sake, or did the acquisition of the title have a meaning? And what did it mean to become a psychoanalyst?

Fulfilling the Equivalency Criteria involved not only the development of clinical work, but also a shift in professional identity. This involved conscious and unconscious processes that will have differed according to our individual histories, personalities, professional backgrounds, and experience. At the same time, although I am not equating becoming a psychoanalyst with "growing up", I think that some of the processes involved in the shift of identity—as well as in the development of our society—have perhaps been similar to those that take place in the course of adolescence in relation to ties to parental objects and superego and ego ideal restructuring (Blos, 1962). As aspects of our transition from psychotherapist to psychoanalyst involved resolution of transference to our training analysts, supervisors, seminar leaders, and, latterly, to the Liaison Committee, all, to varying extents, parental figures, the notion of similarities with adolescent processes of identity formation is, perhaps, particularly apt.

These similarities occurred to me in a BPA society meeting in 2006, shortly after I became a member. We were mulling over the issue of becoming a distinct society of psychoanalysts, and questioned the BPA Executive: What exactly did this mean? Did the Liaison Committee give any specific guidance as to how we could achieve this? We were all analysts, and members of the BPA, so how could we not be a society of psychoanalysts? We could not come up with any specific answers and concluded we would have, for the moment, to sit with "not knowing". I felt that we were like "adolescents" asking how we could achieve the goal of becoming "adults". It was as if we were asking our "parents", the Liaison Committee, to tell us how to do this, how to achieve the necessary identity. It struck me that had there been a road map, a prescription, then we would never have achieved the wished-for identity, that we would have, at best, achieved a pseudo identity based on continuing dependence as opposed to independence. Just as a parent cannot prescribe how an adolescent achieves an independent identity, the Liaison Committee could not prescribe for us.

In their IPA roles, Dr Haesler and Mme Godfrind-Haber acted as facilitators, gatekeepers, information-givers, assessors, and sounding boards. Interwoven through all the functions of the Liaison Committee was the function of models for identification as psychoanalysts, as well as models for identification with the standards and tenets of the IPA. Here, I am not referring to the specific personalities of the members of the Liaison Committee, though these, of course, played a part, but rather to the Liaison Committee as representatives of the IPA and psychoanalysis. The presence of the Liaison Committee was registered, regardless of how much contact any given individual had with the committee. Clearly the Liaison Committee was also the recipient of transference manifestations, as was the BPA Executive.

In the consulting room

In becoming psychoanalysts, the clinical experience in the privacy of the consulting room was pivotal. Although many of my colleagues had already worked with adults at an intensity of four-to-five times weekly, and I had worked with children and adolescents at this intensity for many years, I had not seen adults at this frequency. There was, of course, no one who said I could not see patients for more than three times per week. However, in retrospect, I feel my awareness that I was qualified and, therefore, endorsed to practice three times weekly had had a somewhat inhibiting effect upon my capacity freely to think about what might be in the best interests of my patients, and, therefore, on how I approached the question of frequency with my patients. Seeking membership of the IPA had a liberating impact in this area, and the change in me was communicated to my patients through my interpretations and unconsciously. The following example illustrates this process.

P, then in her early thirties and in her fourth year of psychotherapy, became preoccupied with the issue of her three times per week sessions around the time I was pursuing membership of the BPA. Her thrice-weekly sessions became "not enough" for her. The daughter of a depressed mother, P's personality was organized around a wish and need to please the "other", around the maintenance of, and need for, love from an internal object that was unresponsive. Within the transference, her wish to please me took many guises, and her antennae for anything that might actually please me was astute. I tried to be alert to this, but, of course, could not always be. In this instance, however, when P actually spoke in terms similar to those being used at the BAP in discussions about becoming psychoanalysts, I knew careful exploration and understanding of her wish would be necessary before any increase was agreed upon. I think my experience in this was not dissimilar to that of colleagues also seeking to become psychoanalysts, and it would have been easy for our professional aspirations to cloud clinical judgement.

The development and exploration of P's wish to increase her sessions took time. Beyond her wish to please, her feelings that three times weekly treatment was not enough, was a manifestation of the hunger she felt within the maternal transference, a hunger that would not actually have been satisfied regardless of how frequently she attended. At the same time, I think that my changing my attitude towards frequency had contributed to her sense that it might be safe to express her neediness, that there was a person who could contain it, and that it might be that this aspect of herself, together with her underlying rage and disappointment in the frustrating and withholding maternal object, could be more fully expressed and contained within a treatment of greater frequency.

Of this much, I felt we had some understanding. There were other aspects of P that I had, for a long time, felt were not quite in focus, were just out of reach, and seemed to dissipate in the gaps between sessions. Predominant among these was a high degree of anxiety that intermittently permeated the transference, which we had understood in a number of ways but could never quite get close to before it again disappeared. In the context of exploration of the "not enough" issue, anxiety infused the transference, but this time did not dissipate, and she increasingly struggled with the gaps between sessions. I felt that an important meaning, the main message in it, was to alert me to her wish and need to be able to experience her anxiety, and through this to understand it more fully, rather than trying to shore it up as she had previously done. We agreed to increase her sessions to four times per week. For practical and financial reasons an increase to five sessions was not feasible.

The increase in sessions led to an immediate increase in P's level of anxiety and she felt she was going mad. Far from feeling more contained as she had hoped, P felt terrified of me, frightened of what I would do to her. There was a corresponding increase in the intensity of the countertransference, where I felt I did not know what was what and that I was going mad. What had felt to me just out of reach was now fully in the consulting room where, in the transference–countertransference relationship, there was a primitive mix-up between her and me, and terror of what we were each going to do to the other. P was, I felt, re-experiencing within the transference an early and not differentiated experience of feeling at the mercy of both her mother's projections and her own primitive and intense feelings. Through transference interpretations and reconstruction that served the purpose of enabling P to fill in the missing links in her psyche (Chasseguet-Smirgel, 1985), these aspects of her experience could gradually be worked through.

P's response to the increased frequency of sessions had been dramatic. With other patients, I have not found a difference of one additional session to be necessarily so dramatic, but I have always found that it has made a difference. Gaps between sessions can enable dissipation of not only the transference, but also the countertransference. In conversation, Helen Alfille (2009) has spoken of how patients may use the gaps to "regain equilibrium", and, thus, perpetuate their defensive structures. I would add that, as clinicians, we also regain equilibrium during gaps, and that the impact of an intense countertransference during the course of the week makes greater demands on our own psyches.

Ultimately, I found that working at a greater intensity increased my appreciation and enjoyment of manifestations of unconscious processes, in both my patients and myself. Interestingly, I have also found that working at a greater intensity has enhanced my work with patients seen non-intensively. Many colleagues I have spoken with had a similar experience, and feel that working more intensively has added depth to their experience of, appreciation for, and understanding of, the analytic process. It had not been a question of fulfilling criteria, but rather of developing our clinical skills as we began to regard ourselves as psychoanalysts.

Becoming a member

In assessment interviews for membership of the BPA and IPA (conducted by BPA training analysts and Full Members from spring 2006), it was "expected that applicants [would] be able to demonstrate their abilities and qualities at an advanced level of analytic functioning and thinking with the four or five times a week patient being presented", and that "the interviewers [would] not be expected to examine the applicant but [would] engage . . . in an in-depth clinical discussion of [the] work . . . being presented" (British Psychoanalytic Association, 2006, p. 3). The overall task for the interviewers would be to evaluate whether or not the applicant had achieved a level of analytic work deemed at least commensurate to the level reached upon qualification by analysts who have undertaken an IPA training in psychoanalysis.

The process of preparing for and undertaking the interview focused thought not only on one's work, but also on one's professional view of oneself, and, thus, made an important contribution to the shift in identity from psychotherapist to psychoanalyst. If, after discussion of the interview, an applicant was felt to be ready (s)he was invited to join the BPA and to become a member of the IPA. If the applicant was deemed not ready, feedback was offered, and (s)he was encouraged to gain further experience of intensive work if there was a wish to reapply at a later date.

Some of the analysts consulted in relation to the intensive work presented at the interviews were BPA training analysts, but most were psychoanalysts from the BPAS. A couple were BPAS psychoanalysts who had become BPA members and training analysts. The support for our society from these BPAS analysts helped to facilitate our professional transition. This support could be construed as similar to the support and permission to grow, develop, and, ultimately, become "like them" that parents give to their adolescents, a permission that carries the message that the parents are not Oedipally threatened by the development of their children. Although it would have been possible for us to become psychoanalysts with less support from members of the British Society, as, ultimately, the permission to "become" has to stem from within the individual, we are grateful to have had it.

Consolidation of psychoanalytic identity

Consolidation and development of identity, on both individual and group levels, takes time. The minimum length of time for psychoanalytic training is, to my knowledge, four years. Four years is, thus, regarded as the minimum time necessary for the acquisition, development, and internalization of psychoanalytic skills, knowledge, experience, self-awareness, and professional identity formation sufficient for qualification. I think it can be no accident that the minimum length of time for an IPA Society to proceed from provisional to full status is also four years. In a profession that respects the time it takes for unconscious manifestations to emerge and for internal restructuring to take place, and the time it takes to learn to work with one's patients and one's own unconscious forces, there is appreciation for the time needed both to consolidate the identity of a society and to devise its structures.

Working towards each change of status brought its own tasks. For example, in order to move from Interim Provisional to Provisional Society, we needed to devise a Constitution for governance, which took many of months of deliberation. (Alan Hinkley [BPA member] was instrumental in the drafting of the BPA's Constitution in 2006.) Once we became a Provisional Society, at the Congress in Berlin in July 2007, it was necessary to elect a Board through democratic processes and widen the committee structure for, among other areas, training and scientific life. (The following members of the BPA were elected to the first Board [2008]: Sharon Raeburn [President], Helen Alfille [Vice President], Jean Arundale, Debbie Bandler Bellman, Jan Harvie-Clark, Joscelyn Richards, Philip Roys, Jessica Sacret, and Anne Tyndale.) Increasing numbers of members were, thus, able to take an active part in the formation of the society and in contributing to its day-to-day life.

Society meetings were held regularly, and were comprised of two parts. The first was a business meeting, with emphasis on developments within the society, the society's relationship to the IPA, matters from the IPA and Liaison Committee, and the steps we were taking to move towards Component Society status. The second, lengthier portion consisted of a clinical presentation by a member, followed by a discussion among those assembled. Sessions were presented verbatim, in the manner of our interviews for membership of the BPA. That our members were and are willing to do this within a group context suggests that a "background of safety" (Sandler, 1960) is felt within the society.

From early on, it was apparent that one of the strengths of the BPA was its composition of members of differing theoretical orientations, able to join together in the spirit of psychoanalytic enquiry, respecting differences, and learning. The clinical discussions felt freeing, and it was exciting to be part of this new group. One could simply function as a psychoanalyst, thinking about and debating aspects of the material presented. There was no need to feel apologetic about being a psychoanalyst, no need to ask difficult questions about differences between psychoanalysis and psychotherapy; one could, quite simply, get on with it.

In society meetings, we could leave behind the politics of establishing ourselves within the BAP and concentrate on developing ourselves as a group of psychoanalysts. Similarly, at least in the clinical portion, we did not need consciously to think about meeting IPA criteria. One could say that, to some degree, our meetings provided the function of a peer group in adolescence, provided the space to become "ourselves" as psychoanalysts away from anyone authorized to assess our progress.

Inevitably, there were some complicated transference aspects to our relationship to the IPA and Liaison Committee, regarding their positions as authorities who would say "yea" or "nay" to us at crucial points of assessment. Our overall experience, however, was of being facilitated towards becoming a Component Society. There were criteria to be met, but neither the Liaison Committee nor the IPA was prescriptive. Thus, we experienced both as deeply analytic rather than authoritarian.

When, at the end of February 2009, the main task of the Liaison Committee's visit was to determine whether or not to recommend that we put ourselves forward for Component Society status, we felt both anxious and sanguine. We could not know the outcome of the assessment but, in contrast to earlier times when we wondered how far we had come in establishing our identity as a society of psychoanalysts within the BAP, we now felt we had become a distinct society. We also felt pride in having achieved solid structures within our society, and ready to go forward for Component Society status, ready to take the final steps towards becoming a full society within the IPA. At the same time, we felt that if the Liaison Committee concluded we were not ready to take this step, we would feel disappointed but not dispirited, and would continue to work on and through that which was necessary still to do.

The British Psychoanalytic Association as a Component Society: another beginning

In describing some of what I feel were seminal processes in our becoming psychoanalysts and a Component Society, I realize that, at best, I have given an outline, an overview of all that was entailed. Additionally, there are, no doubt, processes that were and have remained unconscious. Reaching Component Society status signifies, to my mind, not a completion, but, rather, another stage in our becoming a society, another beginning. Parsons (2000) writes that "Qualifying as a psychoanalyst is only the start of becoming one" (p. 74). This statement implies that at the core of the profession lies openness to development, integration, and consolidation. Being a psychoanalyst and a society of psychoanalysts can, thus, be construed as being in a continual state of becoming.

We do not, of course, know exactly what we will become, but I would like to end by taking a look at where we are. We have become psychoanalysts and a society of psychoanalysts while remaining within the BAP. I think this was achieved not by trying to "dispose" of our identity as psychoanalytic psychotherapists, but, rather, by developing from and building on it. As psychoanalysts, we are now in a different position from which to relate and contribute to the BAP. This, however, is not a one-sided relationship. The wider BAP greatly contributed to our development as a society and continues to contribute in many ways.

A while ago, our society reflected on what it means to be a psychoanalyst. A number of areas of concordance emerged. These were: trust in, and enjoyment of, unconscious processes; a strong preference for working four-to-five times weekly and within the transference–countertransference matrix; the capacity to be patient; delight in the unknown; appreciation of, and respect for, the difficulties inherent in the work; recognition of the individuality of each patient; a deep sense of the importance of the structure and continuity of the analytic setting; awareness of the personal and ethical responsibility entailed in working analytically within the consulting room.

What emerged corresponds with what many psychoanalysts have written about as central to psychoanalytic identity and psychoanalysis. Parsons (2000), for example, writes about the importance of trust in unconscious processes, and Ferro (2009) delineates three "invariants" he sees as "indispensable" for

> the term "psychoanalysis" to be used legitimately . . . the conviction that an unconscious exists (even if it may assume a variety of forms); second, respect for unvarying elements of the setting; and, third and last, an asymmetry, with the analyst taking full responsibility for what happens within the consulting room. [p. 210]

What was important for us was that we had, in our individual ways, made what is regarded as seminal to the profession our own; that we had, through the processes of becoming psychoanalysts under the Equivalency Criteria, discovered for ourselves, and in this way discovered anew, what it means to be a psychoanalyst. In contrast with early society meetings, we did not define ourselves in relation to psychotherapy, but in relation to the profession of which we had become a part.

Becoming psychoanalysts had taken us back to what can be considered the basics of the profession, basics that transcend theoretical differences. I think this process of back-to-basics is reflected in the chapters included in this book, with its focus on work within the transference–countertransference, understood and viewed from a variety of theoretical perspectives. The capacity to embrace similarities and differences remains a hallmark and strength of our society, and stems, I feel, to a great extent, from appreciation of the complexity of the human mind and unconscious processes, processes that, as Parsons (2000) writes, we work with, while acknowledging the paradox in striving to know about that which is, by definition, unconscious and, therefore, defies certainty.

Lest, however, we become too self-congratulatory, as a new society we can learn from the experience of colleagues who have been psychoanalysts for many years, from long-standing societies (perhaps, especially, from those who have, as we have, adopted the Eitington model for training), and from the literature. Kernberg (2006), in writing of the stifling effect that dominant ideologies can have on psychoanalytic societies, notes that "the very position of plurality may also assume the characteristic of a dominant ideology, passively accepted as such without raising challenges to the incompatibility of alternative models" (p. 1655). We would, thus, be wise to remember that, while finding points of unity that can enable us to embrace theoretical differences, we need to be aware of any tendency to diminish differences that could stem from a wish to avoid uncomfortable discourse, and any pull towards splitting within our society.

We will, however, make mistakes, and, no doubt, have already made them during the formation of our society. The issue, to my mind, as with any given analytic session, is not the making of what we retrospectively consider to be "mistakes", but, rather, the willingness to reflect, rethink, and to learn and grow. Dr Haesler has emphasized the importance of having "ideals without idealization" (2009, p. 4). Maintaining ideals without idealization can be thought of as a model for resolution of transference to one's training analyst, for clinical practice, for the continuing development of an IPA Society, for, to put it another way, important aspects of a psychoanalytic ego ideal. When idealization creeps in and takes over, whether it is of oneself and one's profession, or of colleagues, I think creative thought stops and development comes to a halt.

This brings me back to adolescence. Restructuring of the ego ideal, and reorganization and solidification of identifications, is deemed an outcome of adolescence (Blos, 1962). In so far as this relates to our professional identity as psychoanalysts and our status as a Component Society, I would say we have "made it through".

In adolescence, this process includes mourning, and it does also for us. We have, for example, said "goodbye" to Dr Haesler and Mme Godfrind-Haber in their capacity as the Liaison Committee, and this leave-taking will lead to increased identification and internalization of psychoanalytic premises, and involves both sadness and anticipation. We hope for a continuing but different relationship with these colleagues, just as we look forward to a relationship with BPAS members and others in the IPA that signifies both continuity and change.

Thus, we begin to take our place as a Component Society. At the time of writing, membership of the BPA is fifty-two: we have a number of candidates in the process of working towards eligibility for membership under the Equivalency Criteria; a group of candidates who have recently commenced our new and full training in psychoanalysis; a lively scientific life, consisting of both clinical discussions and presentations of papers. At the start we had, as Raeburn put it, "a dream" (2009). We have had the energy to realize this dream, and are in the fortunate position of being able to begin, become, and contribute, while continuing to learn from those who have been there longer.

References

Alfille, H. (2009). Personal communication.

Blos, P. (1962). *On Adolescence.* New York: Free Press of Glencoe.

British Psychoanalytic Association (2006). Policy, procedure and criteria for IPA applications to the British Psychoanalytic Association. BPA Document.

Chasseguet-Smirgel, J. (1985). *Creativity and Perversion.* London: Free Association Books.

Ferro, A. (2009). Transformations in dreaming and characters in the psychoanalytic field. *International Journal of Psychoanalysis, 90*: 209–230.

Haesler, L. (2009). Quoted in: Bellman, D., Minutes of the IPA liaison committee visit, March (pp. 1, 4).

International Psychoanalytical Association (1999). Equivalency criteria and procedures for non-IPA psychoanalytical groups, IPA Document.

Kennedy, R. (2007). *The Many Voices of Psychoanalysis.* East Sussex: Routledge.

Kernberg, O. F. (2006). The coming changes in psychoanalytic education: Part I. *International Journal of Psychoanalysis, 87*: 1649–1673.

Maoutsos, V. (2005). Email communication.

Parsons, M. (2000). *The Dove that Returns, The Dove that Vanishes*. London: Routledge.

Raeburn, S. (2009). Address given at the Business Meeting of the 46th Congress of the International Psychoanalytical Association in Chicago, USA, July.

Raeburn, S., & Alfille, H. (2008). Annual Report for the British Psychoanalytic Association.

Sandler, J. (1960). The background of safety. *International Journal of Psycho-Analysis, 41*: 352–356.

Shakespeare, W. (*ca.* 1594). *A Midsummer-Night's Dream*. In: *The Oxford Shakespeare* (pp. 171–191). London: Oxford University Press, 1964.

In memory of Daniel Twomey

CHAPTER ONE

Why reconstruct? Perspectives on reconstruction within the transference

Sara Collins

> "What we are in search of is a picture of the patient's forgotten years that shall be alike trustworthy and in all essential respects complete."
>
> (Freud, 1937d, p. 258)

Arguably, the place of reconstruction in psychoanalytic technique has not been kept in a central position following Freud. Since his time, there has been a gradual but clear shift in emphasis on to working within what is immediate and present in the material, and that is due, to a large extent, to what has become colloquially known among analytic practitioners as "working within the transference". This term is often used synonymously with another analytic colloquialism—"working in the here and now". I believe that this general swing of the pendulum to working almost exclusively in the here and now is an important reason for reconstruction work to have fallen out of favour. The change of grammar within the consulting room to the present tense rather than the past tense seems to have relinquished reconstruction to the margins of psychoanalytic language.

My view is that reconstruction work can be done within the transference, quite organically, and without producing any sense of diversion from the here and now. On the contrary, reconstructive work can essentially feed into, support, and enhance the work on the transference in the immediacy of the session, as I illustrate later in this chapter.

First, I summarize Freud's views on reconstruction, and briefly explore the differential meanings of reconstruction and construction. I then describe the shifting emphasis to the here and now, and frame the decline in the use of reconstruction as a pivotal psychoanalytic technique within the context of the critiques levelled against it. I also consider the contemporary re-evaluation of reconstruction in the light of fresh perspectives on it.

Freud's reconstruction

The epigraph to this chapter sets out Freud's clear agenda for the psychoanalytic endeavour; it was to have reconstruction at its heart. This flowed from his ideas on childhood amnesia and the return of the repressed, both integrally linked to his great discovery of the unconscious. The patient's attachment to the analyst was helpful in promoting a state of mind in the patient that could be conducive to remembering. This, Freud also facilitated through the analysis of resistance. Altogether, he was looking for anything that could assist in what he saw as the essential task of remembering and reconstruction. In fact, to the extent that the transference was brought into the analytic discourse, it was used as an aid to reconstruction.

"The Wolf Man" (1918b) is a detailed example of Freud's case studies. Muslin (1991) has shown how Freud used this case study to argue the centrality of memory retrieval, to be followed by reconstruction in psychoanalytic technique. This was the main therapeutic tool. In this case, as in earlier ones, the emphasis was not on the technique of interpreting the transference. Although Freud recognized the great importance of the transference, it was mainly as an aid to reconstruction, which was the cornerstone of his analytic technique.

The shifting emphasis to the "here and now"

Stewart (1990) and others (Gill, 1982; Grotstein, 1999; Rosbrow, 1993; Schafer, 1997) have commented on the shift away from reconstruction to work in the here and now. Stewart's (1990) view is that reconstruction has been understood as being somewhat in opposition to the work of the transference in the here and now. According to him, reconstruction would be classified within the general notion of what he calls "extra-transference" interpretations: ". . . extra-transference interpretations which concern the environment of the patient's *past* are interlinked with the therapeutic agent of reconstruction, or construction as it used to be called" (p. 64, my italics). Thus, reconstruction might be seen as a diversion from the immediacy and importance of the transference.

Rosbrow (1993) juxtaposes remembering with re-experiencing. Reconstruction means remembering past events, a technique laid down by Freud as basic to psychoanalytic work. Rosbrow maintains that the work in the here and now is about re-experiencing past events. Therefore, Rosbrow believes that reliving in the here and now has taken over, as a psychoanalytic technique, from remembering the past.

Another form of critique levelled at Freud's concept of reconstruction is that it tends to be an intellectual device on behalf of the analyst. Reconstruction may be pursued in order to satisfy the analyst's intellectual curiosity and need for a coherent rational picture, rather than in the service of the patient's therapeutic needs. In this way, putting a reconstruction to the patient may result in some form of "intellectual insight". This cannot be as effective as an experience in the transference that has a lively, emotional component to it, which would be more likely to lead to real insight born out of an affective, as well as cerebral, experience.

The above claim is supported by Stewart's (1990) reading of Freud's reconstruction. Stewart thinks that reconstruction had a research function for Freud, who looked for some form of validation of his psychoanalytic theories through the clinical material obtained via reconstruction. Freud, as we know, was continually inventing, as well as testing the validity of, his psychoanalytic concepts.

Chianese (2008) chimes in with the view that reconstruction as an analytic technique had encountered difficulties early on.

Reconstructions, he says, "interwoven as they are with reason, might have appeared incompatible with the supposed spontaneity of the analytic act" (p. 8). Moreover, he adds: "A certain amount of unease will have been due to the clear position Freud takes on the reality of infantile traumas at the end of the article. This is one of the most tormented aspects of Freud's theory . . ." (*ibid.*).

Thus, there are two rationales given by Chianese for the fact that reconstruction has fallen out of fashion. The first is the aspect of "explanation" involved in reconstruction that implies an appeal to the patient's reasoning and logic. This supposedly means an interruption to the flow of the analytic process, and a puncturing of the analytic space that should be preserved only for free association and "raw", unreasoned material to emerge. The second aspect is connected to the difficulties over the "historical truth" of reconstruction, an issue which itself has attracted substantial controversies expressed over many pages of psychoanalytic writings.

Though the explanations given by Stewart and others are clear enough in attempting to elucidate the decline in the use of reconstruction, I do not agree with the view put forward by Stewart that reconstruction is essentially "extra-transferential".

Construction or reconstruction

In his seminal text, "Constructions in analysis", Freud (1937d) manifestly used the terms construction and reconstruction interchangeably. It would seem that his focus was to convey how central to psychoanalytic technique it was to lift repression so as to get a coherent picture of the patient's "forgotten years". This, in turn, was the key to alleviating the patient's suffering. It is interesting that the concurrent use of two terms, which could correspond to two different meanings while making one essential point, arguably evaded his attention at the time.

A close analysis of the text reveals that it is only in a particular section of "Constructions in analysis", the one that deals with the archaeological analogy, that Freud uses "reconstruction". Throughout the rest of the paper, he uses the original term contained in his title: "construction".

His comparison with the archaeologist is that "Both of them have an undisputed right to *reconstruct* by means of *supplementing* and combining the surviving remains" (p. 259, my italics). From this quote, it would seem that by adding the prefix "re" to "construct", Freud has in mind that something is being added to what is there in terms of the evidence present in the material, "supplementing" the actual fragments of recovered memory.

In the immediate period following this seminal paper by Freud, the two terms have largely been used interchangeably, much in the same way that, as I maintain, Freud did. However, an analysis of the terms used in later psychoanalytic literature reveals a tendency to use Freud's term "construction" in quite a different way from the meaning of construction as contained in Freud's original paper. Chianese (2008), in his recent book *Constructions and the Analytic Field*, revisits the twin usages by Freud of construction and reconstruction, and looks at them from a contemporary perspective. He attributes a substantial significance and a differential application of meaning to the two nearly identical terms, distinguishable as they are only by the prefix "re". Chianese argues that not only was Freud fully cognizant of a disparity between the two words, but that the difference goes to the heart of a debate over what is historically true and what is narrated in an imaginative, story-telling fashion, and, therefore, is "untrue" in psychoanalysis. According to his differential allocation of meaning, "construction" would stand for the creatively narrated story, compounded by fantasy, whereas "reconstruction" would be closer to the historical, factually correct, and therefore true.

I agree with Chianese that Freud was occupied with issues of truth and its verifiability in construction throughout his work. However, I do not feel the text of "Constructions in Analysis" (Freud, 1937d) provides any substantial evidence that Freud was making a deliberate attempt to assign two separate meanings to construction and reconstruction. Quite the opposite, when he writes about "the analyst's work is one of construction, or, if it is preferred, of reconstruction . . ." (pp. 257–259), he suggests an ambiguity of usage that he is quite happy to leave alone.

Emerging distinctions

Sandler and Sandler (1994), while recognizing that the two terms have been used synonymously, argue that construction and reconstruction are different. They also make a link with their own conceptualization of the "past unconscious" and the "present unconscious". In general terms, their understanding of construction is linked to the work of the present unconscious, referring to memory structures present in the unconscious as they are revealed through the work of the here and now in the transference. Reconstruction is linked to their notion of the past unconscious.

They believe that confirmatory material through past reconstructions is not always available. However, their view is that links with the past provide an important added dimension to the understanding of the present. The work of construction is done in the present of the transference relationship, and linked to the present unconscious. New memories become available for reconstruction in the primitive layers of the present unconscious. This strengthens the insights gained in the work, such as the patient's understanding of his "child part". Their conclusion is, therefore, that what Freud termed "constructions" is what has come to be referred to as "reconstruction".

Generally, when construction is used in psychoanalytic literature, it can refer to any idea, description, or picture of a particular constellation of relationships present or past, internal or external, and held by either the analyst, the patient, or both. Construction would often mean any structure or understanding that has been developed in the course of an analysis. It could imply the patient's own view of his life history, and not necessarily one that conforms to that of the analyst. It could also stand for constructing an understanding of a current problem in the patient's life that has to do with current relationships, but is not necessarily yet connected to past history, or even to the inner world. Thus, it can be synonymous with "the way a pattern of behaviour is understood", leaving out analytic scrutiny in connection with past history at that particular juncture in the analysis.

Reconstruction, composed as it is of the word "construction" with its prefix "re", has more easily lent itself to mean a revisiting of an old familiar psychic place, a rebuilding, albeit with the benefit of a new understanding of previous psychic experiences. In this chapter, therefore, I use the term "reconstruction", so as to conform to the emerging consensus. That is, "construction" refers to experiences, whether external or internal, perceived by the patient to have taken place in the past. However, towards the end of the paper, I expand the notion of "the past" in the light of contemporary perspectives on temporality.

Transference and reconstruction: the salient link

In discussing comparative technical uses of transference and reconstruction, it is important to note that the notion of transference itself is complex. The original idea of transference, as formulated by Freud, rested on the essential ingredient of *transfer*. Some element of relatedness is transported from one person to the other. Classically, as in Freud's work, this was from a parental figure to the person of the analyst. It was considered by him to be "a neurosis", akin to an illness, from which the patient should be helped to recover. Recovery would be aided by showing the patient that his intense feelings towards the analyst were feelings that originated with another person. The idea was to relocate those feelings in their "correct" place, as it were. In this way, the relationship with the analyst would be freed from the burden of the "transference neurosis".

Clinical practice subsequent to Freud has proven that it was not always the case that a transference neurosis developed as it did with Freud's patients. In most cases, the awareness of the transference by the patient has to be encouraged and worked upon. Patients cannot be expected to be conscious of the fact that their discussions of experiences outside the analytic session are conveying aspects of their feelings about the analyst. Thus, analysts have sought to facilitate the transference by making comments which link the material the patient brings about objects in the past—or in their lives outside the session—to the relationship between the patient and the analyst, thus encouraging patients to transfer their affects to the person of the analyst.

Following Freud, psychoanalytic theories of technique have promoted a variety of perspectives on what a "transference interpretation" actually is, perspectives that reflect the divergence of theoretical orientations. These differences, put at their simplest, are expressed by grammatical uses of past and present. For some analysts, a transference interpretation means a reference to the patient's unconscious *present* fantasies in the here and now in relation to the analyst. Their underlying assumption, which is kept in the analyst's mind but not necessarily expressed to the patient, is that these fantasies are the modern representations of earlier object relations. For others, a transference interpretation is only that if the analyst articulates to the patient, or, at the very least, implies, the essential element of "transfer" from the *past*. That means that what the patient is experiencing in the here and now has been *transferred* from, or has its roots in, another, *past* relationship, where the focus of the discourse should be.

With the advent of what is commonly known, within psychoanalytic practice, as "working within the transference", there has been a fair bit of further obscurity over the definition of transference itself. Often, transference is synonymous with comments about the here and now. Thus, working within the transference stands for any comment that relates to the person of the analyst, whether or not the interpretation includes a reference to the fact that the person of the analyst actually stands for a projected internal object.

Two clinical illustrations

Shame in the classroom: the case of P

The following clinical material helps to highlight the emerging contemporary distinction between construction and reconstruction in the light of the earlier discussion. It shows how the building blocks of a construction are made up of various interpretations, which, put together, form a construction. It then demonstrates how, with the addition of childhood material, the construction leads to a reconstruction while continuing to work within the transference.

P started his analysis feeling intensely anxious and desperately needing to control me. For the first few months, he arrived with folders, lists, drawings, and sometimes his laptop. These were used as props in his communications with me. At the beginning of each session he laid out his materials and proceeded to talk to me with the aid of what he had prepared.

During this initial phase of the analysis, he once talked about an incident at work that had upset him. He was preparing to go to an important meeting that involved a presentation of his institution's specialist skills in designing outdoor furniture for a specific international event. If successful, this could result in a large contract for his company, as well as an accolade for him. He had prepared all the presentation materials well in advance, went into the meeting room ahead of time, and hung posters on the wall so that when the others arrived they would see them. When his manager arrived, he looked at the posters, did not like them, and ordered my patient to take them down. Feeling deflated and shamed, my patient did as requested, and moved to a corner of the room to tidy up the posters. He looked around, saw other people talking together in groups, and experienced himself as being apart from everybody else, nursing his humiliation in the corner, on his own. Then the meeting started, and he reported that this time, unlike during similar incidents in the past, he was able to collect himself and make a useful contribution despite what he termed the *disastrous* pre-meeting incident. Making the contribution had helped him to recover a good sense of himself, and to notice that his manager was amiable towards him during the actual meeting, despite the request to take the posters down.

In my interpretations, I linked the reported meeting and his relationship with me in a twofold way that addressed both his defence and his anxiety. Before the meeting, the defence was expressed in the obsessional preparation of posters; before the meetings with me, he prepares documents that he then brings into the sessions, wanting me to be "the audience" to his presentations. The other link pertained to the intense underlying unconscious anxiety that underpinned the obsessional behaviour. This interpretation was about his terror of being ignored and unnoticed, and how, therefore, he needed to ensure that what he produces is seen and heard. To that end, he prepares his materials immaculately and controls my attention. (There are, of course, other unconscious aspects to the obsessional preparation and control, such as aggression, but, at that stage of the treatment, it seemed too early to refer to them.) His emotional response to the manager's demand that he take down the posters was that of profound humiliation, experienced as though he was "sent off to stand in the corner" as a punishment. I linked this to how he experienced my speaking to him in the sessions. Since I did not always wait until he finished showing me all his prepared drawings, diagrams, and photos, but, rather, spoke during the course of his presentations, he felt as though I was stopping him and undermining what *he* had wanted to show me.

Each of the links mentioned above would be an interpretation. Put together, these interpretations become a construction, and then, as I will describe, become a reconstruction.

P recalled memories of school, including an episode of intense shame when he was caught copying in an exam for which he did not feel well prepared. He recalled the chorus of his classmates' low whispering voices repeatedly chanting at him, "cheat, cheat, cheat", and he could hear that sound reverberating in his head as he spoke to me. The link to the contemporary experience at work, which the patient had brought to this session, was obvious.

Also present in this material were other allusions to school life, touching on much deeper and earlier Oedipal issues of rivalry and success. The allusions that reverberated in my mind and in the patient's mind, and that linked his experience in the present with his earlier experiences of the past, provided the basis for a reconstruction.

Pink boy: the case of B

This case material illustrates how comments about the transference relationship in the here and now, particularly an interpretation that helps the patient contain anxieties, facilitates the work towards reconstruction. Equally, as will be shown, reconstruction can inform the transference and deepen the understanding of its here and now aspects within the session. It is, thus, possible to combine attention to the changing underlying unconscious fantasy in the here and now with attention to reconstructive work.

B was going to visit his old and frail uncle over the weekend. In anticipation of this important visit, which he feared could be the last, he talked about what it would be like to see his uncle in a "diminished" state, and wondered how he would feel if he found the uncle unable to communicate with him or even recognize him.

I commented on his fear of what it could feel like to him to be out of communication with me over the weekend ahead, and that, as a result, I might become a diminished figure in his mind, with whom he could no longer communicate in the same way as he does at the present moment.

With this comment, which drew his attention to his ability to talk to me in a meaningful manner in the session at that particular instant, he launched into floods of memories about the uncle, recapturing the uncle of years ago with renewed vigour and liveliness. He talked vividly about how this man, who owned a farm, had hoisted him on the top of a tractor as a young boy, and how he was able to be adventurous, running round freely and playing pranks on members of the family. Once, he and his friends exploded a milk churn that they had filled with powder extracted from leftover fireworks. On another occasion he fell into pigs' manure and ran home covered with pigs' excrement, but he did not mind it much; he loved pigs.

I commented on how this was also a time and place in his childhood where he could express some messy, explosive feelings. He agreed. There was a silence.

During his silence, I thought that a question was hanging between me and the patient as to what the real current anxiety could be in relation to this visit, given that he had recovered such positive memories about the uncle, and that he had been prepared for his uncle's deteriorating health for some time.

The patient then continued, "I am afraid I might be very angry with him when I see him because once, by mistake, he introduced me as his brother's 'daughter'." This was followed by a detailed description of the event. It had happened about three and a half years prior to the time of that particular session. His uncle, he said, had started suffering from a series of minor strokes at this time, and he would often make mistakes relating to details about people. He continued to describe the events surrounding his being referred to as "a niece". It was just as they were leaving church, when people were milling around and chatting. A congregant came over to greet the uncle. My patient was standing by him. The uncle said, "This is David's daughter." The effect of the uncle's comment had been devastating on my patient. He had to escape from the church, and subsequently had difficulties looking in the direction of the church, let alone going into it. He was struck by the severity of his reaction, stating that the church dominated the village landscape and it was difficult to avoid seeing it.

I commented on how deeply shaming it was for him to be presented as "a girl", and linked it to his insistence with me that I get all details of what he tells me precisely right. I referred to his intense anxiety about being wrongly perceived by me.

This led to more memories about his uncle and his childhood holiday experiences with him, into which I interspersed transference interpretations. These, in turn, seemed to lead to more memories and then, eventually, to connections with his father. Later on in the session, this unravelled an extremely important new memory about his childhood, and this, again, fed into the transference, as I summarize below.

The uncle often referred to the patient's summer visits to the farm since the age of one. In one of his anecdotes, he told how the patient was brought over by his parents, aged one, dressed up in a pink cardigan. At that, B felt a shockwave going through his whole being, consuming him with shame and rage.

The patient's angry question followed: "Why was I wrapped in a pink cardigan? This had nothing to do with *my* doing, I was only a baby at the time, and *I* couldn't do anything about it."

To my comment about his need to question his own role in this very painful memory of being treated like a girl, he responded by relaying other experiences when he found himself addressed as a woman, and mentioned a period in his life when he actually grew his hair long and had a beard, suggesting it might have been the long hair, seen from the back, that could have evoked the image of a woman. This, however, was connected to important material about the father.

About seven years prior to the session, the patient, then having long hair, undertook a long journey in Europe, following his father's footsteps as a soldier during the Second World War. In a mementoes shop, he was addressed as "Madam". He left the shop in horror.

At this juncture in the session, rather than making an interpretation, I wondered aloud whether it was particularly wounding for him to be thought of as a woman, especially at a time when he was engaged in the experience of following his father's war, very much an experience for men. Therefore, I continued, it was an extremely shaming episode for him.

His father had said to him, he continued, that he always wanted to have two boys. At his younger brother's wedding, the father made a speech in which he had described how he had gone into a cathedral in one of the small towns he had gone through during the war. In a revelatory kind of moment in this cathedral, he had made a wish to God to give him two boys. Indeed, my patient was the eldest in a family that had *two boys*. The patient shifted uncomfortably on the couch as he recounted this story.

I commented on how terrifying it would be for him to be thought of as the child (a girl) his father clearly did not wish for. I also linked it to the transference by saying it seemed difficult for him to tell me, a woman, about his father's wish for boys; how frightened he was to be the "wrong" person in the past, and now he was uncomfortable about saying the "wrong" thing here, since he always tried to be the good patient he thought I wanted him to be.

This led to another important memory, recovered for the first time during this session. His mother had a miscarriage; the baby would have been a girl. His memory was vague as to when the miscarriage happened. He wondered what this meant in relation to his father's emphatic wish for two *boys*. He free associated to this, and questioned whether his mother had somehow acquiesced to his father's wish by having this miscarriage. Then he corrected himself by saying, "But it was definitely a miscarriage, not an abortion."

He went on to muse about how he would have liked to have a sister; it would have been nice to have a sister to talk to. His mother, he said, was a reticent and reserved woman, and how good it would have been to have someone to talk to freely.

I made a transference interpretation in the here and now as follows: I said that at that moment he felt I was being a bit like the sister he never had, and that he was attempting to find in himself a way of talking to me freely like he imagined he might do with a sister.

He continued with a discussion of how, had he had a sister, this would have altered the nature of his relationship with his brother, and said, "Maybe my brother would not have killed himself."

When the patient said "killed himself", he immediately caught himself and anxiously said, "I have never been able to use that word before about my brother. I have never said: 'killed himself'. I don't understand why I said it!"

I made the following interpretation which linked the here and now of the session with the patient's past: "You are now worried about talking to me as if I was a sister to whom you talk freely, and saying things you wouldn't normally say, as though you were becoming too adventurous here, and letting off explosive stuff, as you did when you were a child on the farm and were allowed to be carefree and adventurous for a limited time each year".

There was a silence. After a while he said, "Maybe I am trying to connect to that child I was all those years ago. Maybe that is what it is about".

In this vignette, I hope I have shown how the transference and reconstruction inform each other. The reconstruction can string together meaningful events from different stages in life, but particularly from early childhood. Reconstruction informs the present transference. In the session, the transference altered to a sister transference as a result of the memory, which, in turn, informed the reconstruction of a childhood restricted by a domineering father and a reticent mother who produced despair in their children (the brother's suicide). It also touched on the wish to be free and its attendant anxieties, with freedom being equated with destructiveness and mess.

Further viewpoints on reconstruction

Reconstruction has not kept its position as an essential therapeutic tool for reasons other than the technical difficulty of keeping the focus on the here and now. Theoretical concerns regarding the truthfulness of patients' reports of their early lives fuelled the debate over reconstruction. In 1956, Kris drew attention to the important function of screen memories in childhood recollections. He maintains that events, thoughts, and feelings that can be reconstructed as historically "true" may, in fact, represent later occurrences that have become linked to earlier times, thus creating a false biographical picture.

Melanie Klein's (1946, 1975) fundamental contributions to the role of unconscious phantasy in the presentation of clinical material have put the debate over historical truth in reconstruction into sharper focus. A patient's emotional interior, comprising internal object relations, is subjected to a consistent process of projection and introjection. Between the point about unconscious phantasy on the one hand and projections and introjections altering internal object relations on the other, it seems that it would be difficult to argue in favour of an objective external reality.

However, I maintain that contemporary clinical practice can accommodate both the perspective of historical truth and subjective reality. It allows for a keen awareness of internal psychic life and subjective reality as manifested in the here and now, while maintaining attentiveness to "real" events in the patient's early life. These can be linked through reconstruction within the transference.

Blum (1980, 1994, 1999) has sought to re-emphasize the pivotal place of reconstruction within psychoanalytic technique. He stresses the indispensable value of reconstruction for the *analyst* in understanding "how that adult had remained a disturbed child with that particular psychopathology" (1980, p. 50). In this respect, the analytic session serves as an opportunity for *the analyst to refine his own developmental theories*. However, Blum adds another focus for reconstruction, a focus essentially relevant to the *patient*, and that is its integrative value. As the analysis progresses, it is invaluable for the patient to locate, with the help of the analyst, the source of his unwanted patterns of behaviour, both as expressions and repetitions of early object relationships.

The strength of Blum's position, to my mind, is its emphasis on the value of reconstruction for the patient's integration and its implications for ego strength. Nevertheless, there are two main problems with his other views. The first problem is that he stresses the importance of reconstruction as being essential for the analyst's theoretical understanding of developmental theories. The critique here would be how to justify, within the contemporary context, the analyst getting value out of the analytic situation for a purpose that does not essentially concern the patient. The second problem is that he locates the work of reconstruction outside the work of the transference. Alongside others, such as Stewart (1990), he designates the work of reconstruction as extra-transferential.

What we know about the universality and omnipresence of transference means that the claim of working on reconstruction extra-transferentially makes little analytic sense. It implies that, at certain points in the process, the transference stops, or, at the very least, it stops being attended to, and attention is diverted towards the patient's past. My argument is that the reconstructive work is done within, and as part and parcel of, the transference.

In practice, this is manifested in patients gaining insight and seeing connections between their symptoms and their causes in the forms of underlying conflicts, anxieties, and defences. I think it is important for the patient to be active in that part of the thinking process, together with the analyst. Thinking being a function of the ego, it is that which turns an analysis from a mere experiential process into an integrative thinking process as well. Most patients would want to understand not only the dynamic process of their difficulties, but also, importantly, what caused them and how they started. Patients with intense and debilitating symptoms would like to feel that, at least to an extent, they can be "restored" to a pre-troubles phase that, for most of them, *is* their childhood. It is here that reconstruction serves a crucial part, be it *true* or *true enough*.

The nature of repetition compulsion is such that patients have no choice but to manifest their problems repeatedly within the transference. Analysts will follow those repetitions with appropriate interpretations within the transference. But, unless another dimension of understanding is opened up, there is a danger that both patient and analyst will get locked into engaging in a repetitive process of a reported event, be it external or internal, followed by interpretation. This could become a compulsive process of repetition. What is required is for the analyst to be aware of the pattern and to open another avenue of exploration that will answer the obvious question of, "Why are we in it again?" "What have we not understood so far?" I think this is where reconstruction can offer an opening for the analyst to get away from the danger of impasse.

Reconstruction in cases of trauma

The work of reconstruction, in terms of the patient's emerging ego strength and the integration of the child and the adult, is of particular significance in cases of trauma and suspected abuse. This has been stated by a number of authors, and recently reiterated by Leuzinger-Bohleber (2008) and Werner Bohleber (2008). The point made is that it is important to allow patients, at an appropriate time, to talk about their *past as they remember and perceive it* without inevitably inserting comments about the here and now. As long as the transference is kept in the analyst's mind, one still works within the transference whether or not it is articulated.

The work of reconstruction in cases of abuse and trauma demands particular sensitivity, especially in relation to when to draw the material into the transference. Minute alertness is required of the analyst as to whether and when to address comments to the here and now or to a historical past. Moreover, any connections between a story of abuse and the relationship with the analyst should be made with the utmost delicacy. The material of abuse may be triggered by the patient's re-experiencing in the analysis a form of abuse in terms of either the analyst's lack of understanding or over-intrusiveness. However, these considerations are at times best borne in the analyst's mind rather than immediately interpreted. Eventually, a here and now comment relating to the reported trauma may be formed in the analyst's mind, but it will then be a processed and nuanced version of it. This emerging comment may not necessarily be verbalized, but could lead to modification of the analyst's interventions. When it is appropriate to verbalize the metabolized transference interpretation, it can help the patient to tolerate the memory of the trauma as it breaks into the present.

Clinical material

The snake and the drawer: the case of A

A was troubled by her relationships with men. An attractive woman, she came from a country that in some quarters treated women differently from men. Religion was a strong political force, and women were expected to wear modest dress. According to her, it was also expected that she should act in a timid and passive fashion.

An extremely bright person, she had found the suppression of women, and "needing to pretend to be a half-wit in order to get a husband", unbearable. She came to live in the UK, where she gained a degree and built up a successful career in a field of applied arts.

Some while into treatment, she confided her disturbing worries and frightening suspicion of having been sexually abused by her father. Her memories were vague, but were centred on fears that her father had exposed himself to her.

Aged about six, while being half asleep, she was vaguely aware of seeing a shadowy figure near her bed. She was not sure whether this really happened or whether she might have invented it, but her recall of her own reactions was quite clear. She developed a fear of falling asleep because she dreaded that an animal shaped like a snake's head would come at her. She feared that, while asleep, the animal would move backwards and forwards towards her in a rhythmic motion, coming at her and then withdrawing. She thought this had happened, but tried to dismiss it as a dream. She would wake from sleep in a state of panic, and check under the bed and inside the cupboard next to the bed. She also recalled feeling panicked during the day by the sight of the cupboard drawer's rounded, sausage-like beading. She avoided walking past the cupboard or even entering the room. She talked to her mother about "a snake in the night", but her worries were dismissed.

In her childhood, she spent a long time trying to work out what had happened to her. She eventually settled on a "theory" that someone might have tried to open a drawer next to her bed in the night, a drawer that had rounded beading on it, which, in the mist of sleep, might have given her the impression of a snake coming at her. Still, the opening and shutting of the drawer could not emulate the direction of the movement of "the snake".

In her analysis, she tried to work out whether there could be any basis in reality for these disturbing memories, and became particularly concerned about her state of sanity. Later, as she began to feel stronger and more able to contain her anxieties, she allowed herself to free associate about her father as a person, rather than focusing solely on her suspicions.

In one of those sessions, A described her father as a once vivacious person whose life went downhill. He had once been a political figure, but that was long before she was born. At the time of her early childhood he had already become marginalized in their particular community, no longer holding a public office. After being dismissed from office, he had tried his hand at various occupations, from being a salesman to owning a small retail shop, but none had succeeded.

Though very fond of her father, my patient described their relationship as practically non-existent. He worked in his shop for long hours, and never had time for her or her siblings. This was partly to do with the culture, as men were not ascribed responsibility for raising their children, apart from providing for them financially. Nevertheless, she thought her father had been warm to her when she was very little, and would occasionally address her in endearing terms, like calling her "my little lamb". As she grew and was considered capable of work around the house, aged about five, he began to demand that she do things for him, like fetch his drinks. His demands would often be made through gesturing rather than words. As she described her childhood relationship with her father, A also remembered another, wholly different and extremely disturbing aspect of their relationship.

The older she got the less talking would take place, and gesturing and body language became the main form of communication. My patient, like other young girls in her community, became very attuned to this. My patient thought that this form of communication had to do with a culture that separated men and women into two subgroups, even within their families, a culture which frowned upon open contact between the two groups. Men saw it as their duty to distance themselves from the feminine side of the family and embrace male company in order to keep themselves "clear of sin". The women were adept at reading communications from men through signs like a look, a raised eyebrow, or a bending of a finger. For young girls, this was essential in order not to get into trouble, as obedience was fundamental to getting along and getting what they needed.

A's father would put his hand into his pocket, and would seem to touch his genitals through the trouser pocket while, reportedly, looking intently at my patient and keeping her in his gaze. She recalled that gaze as "a thing" that kept her inexorably linked to her father in an experience that was extremely confusing and disturbing in its mix of unworthiness, secret excitement, and indignation. She recalled how she felt shocked and paralyzed, wanting to escape, but feeling pinned down by the gaze that held her and her father together in a shameful, knowing bond. It felt as though he was saying and doing something to *her* and *only to her*, which felt at once special and humiliating, and it was as though merely by staying there and registering what was going on, she was participating in a disgraceful, sinful act.

For many sessions in the analysis, she wondered whether she was making it up, whether the father did it accidentally for himself while she *happened* to be there, but concluded it was something *between them*. It was intended for *her*.

There followed another memory. When she was about fifteen or sixteen, her father came to her bed at night. On a pretext of rearranging her bed-coverings, he would lift the covering high up, look at her sleeping body for a few seconds, and put the coverings back around her. She found it strange and disturbing that a father who had taken no notice of her as his daughter at all during the daytime would be worried about her blankets at night. She remembered being woken up by his meddling with her bedclothes, and feeling deeply ashamed in case her nightgown had risen in her sleep to reveal parts of her naked body. She also recalled feeling pinned down and frozen by that experience, pretending to be asleep and almost suspending her breath while waiting for *it* to go, for her father to go and leave her alone.

A and I eventually embarked on a delicate task of reconstructing her experiences with her father into a coherent picture of what she called, "what *really* happened to me". It was extremely important for her to try to make sense of the plethora of vague perceptions, half memories, dreamlike states, and sensations with which she was plagued. Above all, she wanted some clarity. She struggled to put those near subliminal, perceptual experiences of seeing and being seen in a shameful way into some form of articulated narrative. Shame had been a major aspect of her affect in all her transactions with people, and she wanted to put her pervasive sense of shame into perspective. At the same time, she desperately wanted to delineate for herself aspects of her memory that she could rely on as *probably* true.

There were two important elements to the original memory of the "snake's head": one was its very appearance, and the other was the rhythmic movement of thrusting. Here, both analyst and patient knew this could imply a masturbatory activity simulating intercourse. A young child would not necessarily know about intercourse unless she had witnessed it, which she was certain she had not. As a girl, she recalled, she had a clear notion of the anatomical differences between boys and girls. She had two older brothers, one of whom was twenty months her senior. She remembered their cots being adjacent to each other and how her mother would clean up her brother when they woke in the morning. It was quite common in her country of origin for men to urinate outdoors, in front of passers-by, which would have made her aware of male anatomy from an early age. What she thought she could not be aware of was actual sexual intercourse.

A embarked on a painfully delicate and cautious process of trying to piece together the different shards of memories, from different ages and stages in her life, into a picture of the nature of her relationship with her father, and what it was that did or could have happened that accounted for her earlier frightened responses to the "snake's head in the night".

The conclusion we arrived at was that it was a possibility that her father might have exposed himself and masturbated by her bedside, but that this was a *hypothesis only*, and that she would never know the *actuality* of it. What we then proceeded to explore was the *impact on her of knowing this was a possibility*. Though the actual facts remained a mystery, she concluded by saying, "My father definitely had a problem with his sexuality. He could not keep it to himself."

In the period when I listened to and witnessed her discussions of the past relationship with her father, who was I, in her mind, at the time of those discussions? And why was it so important not to inquire further or attempt a reconstruction? The answer is that I could have become equated with the transgressing father, who watches her discomfort as he performs his impulsive acts, and that her experience in analysis would have become close to an abusing one. In the transference, my impulsive act would be *my* intrusive need to know exactly what happened to her as a child as, in her mind, this was what analysts wanted, they always wanted to know about childhood, it was their "obsession since Freud", she once commented, while she, on the contrary, for many years "did not want to know about [her] childhood".

Countertransference in reconstruction

What role does the analyst's countertransference, available as it is in the present, play in informing the reconstruction of the past? If, for example, the analyst feels impatience, irritation, or even hatred, this could be seen as a projective identification, in as much as the analyst absorbs and experiences a part of the patient that is denied and projected as an unwanted, or even dangerous, experience. Although this would be a contemporary experience in the analysis, the projected part is likely to represent an aspect of a historical object relationship. For example, the patient may identify with an impatient and hating parent who wants the child to develop more quickly, but projects this impatience and hatred. It could be that, historically, the patient has introjected an object experienced as impatient and hating. The introjection may have survived all the transmutations of object relationships through the developmental processes, and reappeared in an analytic moment in the "here and now" of a session, perhaps in an unconscious attempt to enlist the analyst's help through the countertransference. The work of reconstruction, in this instance, would give a historical perspective and explanation for the patient's masochistic need to provoke sadistic responses.

Clinical vignette

"I need to get on with it, therefore forget it": the case of C

The following clinical vignette reflects the notion of countertransference employed in the service of reconstruction.

C was sent to a private school from the age of nine. His father and his grandfather before him had gone to the same school. C was the eldest of five children, three of whom were boys, and it was understood all children would be sent to be privately educated in the same way. At the age of sixteen, he had a serious breakdown. He was overwhelmed by anxiety and depression, and felt his world had collapsed. From then on he saw his life as divided into two parts; the life before the breakdown, his "happy childhood", and his life after it, which was dominated by being ill. He came to me two years after his breakdown, having tried various treatments, all of which he did not find helpful. He was beset by intense guilt about becoming ill and about letting his parents down.

During the first two years of treatment, he regularly missed sessions and was habitually late. At the end of sessions, he often said that when he left he never knew if he would turn up for the next session, or even unilaterally decide to terminate the sessions, therefore never seeing me again. He told me he thought that if he decided not to come again it would probably be a "good thing", since it would follow the conclusion that the treatment had been a "bad thing" for him, and he would, therefore, be better off walking away from it. Predictably, these uncertainties were acute before breaks. He found it impossible to register the date of the first session after long breaks, and needed to call me a few days before the first session to confirm the date of return. When he did come to his sessions, he could never remember what went on before, and claimed he forgot the session the minute he was on the other side of the door.

Although I registered the elements of aggression and contempt in what he told me, my countertransference was predominantly that of anxiety, born out of extreme uncertainty as to whether I did or did not have a patient. I saw it as reflecting his panic and terror at the fragility of his mind, at being unable to keep any object as constant and safe. I had thoughts about links between his openly cold, calculated discussions with me about the treatment being a "good thing" or a "bad thing", his fear that he might compulsively walk away from it, and his childhood experiences of repeatedly being sent off to school from home and having to consider it "a good thing".

Parallel to his own uncertainty as to whether he could bring himself back to the first session after a break, he also held a belief that I used my breaks to consider whether or not I wanted to continue to see him. Consequent to this belief, he felt certain that when he came back to the first session he would, one day, find my house "boarded up", and would have to realize that I had moved away during the break. The connection with "boarding school" and the sense of displacement it had given him was apparent.

As he began to let me know in more detail the contents of his terrifying fantasies about the imminent breakdown of his treatment, either due to his disappearance or mine, I learnt more about why he felt it necessary to attempt to obliterate what he got from me. On one occasion, he explained that it was important to try and forget the treatment each time he left my consulting room because, "I need to get on with it, therefore forget it". It was a mantra-like saying he repeatedly told himself.

At this point I felt very moved and sad by this revelation of his intimate and habitual way of self-destructive thinking. I pictured a distressed little boy who tries to be "brave" and get on with his life each time he is sent away to school by forgetting his mother and his home life. My reconstructive interpretation, relating his habitual cutting off his links with me to how he had trained himself to cope with repeated separations from his mother—"You would just have to forget it and get on with it"—led to detailed accounts of this part of his history.

It was my countertransference experience of sadness, alongside a reverie that pictured him as a vulnerable young boy, not the initial verbal content of the material at the beginning of the session, that was the clue that led to what was a very important piece of reconstruction about this patient's life. It immediately fed into the transference in the here and now in throwing light on a central defensive pattern that was prevalent in the sessions and caused the patient a great deal of psychic pain.

Fresh perspectives on reconstruction

Feldman's (2007) paper, "The illumination of history", revisits the role of understanding past history within the work of the transference and its manifestations of early internal object relations. Although Feldman does not refer to reconstruction by name, he does show how keeping in mind historical material can help the analyst understand contemporary object relations as they are revealed in a current version in the here and now. He refers to history as *illuminating* the present. At the same time, he turns the idea of *history* on its head by calling developments within a session the "history of the session", and referring to the "history of the treatment". This contemporary Kleinian development shows, if nothing more than in the form of a nod in the direction of reconstruction, that understanding early history has been reclaiming its place in the "tool kit" of modern psychoanalytic techniques. However, in my view, Feldman's thesis on early history and its illuminative powers also supports the postmodern notion that temporality itself has become rather more relative and flexible in comparison with its original use by Freud.

Westen and Gabbard (2002) have looked at the link between transference and reconstruction from a recent perspective of cognitive neuroscience. They have proposed to redefine the meaning of transference in the light of contributions on memory in a manner that wholly integrates "transference", "construction", and "reconstruction" at a theoretical level. Accordingly, transference can no longer be portrayed as shifting libidinal aims on to the analyst, as Freud maintained, nor is it "the activation of an old representation lying in wait" (p. 130), since memory, we now know, no longer gets stored in that static manner that can lend itself to being transferred.

My own view occupies a middle ground between the more traditional and the postmodern extreme outlooks. I believe that patients benefit from addressing both past and present. I would define the present as working within the transference in the here and now. The past would be the work of reconstruction, an attempt to have a view of the past, whether real or fantasized, and connected to the present. In a way, the more temporalities are present in the discourse and in the minds of the patient and the analyst, the richer, freer, and livelier their interactions and communications can be. One could view the use of temporality in psychoanalytic technique as an idiom of psychic reality, rather than, necessarily, a specific representation of a particular real time. In the end, both uses of the past and the present lead in the same direction; that is, to the internal life of the patient and its salient role in determining his experiences. Internal life consists of internal objects that are amalgams of the past and the present. The composition of those internal object relationships heavily relies on projection and fantasy, processes closely linked to the unconscious that, as we know, is, itself timeless.

The purpose of the above contention is not to trivialize the debate over issues of technique in relation to reconstruction through reductive theoretical considerations. Indeed, the consulting room realities are such that, when talking to their patients, analysts constantly make choices about which point in time they address. Rather, it aims at adding a unifying perspective over temporality that, in turn, could lead to greater flexibility in the employment of reconstruction within the transference.

References

Blum, H. P. (1980). The value of reconstruction in adult psychoanalysis. *International Journal of Psychoanalysis, 61*: 39–52.

Blum, H. P. (1994). *Reconstruction in Psychoanalysis: Childhood Revisited and Recreated*. Madison, CT: International Universities Press.

Blum, H. P. (1999). The reconstruction of reminiscence. *Journal of the American Psychoanalytic Association, 47*: 1125–1143.

Bohleber, W. (2008). Remembrance, trauma and collective memory: the battle for memory in psychoanalysis. *International Journal of Psychoanalysis, 88*: 329–352.

Chianese, D. (2008). *Constructions and the Analytic Field*. New York: Routledge, The New Library of Psychoanalysis.

Feldman, M. (2007). The illumination of history. *International Journal of Psychoanalysis, 88*: 609–625.

Freud, S. (1918b). From the history of infantile neurosis. *S.E., 17*: 3–122. London: Hogarth.

Freud, S. (1937d). Constructions in analysis. *S.E., 24*: 257–269. London: Hogarth.

Gill, M. (1982). *Analysis of the Transference: Theory and Technique, Volume 1*. Madison, CT: International Universities Press.

Grotstein, J. S. (1999). Review of: *The Contemporary Kleinians of London*, R. Schafer (Ed.). *Psychoanalytic Quarterly, 68*: 643–648.

Leuzinger-Bohleber, M. (2008). Biographical truths and their clinical consequences: understanding "embodied memories" in a third psychoanalysis with a traumatized patient recovered from severe poliomyelitis. *International Journal of Psychoanalysis, 89*: 1165–1187.

Klein, M. (1946). Notes on some schizoid mechanisms. *International Journal of Psychoanalysis, 27*: 99–110 [reprinted in: *The Writings of Melanie Klein, Vol. 3: Envy and Gratitude*. London: Hogarth, 1975].

Klein, M. (1975). Envy and gratitude and other works 1946–1963. *International Psychoanalytical Library, 104*: 1–346.

Kris, E. (1956). The recovery of childhood memories in psychoanalysis. *Psychoanalytic Study of the Child, 11*: 54–88.

Muslin, H. L. (1991). The role of transference in the Wolf Man case. *Journal of the American Academy of Psychoanalysis, 19*: 294–306.

Rosbrow, T. (1993). Significance of the unconscious plan for psychoanalytic theory. *Psychoanalytic Psychology, 10*: 515–532.

Sandler, J., & Sandler, A.-M. (1994). Comments on the conceptualisation of clinical facts in psychoanalysis. *International Journal of Psychoanalysis, 75*: 995–1010.

Schafer, R. (Ed.) (1997). *The Contemporary Kleinians of London*. Madison, CT: International Universities Press.

Stewart, H. (1990). Interpretation and other agents for psychic change. *International Review of Psycho-Analysis, 17*: 61–69.

Westen, D., & Gabbard, G. O. (2002). Developments in cognitive neuroscience. *Journal of the American Psychoanalytic Association, 50*: 99–134.

CHAPTER TWO

Here and now interpretations

Jean Arundale

Contrary to what one suspects is the general view of psychoanalysis in the public eye, the ultimate aim of analysis is to enable the individual to live in the present. With its apparent emphasis on past experience in the formation of the mind and the very consciousness of an individual, it is easy to make the mistake of thinking of psychoanalysis as a dwelling place of the past. This view can be associated with the psychic determinism within which Freud's theories originated and developed, along with its idea of an unconscious that records and preserves all experience. Moreover, clinical psychoanalysis as a procedure is known to involve reawakening memories of the personal historical past, both near and distant, so that those not in the profession can be excused for believing that the analyst's consulting room is an archive to past experience.

Within the profession there are many clinicians who work primarily with memories and reconstructions of the past, or with events occurring in life outside the sessions, and these certainly play their part in understanding the patient, and are kept in mind. Michael Feldman, in his paper "The illumination of history" (2007), discusses how we are all still influenced by Freud's original theories of the therapeutic value of the recovery of repressed memories and the need to build up a coherent picture of the patient's past history and fill in the gaps, together with linking the past to the present. However, Feldman states that this does not, in itself, promote psychic change. Nor does working at the level of conscious conflicts or problem solving bring about structural change in unconscious patterns. As he understands it, the historical objects from the patient's past are alive in the present moment as internal objects, so that they are available as transference objects; the patient's history is embodied in these internal objects, and when the present transference relationship is experienced and understood, the past becomes clearer and internal objects are modified.

Clinical theory has evolved since Freud to the degree that it is now widely believed that emotional and mental events must be alive in the present moment, in exchanges between the patient and the analyst, in order for there to be psychic change. Strachey (1934) must be greatly credited for focusing the attention of his generation on the here and now as the locus of psychic change with what he termed the "mutative transference interpretation". He carefully demonstrated that the severe superego could only be modified if "caught in the act" in the present moment, when it is projected into the analyst. Strachey's mutative transference interpretation became a template for psychic change for future generations of all schools of analysis.

Although many psychoanalysts have contributed to advances in clinical theory, I take as my starting point aspects of the work of Betty Joseph and Michael Feldman, who have been at the forefront of the tradition of "microanalysis", the analysis of small shifts in the patient's experience in the here and now that lead to longer-term changes. For Joseph and Feldman, a focus on the past defuses the intensity of the patient–analyst relationship in the present; the here and now needs to be clarified first before explicit links are made with the past. Their emphasis is on depth in the analytic relationship. This allows the past to be discovered in a new way, often changing long-held assumptions and beliefs about object relationships derived from early stages of development. Joseph writes in an early paper, "The patient who is difficult to reach" (1975), there is a

> need for the analyst to keep interpretations in constant contact with what is going on in the session ... Useful understanding usually

> comes from an interpretation of events that are immediate. If it is too far from the actual experience going on in the room, it leads only to verbal understanding of theory. [pp. 59–60]

She has gone on to hone her technique into a sensitive instrument to detect complex defensive structures, and projections of parts of the personality, that are experienced as enactments and projective identifications emotionally affecting the analyst.

As I see it, the essence of the approach of both Joseph and Feldman, and what characterizes their work, is a consistent effort to trace the process within the session in order to identify the nature of the unconscious phantasy alive here and now in the patient in the form of a maladaptive or malignant object relation. If there is a theoretical distinction to be made between the two analysts, it is my impression that this would be around a particular interest on Joseph's part in the method of reaching insight through moment-to-moment shifts in the session, whereas Feldman focuses slightly more on projected unconscious phantasy. However, their methodology is similar in the way they track the effect patient and analyst have on each other. Both emphasize that object relationship patterns, if not made conscious, will be lived out in actions in life, to the detriment of the patient.

I would like to emphasize in this paper that interpretations that make contact with the patient's mental state alive in the present provide a moment in which the patient can see himself more truly in the analytic mirror, or, as Bion puts it, a moment in which the analyst introduces the patient to him or herself. By means of this truer picture, distortions in psychic reality can be corrected or transformed. Thus, the fundamental aim of here and now interpretations is to make contact with the psychic reality of the patient. Emotional contact necessarily takes place at different levels ranging from the surface to the depths, including defence mechanisms and projective processes, as the analyst works to bring the unconscious into view. An exposition of the various levels, however, is beyond the scope of this paper (see Roth, 2001).

Following from Feldman and Joseph, what I want to propose is that when the analysis approaches the area of contact with persecutory archaic objects at the most primitive level, the here and now interpretation attains its most vital and important function. At this level, there is, as Strachey observes, a fear on the part of both analyst and patient that the situation will disintegrate into a real situation, which generates a fear of making mutative interpretations. Strachey writes, "the analyst is courting an outbreak of anxiety which can make him anxious himself" (p. 141) when there is a charge of id energy that is unambiguous, actual, and aimed directly at him, testing his capacity to withstand the patient's primitive emotional impulses, as well as his own. Yet, it is, I believe, this level that provides the best opportunity for the patient to become aware of a distinction between his archaic phantasy object and the real external object, a mutative moment in which a new, less persecutory object can be internalized in small doses of reality to modify what is essentially a phantasy situation. Many have noted that there has been insufficient emphasis on Strachey's notion of the difficulty in making mutative interpretations, which are attested in this paper as being due to the felt proximity to action, or "acting in", that accompanies work in the here and now for both participants.

Before looking at these processes in detail in a clinical context, I would like to elaborate on Joseph's views, which inform my technique. Joseph writes about the importance of the rediscovery of a good object to help the patient to face the difficult truths of psychic reality met with in the session. A co-operative alliance with the analyst is essential, but the analyst as a good object is often lost when the patient is in the grip of deep archaic objects, so that interventions can be felt to be persecuting, to be coming from an unsupportive, uncomprehending, primitive object. The patient will inevitably experience the loss and refinding of his good object again and again.

Close attention to how the patient uses the analytic relationship is the keystone of Joseph's method, and she has focused on this since her published papers in the 1970s. The patient uses the analyst in various ways: for example, to project anxiety into, to collude with to deny anxiety, to collude with manic and other defences, or to carry various parts of his internal world. Helpful clues to how the patient is using the analyst can be found in non-verbal aspects such as tone of voice, mood, the atmosphere, the words used, strange feelings or lack of feeling, based on Melanie Klein's idea that the transference is "memory in feeling" (1957). As she notes the textures, colours, and small enactments taking place, Joseph encourages work from the intuition, from the gut, not from the intellect, with a keen sensitivity to where the patient is in the present. Close attention to the response by the patient is essential, whether after the intervention the patient becomes, for example, sadder, more thoughtful, calmer, aggressive or angrier, closer or more distant. From this response, a better view of the internal world is possible.

Joseph maintains that her work is descriptive, not theory-led, and relies on not knowing beforehand. She is always alert to contacting hidden emotional states in the here and now, such as anxiety, depression, manic or paranoid states, bringing them into consciousness. Her eye is watchful for the character elements, for the person behind the material, for the dreamer behind the dream.

Case studies

The first patient I would like to discuss is a male in his sixties, who, due to inauspicious circumstances around his birth, never knew his father. His mother was often unavailable. Precocious and gifted at school, rebellious, highly energetic, and manic, able to speak brilliantly on numerous topics, he had never reached his potential, essentially because he feared his sexuality and, consequently, any real, potent interactions with the world. His brief relationships with women have ended unsuccessfully.

When he began his ten-year, four-times-weekly treatment, he was scarcely working, suffered from a variety of paranoid anxieties, and it was clear that he lived in an omnipotent, narcissistic world of phantasy and magical thinking, feeling morally superior and barely aware of the existence of others. Our early work was around achieving insight into his narcissistic world and his omnipotence of thought, and what this meant in terms of his belief that he did not have to make efforts to actually put his ideas into practice in the real world, to realize and actualize his thoughts and intentions. Partly this was arrogance, but mostly this was due to unconscious magical thinking: he believed he had only to think something and it would happen automatically.

From the beginning he was anxious about coming to sessions and being alone with me, although at the same time, in a split way, he found the sessions helpful and felt they were a haven of safety and protection from a frightening world in which he was under attack from his enemies. Much of his spontaneous phantasy was about finding a place to hide away. His psychotic anxieties and paranoia took the form of threats from authority figures, whom he hated, and from spies that he saw everywhere, which formed much of the content of work in the transference in the here and now, with me appearing in his mind as an authority figure or a dangerous government spy. However, I would like to focus in this material on the area of the sexual transference and destructive primal scene phantasies, abundant and alive in his analysis. As a child without a father, he had no opportunity to work through Oedipal issues afforded by the real presence of a sexual parental couple, and, furthermore, his mother was puritanical and anti-sex, having been brought up in a fire-and-brimstone Christian fundamentalist family. There was little physical closeness to her, and he grew up feeling his mother disapproved of his masculine sexuality, engendering a fear in him that were he to become too close to her, the situation would become dangerously erotized.

As a rule in the sessions, he tried to use me to collude with his intellectual defences, wanting a protective relationship with me without emotional contact. He would deny any feelings of affection or care towards me, keeping me at a comradely impersonal distance, stripped of emotion, which I understood as a defence against closeness that might threaten to erupt into sexual excitement. As I entered into his internal world and identified with his object relationships, I often found myself cast as partner in a scary sexual encounter, originally with one of the women from his past, and I regularly interpreted these moments as his erotic feeling towards me, with which he agreed. It was apparent from his responses that these interpretations decreased his anxiety in the sessions.

For him, sex was vile, disgusting, and subhuman. He told me a phantasy in which he imagined half of the population of the world, at any given moment in darkness, at night, fornicating like animals, in a violent grasping for pleasure. His next association was to a primitive tribe in Africa that he had heard about, which had the disturbing practice of ritually sacrificing a goat, after which there was a wild dance, blood everywhere, ending in orgasm. I interpreted that the idea of sex was frightening for him, and that he was curious about sex between me and my partner.

A few sessions later, he was ashamed to tell me of an incident that had occurred with a woman with whom he had had a business meeting the day before: there was an attraction between them that ended in a "grope", as he put it. He felt afraid to tell me this, feeling that I would disapprove. He went on to talk of the anxiety he still feels when coming to sessions, feeling unsure of what this anxiety is about. Putting himself into places where he feels disapproved of makes him feel anxious, he said. In the countertransference, I felt the tension between us escalate, as if there was something like a grope taking place as I tried to make contact with him, or he with me. I did not want, at this point, to repeat once again his belief that I did not approve of his sexuality. Near the end of the session, I made an interpretation that I felt was closer to his unconscious phantasy, about how afraid he was of coming to the session and penetrating into my space. The next day, the last session before a week's break, he arrived calmer and less anxious, saying he did not feel his usual insecurity about the business he operates. The setup depends on grants from institutions, and he is usually frightened that they will be withdrawn, but today things feel more secure. He spoke of how surprising it felt that I had not shown disapproval the previous day about the groping incident; he felt reassured. He told me he did not feel so anxious, as he usually does, about the following week when we would not be meeting.

In the first session after the week's break, he started by speaking of a woman at work, his assistant, with whom he usually had a good working relationship. Oddly, he told me, this morning she had appeared cold, distant, and hostile; he felt it was strange. Noting that the break had affected his contact with me as a good object, I said that my being away last week made him feel estranged from me, that I felt like a distant and hostile person today. He said that whenever I brought up something about our relationship, he became aware of how much he does not want to deal with me as a person. "I would rather think of you as . . . well . . . a mechanism, something impersonal. I don't know what to do about the blockage I feel here. I can feel emotions in relation to others outside, but here I can feel only an intellectual relating, as we have often talked about. I don't know what I feel towards you. I feel a ghastly embarrassment when I am with all women. It's the sexualization of women we've spoken about, men too; I go all staring and transfixed." I was aware of the distance he created by generalizing his discomfort to apply to everyone, and I brought the sexual feeling into the present with me, and said, "The sexual feelings you have here towards me are embarrassing." He moved away, changing the subject, and said "I haven't visited my mother in a long time. I may go next month." I said, "You feel two ways about me, one is sexual and the other is as a mother who nurtures, comforts, and gives security," He said, "Yes. But there is some sexual element towards my mother as well. It's dangerous in proximity to her. I see my mother as a sexual figure; this wasn't conscious before. It's linked to other things I don't understand. Being close physically to my mother is repulsive and horrible."

Remembering something he had told me previously, I made a link to the past and said, "You've told me of a memory from childhood of looking at your mother sitting on the stairs, seeing her genitals under her skirt, feeling they were frightening and dangerous." He responded, "That explains my fears, but it's inconsistent. I have had sexual relationships." The patient's matter of fact demurral to my linking with a previously mentioned childhood incident, although I had thought it was an instance of the past alive in the present, showed me that my interpretation was of no use in bringing the patient closer to his present emotional state, illustrating how explanatory interpretations are ineffective and that I should have taken up the repulsive feeling of being close to me physically in the here and now. He went on to say, "For my mother, sexuality is a menace. Even now, at ninety-seven, she has delusions that the orderlies in the care home trying to undress her want to have sex with her. This is a curiously powerful, dangerous subject. I think I turn you into her." I responded, having recovered a feeling of connection to the patient in the present, albeit accompanied by an anxious sense of risk, saying, "Yes. You feel my sexuality is a menace to you and that I want to pull you into something sexual." I felt a tense darkening of the atmosphere as he said, "This reminds me of a previous time when we were talking about this; I didn't tell you at the time, but I thought you were going to reach out and touch me." I felt we were on dangerous ground. Awkward and uncertain about what to say, I thought of asking more about his fear, but instead commented rather too generally and intellectually, an option that moved us away from the primal terror, "Talking about sex or having sexual feelings in your mind equals action; it's hard for you to tell the difference between a phantasy about sex and what is real." He responded, "This subject is difficult for me, anathema. There's something very disquieting. I just had an image of being on an aeroplane and noticing an unusual wing formation." I felt a loss of the vitality and the thread of emotion between us; I said, "Your thoughts fly away and escape from what we are talking about here, from the fear that sexual feelings here will develop into actions and that I am trying to seduce you into a sexual relationship." There was a moment of silence, during which I felt anxious about how he would respond. Then he said, "Sex is a mystery, like the weather; there are tornados, storms, dangers of retribution. With A and the mating ritual [A is a woman of whom he often speaks with longing, with whom he had a brief intense flirtation, during which she had given him a whack to get his attention] . . . with A I had a fear of being attacked; it felt wonderful and at the same time frightening; afraid I'd be hurt if I got involved. My whole adolescence was made up of fearful potential sexual adventures, each more menacing than the last." I was aware of his projection of exciting, dangerous sexual feelings into A and into past relationships, so, to bring it back to the here and now, I said, "Being here with me is sexually menacing and at the same time an exciting adventure, but you're afraid your involvement with me will hurt you." He hesitated, and then went on to talk of two episodes from the past that involved couples, in which he was attracted to the woman, and at the same time her partner's physical presence posed an angry threat.

In the next session, he continued this theme, speaking of being with a woman where there was a sexual element and he was afraid that a male who was present would attack him. I felt it was important to make a here and now interpretation to help him with his anxiety in my presence, his fear of being close to me, and to put him in touch with the frightening unconscious phantasy that because he and I are together here, my partner will be angry and attacking towards him. When I said these things to him, he replied, "You have said similar things before, and it resonates . . . yes, I can see the truth in it."

These passages illustrate, in my view, an approach to a disturbing, archaic configuration of dangerous Oedipal sexuality, wherein personal potency and sexual impulses give rise to terror of attack from the return of an absent, jealous father. Feldman describes, in his 1994 and 1997 articles on projective identification, how disturbing mental contents or phantasies are expelled into the object as a defensive manoeuvre. He writes of

> . . . the patient's use of a particular omnipotent phantasy as a defense against primitive anxieties. The most important aspects of this defense mechanism involve those internal elements, or "parts of the self" that are experienced as threatening and "bad," being split off from the rest of the self and projected in phantasy into an object. The object (prototypically the breast, and subsequently the mother) becomes transformed by the projection, and is experienced as possessing these bad elements as its own. [1994, p. 437]

Thus, a part of my patient's self, made up of his sexual curiosity, his erotic impulses, together with anxiety around a destructive primal scene, was projected into me so as not to recognize these as his own, in an attempt to deal with the intense anxiety stirred up. He believed I was the dangerous, sexual mother who wanted to seduce him, to touch him, and draw him into a sexual situation, which, when interpreted in the here and now, reduced his anxiety and modified the archaic persecutory object. Further, mutative exchanges took place when he internalized an aspect of me that accepted his sexuality, which acted to modify his persecutory superego and his fear of an angry, jealous father returning to attack him. As these exchanges took place repeatedly over time, he became less frightened of archaic internal figures, less frightened of me and of his fellow humans, and all his relationships and his work noticeably improved over the years, even though his basic feeling towards the world was still one of antipathy.

* * *

The next patient I will discuss is a thirty-five-year-old woman, who has come for five years, four times a week. She is an only child whose mother suffered post-natal depression after her birth, during which time she was cared for by her maternal grandparents. She remembers terrible loneliness during childhood. When she was four, her parent's marriage broke up, and she was passed back and forth between them as they formed relationships with new partners, whom she bitterly resented, feeling jealous, unwanted, and victimized. She became a problem child, to the distress of her parents, refusing to work at school even though she was highly intelligent. In early adulthood, she had a series of unhappy relationships with partners who bullied her and made her miserable; she would go to her parents, complaining and crying, begging to be told what to do, then never doing it. She eventually went to college, then got a good job, but continued to complain bitterly to her parents, making them feel guilty, showing them what failures they were as parents.

In the initial period of the treatment, she responded well to the containment and understanding afforded by the analytic situation; her relationship with her parents and her current boyfriend improved, and she got a better job. Nevertheless, it slowly became apparent that there was an underlying grudge and a wish for revenge on her objects, entailing repetitive, obsessive, omnipotent control and withholding, and, at the same time, clinging, fearing to lose her object. The analysis settled on to a plateau that felt flat and without spontaneity as she maintained sameness and equilibrium, with a feeling of emotional isolation. In relation to me, in the transference there was revenge, resentment, attack, and triumph, all carefully covered up and hidden by submissive, compliant behaviour. Typically, in a quiet, uninflected voice, she would speak briefly, giving a headline relating to something in her life, then pause and move on to the next, usually unrelated, association, only touching on subjects, without going into any depth. When I attempted to engage her, she compliantly went into the issue, but in a sterile, intellectualized way that led nowhere. She was in control. She often cancelled sessions, pushing me aside as she felt pushed aside as a child. She said she liked coming, that she did not want to stop, while I struggled to make emotional contact with her and consistently felt useless, helpless, and unwanted, as she felt unwanted by her parents. When I interpreted from the countertransference, she said she felt guilty and sorry about cancelling sessions and devaluing our work, but nothing really changed. Terrified of object loss, she wanted to keep me, but mostly in order to control me and to torment me by projections of uselessness and inferiority, getting her revenge by secretly triumphing over me (which she often admitted). The violence and chaos of her internal world were confirmed by occasional terrifying dreams.

With so many of her authentic feelings hidden away from me, I was constantly aware in the sessions of how slippery she was, how hard to reach, and, thus, of how important it was to contact her in the here and now. When I interpreted in the transference, particularly in relation to what I sensed as criticism of me, or the analytic work, she would deny these feelings and quickly slip away. Or she would respond, "Oh, you know I think of you as S", who was her hated stepmother, who, according to her accounts, criticized and bullied her ruthlessly as a child. Describing a similar situation, Feldman, in his 1993 paper, "The dynamics of reassurance", writes of patients who are reassured by the repetition of a bad object relationship. Although the quality of their current relationship may be good, they make the object into a more familiar bad one. Feldman writes,

> . . . by evoking the familiar version of a critical and unsupportive parental figure . . . projected in phantasy into (her) representation of (her) analyst. While we might think this created a painful and difficult situation for the patient, (her) actual response in the session seemed actually to make (her) feel comfortable, by restoring a version of an object relationship that was familiar, and over which she felt she had control . . . there was a sense of grievance and blame, with the patient adopting the role of a well-meaning and innocent figure who was being abused . . . with no reference to the possibility of another perspective. [1993, p. 280]

Feldman's account applies to my patient, in the manner in which she projected S into me, and believed I was S, and did not take the perspective that she was with a person who was different from S, who cared about her and thought about her and her life. As long as she thought of me as S, her hated internal object, she was in a repetitive situation from the past and rejected present experience with me that gave her a better experience to internalize, thus modifying the persecutory psychic object.

Joseph, too, is interested in the way in which projective identification is used, writing in her 1988 paper that not only is it used to repeat the past, but also for the purposes of maintaining the patient's narcissistic omnipotent balance. When my patient thought of me as S, she maintained her moral superiority over me, her sense of grievance, and particularly her control of me. When she avoided the relationship between us, she avoided, as Joseph points out, the experience of dependency, anxiety about loss, and the awareness of envy, or guilt.

The material I will discuss followed a session in which I told her that I would be away for a week at the end of the month. Quite unusually for this patient, her equilibrium had been disturbed by this session, in which we had also touched on her "baby feelings". She phoned to cancel the next session, then came in for the next one, in an agitated state, to report how very angry she had been after the last session. When was she going to be better? Why does she still have baby feelings? She was so angry after she left, she told me. I commented that she cancelled the session instead of coming to tell me she felt angry, to which she responded, "I know, I like to play chess with you, to put you in your square, when I don't come."

Then she told me about a blazing row with her boyfriend over the weekend; he had criticized her and called her a bitch and he would not apologize. She shouted and shouted at him, then cried and sobbed, she was so angry. She also told me she felt angry with her supervisor at work, who had criticized her for being out of the office so frequently.

My reflections on this material were around how rarely she was in touch with real emotion, ordinarily rationalized or denied, and, as I expected, when I tried to interpret present anger with me about the break, she said, no, she was going to be away as well, and anyway, I have helped her a lot and she is better in many ways. As for her boyfriend, that's how relationships are, up and down. "Most of the time we are good company, he's very loyal and there's lots of love. He thinks about me all the time." While I was trying to clarify in my mind her present emotional state, and something about whether I will think about her during the break, she said of her supervisor in a choked voice, "I have worked so hard for the company, how dare she?" This last bit she muffled, as if to cancel it out. At this point, I felt connected with the crux of her mental state, which I felt was omnipotent outrage towards her objects that she attempts to stifle, and I responded with, "You do think, how dare she criticize you, someone who works so hard. You feel outraged when I comment on your cancelled session, angry with anyone who questions or disagrees with anything you do." She said, "Do I? I do know they will miss me at work when I leave to go to my new job. My supervisor has said as much, and the others too, that they will feel my absence and feel abandoned." I said that she felt abandoned by the impending break, outraged to feel that she needs me, but blotted it out by saying, it isn't so bad, I have helped her, her boyfriend loves her, and her workmates will miss her, denying what she is feeling in the present moment, cancelling it out, like the session. In response to this, she moved away to a generalization, saying, "I'm angry with everyone at the moment", and spoke of anger with a man at work who had failed to deliver her papers, and anger towards her father, who had let her down in relation to a planned holiday trip.

The next day she began the session by saying she felt angry towards her father for being annoyed with her on the phone the previous night. She had told him about the important business trip she would be going on that would also be somewhat arduous and exhausting. She had thought he would be pleased and proud of her, but instead he had told her off for doing too much. She said, "I felt so furious with him. I get upset and anxious when people have negative thoughts of me." I said, "I'm not sure you know what anyone really feels about you. You don't seem to think he gets worried when you tell him how exhausted you get and now you are going on another long trip. You feel outraged when anyone thinks differently or questions you. You think, how dare he tell off someone who does such important work." She said she felt sheepish when I said that, so it must be true. She tried to notice when she feels egotistical. At this point, I moved forward in my chair to get a tissue, and she said, "I feel attacked; you moved nearer me and I thought you were going to hit me." I waited for what was to come next.

After a pause, she said she felt resentment and envy coming from J and R at work, and that she was running around in an important way trying to get everything done at once, but she did not want to turn down the exciting trip. However, she did feel embarrassed about feeling so important. I interpreted at this point that she felt that I envy her and wanted to attack her and hit her for being so inflated and for being away next week on a trip, missing our sessions. She responded with, "Dad was really cross with me." I said to her that we were speaking of what was happening between us right now, the feeling she had that I was going to hit her, and why did she put the anger into her Dad when she felt I was angry with her. She said, "I know, I feel fear and anger. I experience what you say as an attack. I was angry with K [her boyfriend] on Sunday and I had a right to be. I'm more angry with K than with you." I said that it was hard to tell me how angry she is with me for thinking about her problems rather than praising her for her accomplishments. She responded, to my surprise, by saying she is angry with me for being away for a week at the end of the month, and this sounded genuine. She added that she felt upset and left out lately at work. I said she did not like me being away and felt upset and left out of my life when there was a break. Later in the session, returning to her high self-regard, about which we are learning more and more, she said, "Do I really have such a huge ego?" She then spoke in a more accessible, open way about how going abroad on the important work trip is terrifying, and spoke of a number of things that could go wrong. But she did feel proud of being asked to do it. She did see she is full of herself, and wanted to come and work on this. She saw that what she wants is praise and reassurance, and that she can never get enough of it.

Discussion

The above material represents my struggles to put my two patients in touch with split off, denied, and projected emotional aspects of the transference. With the first patient, I became identified with the dangerous, erotized mother who, along with the demonized father in the destructive parental couple, was part of an Oedipal constellation in which emotional closeness or sexual impulses towards me (or anyone) are dangerous, and will bring on an angry attack from the partner/father. Thus, any potent penetration into my space or my mind evoked anxiety. I felt anxious speaking to this patient about sexual thoughts and penetration: the incipient attraction between us felt real, which made me feel I was breaching an Oedipal boundary, so that I had a sense that I was speaking the forbidden, but numerous repetitions showed that verbalizing his libidinal impulses in the here and now brought relief; that, for him, although action felt imminent, nothing actually happened.

The second patient equated me with her hated stepmother, repeating a familiar past relationship in order to maintain equilibrium, while making me experience the rejection she felt as a child. Her fundamental terror of abandonment brought with it a fear of overt angry feelings towards her objects in the here and now. For this patient, there was the complicating factor of a perverse character development, with an omnipotent self that inflicted rejection on the transference object in revenge for the cruel treatment she felt from her parents, using me for this purpose. The belief she expressed, that I was about to hit her, was, in my view, a fear of retaliation from her hated internal parental object on whom she depended and towards whom she felt anger and outrage. She believed that to approach the brink of anger towards me in the here and now meant that our relationship would disintegrate into mutual rage, physical attack, and rejection. There was anxiety on my part in speaking to her, particularly in view of my very real frustration and irritation about her elusiveness, which echoed her fear that the relationship would come to an end; I felt anxious that she would perform the final rejection and end the analysis before she had sufficiently improved.

For both patients, I represented a terrifying archaic figure at an unconscious level. Here and now interpretations in the transference were attempts to incrementally modify the archaic figure, in the first patient, the dangerous, sexual, Oedipal mother, and in the second, the cruel, abandoning, hated parent figure. Modification took place when the flow of libido or hate towards the transference figure was experienced as occurring at the same time towards an analyst who had good, caring aspects and was essentially a good object.

Thus, in conclusion, the point of interpreting in the here and now is not only to maintain an ongoing contact with the patient, but, most importantly, to link with persecutory archaic figures in the transference to loosen their grip. This happens when the patient can make a distinction between the phantasy object and the real relationship with the analyst, modifying the terror of the internal object world. The aim is that a desirable state will follow in time, when the patient can relate in the present, freely able to move about in his mind without the danger of triggering primitive anxiety, with the ultimate aim of forming ordinary, good object relationships.

References

Feldman, M. (1993). The dynamics of reassurance. *International Journal of Psychoanalysis, 74*: 275–285.

Feldman, M. (1994). Projective identification in phantasy and enactment. *Psychoanalytic Inquiry, 14*: 423–440.

Feldman, M. (1997). Projective identification: the analyst's involvement. *International Journal of Psychoanalysis, 78*: 227–241.

Feldman, M. (2007). The illumination of history. *International Journal of Psychoanalysis, 88*: 609–625.

Joseph, B. (1975). The patient who is difficult to reach. In: E. Bott Spillius (Ed.), *Melanie Klein Today: Developments in Theory and Practice, Volume 2, Mainly Practice* (pp. 48–60). London and New York: Routledge.

Joseph, B. (1988). Projection and projective identification: clinical aspects. In: E. Bott Spillius (Ed.), *Melanie Klein Today: Developments in Theory and Practice, Volume 1, Mainly Theory* (pp. 138–150). London: Karnac.

Klein, M. (1957). Envy and gratitude. In: *The Writings of Melanie Klein, Vol. 3, Envy and Gratitude and Other Works*. London: Hogarth Press, 1975.

Roth, P. (2001). Mapping the landscape: levels of transference interpretation. *International Journal of Psychoanalysis, 82*: 533–543.

Strachey, J. (1934). The nature of the therapeutic action of psychoanalysis. *International Journal of Psychoanalysis, 15*: 127–159 [reprinted (1969) *International Journal of Psychoanalysis, 50*: 275–292].

CHAPTER THREE

Sexuality and the analytic couple

Viqui Rosenberg

> "The darkest place, according to a Chinese proverb, is always underneath the lamp."
>
> (Barthes, 1979, p. 59)

In the *Three Essays on the Theory of Sexuality* (1905d), Freud postulated the centrality of infantile sexuality in the structuring of the human psyche, describing sexuality as a pleasure-seeking instinctual energy. Admittedly, he was expanding the concept of sexuality to define

> a whole range of excitations and activities which may be observed from infancy onwards and which procure a pleasure that cannot be adequately explained in terms of the satisfaction of a basic physiological need (respiration, hunger, excretory function, etc.). [Laplanche & Pontalis, 1985, p. 418]

As it was for Freud's readers then, nowadays we continue to struggle to accept that there is a connection of a sexual nature between the baby nursing at the breast, thumb-sucking, the complex vicissitudes of anality, childhood and adolescent masturbation, and adult sexual life. Many of these activities, being as they are an integral part of universal human experience, are often surrounded by secrecy, apprehension, shame, and even repulsion. Recognition of these early experiences as generating from, and expressing, our sexual life helps us to get the measure of this instinctual force, but this recognition would not be complete without the understanding that sexuality is always curtailed by the necessity to engage with others, and that, retrospectively, we experience sexual excitement from a perspective illuminated by the Oedipal dilemma. That is to say, sexuality is always linked to a sense of loss and absence, and the fantasy of sexual fulfilment inevitably leads to the notion of prohibition and guilt. Furthermore, with the question, "where do I come from?", the child faces the fact that there is a sexual relationship at the beginning of each life (Green, 1995, p. 880; Laplanche, 1999, p. 171) and, with this knowledge, the painful reality of exclusion from that original union.

The specific ways in which the conflict between sexual impulse and the demands of relatedness are negotiated from infancy to adulthood constitute, as well as give shape to, the structure of the psyche, and make human beings human. It is the singular destiny of sexuality to lie at the crossroads where body, fantasy, and emotion meet. This might account for the intensity of sexuality, and perhaps explains why we perceive it as dangerous and potentially explosive: sexuality makes babies, cements intimacy, sparks and maintains love between two people, and inspires creativity. Paradoxically, however, in the pursuit of relatedness, sexuality is—and must be—repressed, even if not ever fully dispensed with. Our lives are devoted to mastering our sexuality, harnessing it, and finding ways of deriving pleasure and satisfaction from it. In the process, the psyche is shaped when—of necessity—we renounce and transform some aspects of this drive, while some others fall into the unconscious as repressed ideas and fantasies. Much of our cultural production attests to the human attempt to shift sexuality from its original physical root into the symbolic realm, and yet a great many cultural artefacts (in literature, visual arts, music, advertising), express and denote that ever-present preoccupation: the pain and the pleasure, and the intense engagement we sustain throughout life with our own sexuality and that of others.

Very early on, Freud (1905d) saw sexuality as rooted in the biological body and obeying the rules of the pleasure principle:

aiming at the discharge of built-up tension, and seeking an object that would enable the fulfilment of this aim. At the same time, he also understood that, at a variance with pure animal instinct, human sexuality was capable of a plasticity that raised it to another plane. Formulating his instinct theory, he used two different words: *Instinkt*, to define a most basic, biological, and over-determined impulse, and *Trieb*, to refer to its more plastic and adaptive aspect. This distinction was not sufficiently emphasized in the English translation, but, nowadays, *drive* has come to be recognized as closer to that second meaning. The British Object Relations School elaborated on the original notion of an *object* (to which the sexual instinct is aimed) as defined both by its exteriority to the subject and by all that it evokes in the subject. That is to say, the human subject has an external as well as an internal relationship with its so-called objects: we perceive the other, but we also fantasize and react internally to the other in ways that transform the *objectivity* of the object. Thus, sexuality becomes *love* when we are able to recognize not only that we have an internal relation with the object of our sexual drive, but also that the object is capable of its own subjectivity. Green (2000) wrote about a process in which "the search for pleasure [is] replaced by that of the [search for the] object", and called this a "programme of domestication" (p. 72). Therefore, when we talk today about human sexuality, we should know that we are drawing a wide circle which can include love, but, at times, does not. Within the psychoanalytic discourse, we are concerned with a definition of sexuality as driven by instinct, affected by the finding of an object, and transformed by fantasy.

French authors developed the concept of *drive* into the notion of *desire*, and, in this way, firmly moved sexuality from the instinctual–biological arena to the strictly human realm. For human beings, the central characteristic of desire is that it can never be fully satisfied, both because the first (maternal) object must perforce be renounced, and also because the new (re-)found love object must be recognized as a subject in its own right. Thus, desire is always inconclusive, and destined to confront us with the inevitability of a vacuum, an impossibility, a gap. This is the process through which desire becomes the key to both pleasure and pain. In this respect, Lacan gave *jouissance*—the English word "excitement" is a poor translation—an important place in the continuum of sexuality from pleasure to pain. The idea of *jouissance* elaborates on Freud's original observation that the symptom offers a secondary gain by providing a source of sexual pleasure. Lacan reminded us that this gain, or gratification, is yet another manifestation of sexuality in search of discharge. As Evans writes,

> The symbolic prohibition of enjoyment in the Oedipus complex (the incest taboo) is thus, paradoxically, the prohibition of something which is already impossible; its function is therefore to sustain the neurotic illusion that enjoyment would be attainable if it were not forbidden. The very prohibition creates the desire to transgress it, and jouissance is therefore fundamentally transgressive. [Evans, 1996, p. 92]

The symptom, we know, represents a compromise—and the need to compromise refers to the unconscious knowledge of impossibility. Furthermore,

> There is an element of horror present in *jouissance* to do with its painful intensity and the impossibility of its full expression or discharge, which places it beyond the pleasure principle and connects it to the death drive. [Levy-Stokes, 2001, p. 101]

We could say that the presence of *jouissance* goes some way towards explaining the resistance that both analysand and analyst experience in recognizing the sexual register in the consulting room.

Just as sexuality operates from the earliest moments as a binding agent in the mother–baby relationship, in the consulting room the analyst also cathects *the idea* of the analysand with a passion that is already in place before he or she actually arrives. Curiosity and excitement— staple companions of sexuality—find expression in the analytic vocation. The care invested in the setting, the quality of listening, the reliability of the analyst—all these elements enhance a process that simultaneously mobilizes and erodes repression in the analysand, and contribute to the emergence of sexual feelings. Moreover, it is precisely the state of "helplessness" (Freud, 1926d) evoked by the analytic situation that becomes a key referent to the original state of complete dependency, where the omnipotent mother has everything that the baby needs in order to survive. Describing that nursing paradigm, Kohon wrote,

> The importance of this first experience of satisfaction (which will determine all future experiences of pleasure) resides in the fact that the hallucinatory process does not deny reality. Just the opposite, it helps to recognise the existence of a reality outside the self, different from it, which needs to be found. [Kohon, 2005, p. 65]

In much the same way, the analytic setting fosters the emergence of hallucinatory experiences, and recreates instances of the initial formation of the analysand's psyche, but this time orientated towards the person of the analyst. Laplanche (1992) drew a parallel between the *scene of seduction*, defined by the fact that the mother cannot but seduce her baby with the care that she takes of his or her body, and the analytic relationship. He did not believe that the *primal scene* could be comfortably thought about as a *primal phantasy*, which would imply that this is principally an innate notion, and he postulated that the actual fact of the parents' sexuality is integral to what the infant receives in its engagement with them, and that this early dynamic is reproduced in the analytic relationship. In the analysis, both parties invest, in varying degrees, a sexual charge in what is about to happen—in what begins to happen even before an actual encounter takes place. The analyst's role elicits regression and dependency in the analysand, while the analysand as an idea evokes the maternal function in the mind of the analyst.

Can, however, the maternal function legitimately be located within the parameters of sexuality? Perhaps to answer this question, we need to return sexuality to its instinctual cradle, governed by the pleasure-seeking principle. Although there is a risk here of equating sexuality with instinct (Eros), this admittedly wide definition might help to open up and facilitate an exploration of sexuality in the transference. Alternatively, too narrow a definition can harbour a reductionist approach, where every manifestation of sexuality is understood as either perversion or regression, thereby doing away with the notion of ordinary sexuality in the analytic transaction. From the wider instinctual perspective, we might not find it impossible to recognize the sexual impulse that turns a woman into a mother, since becoming pregnant and giving birth are both rooted in the instinctual body, and they both represent an attempt to satisfy a desire that, as is the case in the nature of desire, cannot be fully satisfied. It is not pertinent to include in this discussion the complexity and ambivalence that surround these processes, being, as they are, not just guided by instinct, but also inserted in relational and cultural dimensions. But even then, maternal love, shaped by adaptation, identification, and mirroring, becomes invested with all the passion that a lover would elicit. It would be true to say that the mother–baby relationship can be singled out—within the rules that govern the sexual instinct—as one where the orientation towards the object acquires a very large significance, measured against the original aim of discharge. No doubt, mothers are in love with their children, but once the child is perceived as *another*, with its own needs and desires, the erotic charge of this love is curtailed and transformed.

During the analytic process, the need of the analysand and the desire of the analyst lock together, and, although much has been written about the dependency of the analysand on the analyst and on the process of analysis, the desire of the analyst appears more elusive and understated in the literature. The analyst's desire is coloured by a number of overlapping aims: embarking once again on the analytic journey, giving shape to professional creativity, earning a living, to name just a few. At a certain level, the person of the analysand will embody a promise of fulfilment of these aims, and, at the same time, the analyst knows that there is an illusory dimension hidden in this promise. The analyst is not the mother and the analysand is not the baby, and this—only retrospectively—idyllic evocation is kept in check by the tension between two facts: that there are two adults in the room and that, like the mother previously, the analyst is required to curtail her own desire. The analytic role demands a constant monitoring in order to ascertain whose sexuality is on the ascendance in the transference. Need and desire emanating from the analysand will take turns to lure the analyst, but the analytic dyad is also exposed to the forces of seduction that each has the power to generate.

Discussing the question of the feminine, Green (2000) concluded that it is the maternal, rather than the feminine, that ultimately results in repudiation from both men and women alike; the passion and enticement that exist between mother and baby will, in due time, give way to Oedipal prohibition, and to the ensuing fears of rejection and castration, which pertain to both sexes. Thus, the analyst's actual gender is not pertinent to the maternal function that is elicited by the analytic setting. The analyst as a sexual object is both elected and circumstantial, but always over-determined by these other factors that gradually come into focus with all the weight of the developing transference. In this way, the full gamut of sexual feelings will unfold in the consulting room, and the style in which they are dealt with, acknowledged, interpreted, or ignored, will open different gates along the journey.

For the female analysand, the analytic setting offers an alluring situation for the recreation of a primitive fantasy: erotic feelings towards the mother, renounced during the Oedipal phase, come to the fore, fostered by the attention of the analyst. It could be said that the female analysand is given an opportunity to surrender to the analyst's passion for mothering. In fantasy, the analysis creates a second chance to skip the always hard and incomplete labour of acquiring a feminine identity, which is achieved through the renunciation of the mother as the object of desire. If the analyst is male, this could be all the better, since the woman would have found an object that could fulfil the pre-Oedipal maternal function without putting into question her adult heterosexual identity. When the analyst is female, there is a temptation in both parties to "regress" the interpretation of the erotic transference, which is indeed already regressive, to an exclusive understanding of it as a mother–baby dependency. And yet, is not regression an element present in all forms of adult sexuality? To what extent, therefore, when the female analyst interprets this transference as pure infantile longing, is she adopting a defensive attitude, thus denying her analysand's and her own adult (homo)sexuality?

The male analysand also faces a sexually provocative situation. In fantasy, the analysis recreates a two-person relationship where he can possess the mother/analyst. However, the balance of power, which often seems to have a bigger impact on the male, may lead to deeper ambivalence and greater anxiety as to whether he should expect to be loved or castrated by his analyst. The perverse solution here is to unleash sexuality in a hostile and controlling manner, to flood the analysis with sexualized and aggressive fantasies—or behaviour—in an attempt to immobilize the threatening figure of the analyst. This, however, is by no means the only possible development, as I will discuss later while following the vicissitudes of one analytic journey. Equivalent dynamics, as they unfold between a male analyst and his male analysand, are not part of this writer's experience.

Awareness and understanding of the sexual register is central to the development of the transference, yet its interpretation often appears dangerous to both patient and analyst, as if verbalization would risk a scene of seduction, thus turning the metaphor of language into concrete enactment. Laplanche and Pontalis stated that ". . . human sexuality, with the peculiar unevenness of its temporal development, provides an eminently suitable field for the phenomenon of deferred action (nachträglich)" (1985, p. 112).

They wrote that, in hysteria, the early seduction scene is initially repressed and then resurrected when, due to the process of maturation, it can be credited with its relevant sexual significance. It is possible that this process does not only take place in the mind of the hysteric, but that it inevitably unfolds in the analytic milieu, as the analysand becomes able to bring back from repression the sexual feelings from early childhood. The emotions that emerge towards the person of the analyst are both regressive, in as much as they are a repetition from the past, and actual, in as much as they can only be sexually charged as a consequence of the maturational process that turns the infant into an adult. As repression becomes eroded by the analytic process, sexuality is once more in search of an object.

Clinical illustrations

I shall now give two brief, and one fuller, clinical illustrations. As is well known, each analysand experiences a variety of complex responses in anticipation of a break, ranging from feelings of hostility and fear of breaking down to a sense of relief and liberation. Once treatment is established, the stability of the setting, and even the regularity and shape of expected holiday breaks, contribute to the frame and help to create a container for infantile dependency. However, a break taken out of step with established routines has an impact on the analysand at a more acute level, and can become a reminder of the lack of control over the analyst. In these two accounts, the analyst's announcement unearthed the ever-painful notion of a third party, rekindling the Oedipus complex and provoking an upsurge of the analysand's desire.

Mr O

Mr O initially reacts with some indifference to my telling him that I plan to take a week off, but, later on in the session, proceeds to tell me that he will be missing the following week's sessions due to a business trip. A few minutes later, he realizes that his business trip is not the next week, but, rather, two weeks on (neither of these weeks actually coincides with mine). Although Mr O agrees that, following my announcement, he now wants to retaliate and leave me behind as soon as possible, he still drops into one of his dark and silent moods, and for the rest of the week cold and dismissive remarks keep me at a distance. Meanwhile, I observe in myself feelings akin to those of the unfaithful lover, experiencing my week away as an open betrayal for which I actually deserve to be punished. Mr O's hostile distance is coated in a self-righteous conviction that I am in the wrong, that I have no right to disrupt our well-established routine, and, more importantly, that I have no right to remind him that I am not entirely his own. The idea of this unexpected break resonates with him at an Oedipal level (whether this is pitched at the level of his discovery of the primal scene, or perhaps the birth of his younger brother, we are still to discover), but it is as a jealous lover that he tries—and, for moments, manages—to impose his will over mine. He is not an analysand who over-sexualizes the transference; neither is he particularly unhappy in his emotional attachments. His analysis has tended to progress in a fruitful way, and there is normally a working alliance between us. What we can now see, however, is the way in which Mr O's sexuality in the transference has gathered around an undisturbed analytic frame that feeds his illusion of having a special and exclusive relationship with me, an illusion brutally fractured by my unpredictable act. It is only as I become aware of my own sense of having betrayed him that I gain awareness of the sexual element in this transaction, operating in a mute way. It is then that it becomes possible to interpret his possessive and jealous hostility.

Mrs A

When I tell Mrs A that I will be away for a week which is outside our familiar and established routine, she tells me that by now, four years into her analysis, she is used to the interruptions afforded by my regular holidays, but that she finds this extra week difficult to accept. Mrs A begins the following week by telling me that she has calmed down during the weekend. "Last week I went a bit mad", she says. During the weekend she lost her mobile phone and felt "disconnected and homeless". I reply that my announcement the previous Monday also made her feel disconnected and homeless. She says that my week off has been very much in her mind. She then reiterates that while she can cope with ordinary breaks, this extra one produces feelings of hate in her. She tells me that she feels betrayed. Mrs A is surprised by the intensity of her reaction; she feels vengeful and she hears herself wondering, "What's the point?" With difficulty, she locates a vivid physical sensation: she wants to pound on my chest, and she is filled with an "all or nothing" feeling that she finds very painful. I say that last week she had wanted to spare me her anger, and she had also wanted to spare herself from the awareness of the passionate feelings she harbours towards me. Later on, she recalls a situation at the weekend, during a large extended family outing, where she suddenly became aware of her parents' wish to spend time alone with each other. This is significant given that, from an early age, Mrs A always believed that she enjoyed an exclusive relationship with each of her feuding parents. The announcement of my short break has shaken her to the core because it makes her fully aware that she is not on her own with me, that there is a "third" between us. Mrs A's desire to pound on my chest conjures up an image where she attacks me while still needing to be firmly held by me. This gives shape to the idea that she could be cradled by the same arms she wants to attack. I think her reaction is fed both by infantile rage and sexual passion. Later on in the session, Mrs A says that perhaps she does not know what the difference between being a man and a woman really is—signalling the opening of new insights into the complexities of her sexuality. In her childhood, Mrs A's exclusive and secret relationship with each of her parents created the feeling in her that she provided both with what she thought they could not find in each other. Her response, when my announcement came to disturb her fantasy of our exclusive and mutually beneficial alliance, illustrates this bisexual transference dynamic: at once lover–mother and lover–father, I hold her in my arms while she gives vent to her Oedipal rage by pounding on my breast–chest—confused in her own mind as to which of us is a man and which a woman, and who is holding whom.

* * *

The following case, cited elsewhere (Rosenberg, 1999), follows in greater detail the presence of sexuality in the transference–countertransference relationship.

Mr S

After six years of analysis, Mr S was no longer trapped in the deep feelings of depression that for many years had kept him in bed when he should have been at work, had made his family life tense and disconnected, and his professional life unfulfilling. His depression had been characterized by anger and withdrawal, which, in the course of treatment, we gradually came to understand as concrete manifestations of mechanisms of repression. Mr S's strictly religious upbringing, being the first child of a frightening, authoritarian father and a very submissive mother, had resulted in his marrying very young. The emotional neglect that he experienced as a child could have led to high levels of auto-erotic activity in an attempt to find some comfort in his own body, but instead a strong identification with his father's superego prevailed, and he kept his sexuality in check with an iron grip. As a result, his very limited sexual experience did not develop significantly during his marriage. Against this background, Mr S had experienced the intimacy of the analytic relationship as a form of idealized platonic sexual intercourse. Because of this erotization, Mr S could hardly ever discuss his very sparse sexual life, be it actual or fantasized. Yet, I came to feel that his masculinity was expressed in the characteristic way in which he made me aware of his presence while waiting to be fetched from the waiting room. He would be standing directly facing the door of my room while vigorously wiping his feet on the mat, the menacing noise that could be heard from the other side of the door reminding me of a spirited horse about to mount his mare.

After the first couple of years, during which his sulky silences and agonizing anxiety were often interpreted in terms of the violence and explosion that he expected to result from our coming together as an analytic couple, Mr S began to feel sufficiently trusting to show some of his potency. In the process, he discovered that he was a fine artist, a keen swimmer, an accomplished cook—and very good at his job. He also became able to get hold of, and to share with me, the manifestations of his own unconscious, such as his dreams and his fleeting thoughts. It appeared as if, in the safety of the consulting room, the desire of his analyst had enabled Mr S to find in himself the personal qualities that made him lovable. I believe that my own desire to create an analytic subject, to witness and to appreciate his capacities, and to avoid colluding with his harsh superego, gradually allowed him to acquire a sense of himself as a potent man. As it became established, this identity began to expand into his relationship to his children and wife, as well as manifesting itself in steady professional progress. In the transference, his growing capacities developed hand in hand with a diminution of his idealization of the analyst, seeming to make a man out of him, and a more ordinary woman out of his previously seemingly all powerful analyst. One enabling element of this treatment was the offer of a space where he could play, both *in* my presence (Winnicott, 1971) and *with* my presence, represented by the "feet on the mat" ritual—which was never directly interpreted. Another was a "passivation" dynamic where—like that of a helpless infant—Mr S's sexuality had initially been engaged in the transference by quietly enjoying my attention from a position comparable to that of a small baby receiving his mother's loving care while only equipped to respond at the level of hallucinatory fantasy. Green described this process: ". . . the analytic cure is not possible without this confident passivation, where the analysand gives himself to the analyst's care" (1986, p. 248). Equally, I believe that it was essential to the development of the treatment to transcend this stage and to be ready to recognize the moment in which passivation would become hostile or sexualized passivity.

As the notion of ending became a reality, and a date was eventually mutually agreed, Mr S returned to his initial stance, remaining almost completely silent for many weeks. But this time, as well as conveying a feeling of great pain, perhaps mourning the end of our work together but unable to express his sadness, there was a sexually hostile charge in the fabric of his demeanour. In this instance, I refrained from taking an active part in guessing or giving meaning to his silence, and when he finally began to speak again he said that, although the decision to end the analysis had been very much his own, he could not believe that I would let him go. He added that he needed to know my "opinion" about the ending. I centred my interpretations on the idea that what he needed to know was what my feelings for him were. In turn, this led to his own realization that he had harboured the fantasy that at the end of the analysis we would at last become lovers. My agreeing an ending date had made him realize that this was just a fantasy. Once Mr S was able verbally to articulate this insight, it became clear to him that, at a different level, he had never really expected to become my lover. For myself, I saw this fantasy as representing a shift from passivation to sexual genitality. During the following weeks I largely listened and accompanied Mr S in his grief, perhaps returning to the quiet position I had adopted at the beginning of his analysis. It seemed to me that his sadness was beyond interpretation once he had discovered the impossibility of his desire, and that it was important to respond in such a way that would avoid both seduction or presumed rejection of his adult sexuality. By the time the ending date arrived, Mr S had gained full ownership of his decision to end, and he was becoming aware of an anxiety that he might soon return to the same depressed state that had originally brought him into analysis. I understood this concern as indicative of an abatement of his erotic transference and recognition of what I had truly been to him: a helpful vehicle in the journey towards understanding his suffering and achieving more of his potential. Interestingly, Mr S had also begun to make plans as to how he would use the money he would soon be saving in analytic fees. Over the years he has periodically written to let me know about his life, where depression seems to have ceased to be a feature.

Described in a different way, this was the analysis of a man paralyzed by the inhibition of his vitality. Longing and dependency were soon elicited in the transference and manifested in the form of sexual feelings and fantasies. Mr S seemed to be conscious of his feelings towards me (the repression of his sexuality having become eroded), but possibly hoped that these feelings could remain concealed in order to avoid shame and humiliation, and also because of the gratification that they afforded. In the countertransference, his sexualization (conscious and unconscious) was evident, and yet it did not feel productive to interpret it. My concern was that interpretation would repeat a trauma and force his sexual drive into further repression. I also felt that there would have been a risk that any interpretation—the actual naming of his sexual feelings—would be sexualized by him, and experienced as a seductive gesture from the analyst. I thought of Mr S's sexual strivings as infantile and tinted by perversion. That is to say, there seemed to be a child inside him who was longing to possess and devour me, but there was also a man who was concealing his feelings while making me responsible for them. In this concealment lay a sense of threat and hostility that was later present in his silence. For a very long time, it seemed impossible to interpret this dynamic without forcing the nascent awareness of his sexuality into retreat. As it was, I was allowing the analysis to coexist with his private fantasy that he was in a sexual relationship with me. And yet, it was during this period that his sense of aliveness and subsequent confidence in himself grew, permeating his marriage, his relationship to his children, and his professional development.

Mr S's initiative to end his analysis probably emerged from a sense that he was now feeling closer to becoming a grown, fully alive, man. He might have fantasized that he was now ready to elicit my desire, and when he finally approached me with the idea of "arranging a date", in fantasy he was, in fact, "proposing" to me. This is the moment where two parallel lines met and, by my saying "yes", I said "no". I confirmed that I was his analyst and not his bride: I was prepared to let him go. However, he was now ready to experience this rejection as a man, and not as a baby. Because of this, he did not retreat into repression with its habitually castrating inhibition; instead, he was forced to mourn the impossibility of his desire, and he entered this process in my presence, using me as an analyst, before and after the completion of our work together.

Instinctual drives were, in this case, manifested in the transference as powerful sexual feelings, even though these originated in infantile need. As is always the case, adult and infantile sexuality could not easily be disentangled, and Mr S felt compelled to conceal both. I am reminded of the game of hide-and-seek that a young toddler plays with his mother, where she is not supposed to see him when he covers his eyes. By my not impinging with interpretations of his sexual feelings, Mr S was able to become less afraid and to tolerate his own emotions; by the time I told him what I could see, he had grown to have a life and a sexuality of his own. Perhaps I am saying here that attention to sexuality does not automatically mean interpretation, but that it requires careful following of the countertransference, and that to neglect this dimension is to neglect another royal road to the unconscious. The sexuality of the analyst (engaged as it is in the analysis) will tempt us to make premature interpretations (in order to freeze it in the room) or omit them (for fear of seduction), or turn a blind eye and overlook our analysands' instinctual drives. Here, timing is of the essence.

I now believe that a very important therapeutic factor in this analysis was my initial restraint in interpreting the most obvious manifestations of the erotic transference. It is possible that interpretations of his sexual feelings—often present in the dream material—would have been experienced by his immature ego as sexual invitations on my part. I did not take this position without hesitation, at times wondering whether, by not interpreting, I was actively colluding and perhaps encouraging the "lovers" fantasy. Retrospectively, I think that this restraint helped to prevent further sexual repression, which would have instituted the analysis—and myself within it—as a castrating agent bent on reproducing his original trauma. Noticeably, it was during the very last stages here described that transference interpretations that openly included the erotic were instrumental in allowing Mr S to leave, to mourn, and to maintain his gains.

* * *

The case of Mr S, especially, poses the question of when and how to acknowledge the presence of the sexual. It has been suggested that interpretation of this form of transference is less likely to be experienced as seduction if the analyst feels contained within a "couple" (Halton, 2006); that is to say, if the interpretation is offered from a position of thirdness, where the analyst feels confidently "married" to a psychoanalytic stance. However, the sexual instinct can never be fully confined or controlled by consciousness, and this may explain why the presence of sexual feelings is often interpreted as an attack on the analysis, or else considered exclusively as infantile longings. Difficulties in the countertransference may result in sexual manifestations being interpreted too soon, and, thus, forced into repression, or else being denied or negated. Green (1986) once lamented how often clinical material is presented where the sexual is not heard about. He wrote that the clinician defends against the sexual by deeming it to cover "deeper meaning"—such as more regressive or else aggressive strivings—and, thus, proceeds to interpret "primal anxieties of a destructive character" (p. 27).

The analyst fears to mark the transference with her own sexual feelings and fantasies. Laplanche (1999), formulating his "seduction theory", locates the inevitability of seduction between mother and baby and describes it as the "presence of a sexual fantasy in the adult" (p. 169). Paradoxically, however, in the countertransference it is the adult sexuality of the analysand that threatens the infantile sexuality of the analyst. Thus, unrecognized sexuality gives way to enactments, as, for example, the emergence of an unconsciously collusive alliance in the repudiation of an analysand's sexual partner, or vicarious and blinding gratification derived by the analyst from the achievements of a successful analysand. Perhaps inevitably, as aspects of the analyst's libido find expression in her work, the analysand has the potential to represent the adored baby, the exciting lover, and the phallus itself. Meanwhile, projective mechanisms in the analysand would, of necessity, pitch for those aspects of the analyst that are beyond consciousness and susceptible to engaging with the analysand's sexuality. Laplanche (*ibid.*) described the "irreducibility of communication" that creates a message that is "opaque to its recipient and its transmitter alike". In these muddy waters, the analyst is wary of interpreting the erotic for fear of articulating what might, in fact, turn out to be her own sexuality.

It is not surprising to conclude that there is fluidity in this field that is hard to pin down. Sexuality is in the fabric of the analytic relationship, and it belongs with both parties. It moves from the most infantile and vulnerable state of need to the reckless and the perverse. Pleasure seeking is at times joined by the wish to control, dominate, or destroy. The analyst needs to contend not only with the analysand's blind sexuality, but also with the avatars of her own infantile needs and adult desires. Interpretation is, therefore, difficult to produce, formulate, and time. Furthermore, within this particular register, the wrong interpretation—or the wrong moment—can change the level of the analyst's utterance from metaphor to seduction. Thus, the sexual register easily remains unnamed and often unthought. The naming of it is a question of technique—not within the scope of this paper—but the thinking is vital. I am suggesting here that to recognize the significance of sexuality in the analytic relationship enables us to understand at a greater depth, and offers a singularly direct line into what is most primitive, intimate, and real in each person. I have deliberately avoided in my discussion specific instances of perversions, sado-masochistic phenomena, and other pathological sexual presentations with their ensuing transferences. This decision was based on the idea that to discuss more extreme formations would have reinforced the belief that sexuality, as it presents in every analysis, does not require all of our attention. If, however, we are lulled by the impression that there is an absence of sexual charge in our interactions, it is only because, as the Chinese proverb says: "the darkest place is always underneath the lamp".

References

Barthes, R. (1979). *A Lover's Discourse: Fragments*. New York: Hills & Wang.

Evans, D. (1996). *An Introductory Dictionary of Lacanian Psychoanalysis*. London: Routledge.

Freud, S. (1905d). *Three Essays on the Theory of Sexuality. S.E., 7*: 1–230. London: Hogarth.

Freud, S. (1926d). *Inhibitions, Symptoms and Anxiety. S.E., 20*: 75–172. London: Hogarth.

Green, A. (1986). *On Private Madness*. London: Hogarth Press & The Institute of Psychoanalysis.

Green, A. (1995). Has sexuality anything to do with psychoanalysis? *International Journal of Psychoanalysis, 76*: 871–883.

Green, A. (2000). *Chain of Eros* (Editions Odile Jacob, 1997). London: Rebus Press.

Halton, M. (2006). Personal communication.

Kohon, G. (2005). Love in a time of madness. In: A. Green & G. Kohon (Eds.), *Love and its Vicissitudes* (pp. 43–100). London: Routledge.

Laplanche, J. (1992). *Seduction, Translation, Drives*. London: Institute of Contemporary Arts.

Laplanche, J. (1999). *Essays on Otherness*. London: Routledge.

Laplanche, J., & Pontalis, J.-B. (1985). *The Language of Psycho-Analysis*. London: Hogarth [republished London: Karnac, 1988].

Levy-Stokes, C. (2001). Jouissance. In: H. Glowinski, Z. Marks, & S. Murphy (Eds.), *A Compendium of Lacanian Terms* (pp. 101–109). London: Free Association Books.

Rosenberg, V. (1999). Erotic transference and its vicissitudes in the countertransference. In: S. Johnson & S. Ruszczynski (Eds), *Psychoanalytic Psychotherapy in the Independent Tradition* (pp. 133–149). London: Karnac.

Winnicott, D. W. (1971). Playing: a theoretical statement. In: D. W. Winnicott (Ed.), *Playing and Reality* (pp. 51–70). London: Routledge, 2005.

CHAPTER FOUR

From Hades to Oedipus: from psychotic to erotic transference and beyond

Irene Freeden

Erotic transference or erotization?

Anna O's erotic transference terrified Breuer in 1882 and caused him to flee. However, her case, and four other cases of Freud's first psychoanalytic patients, enabled the founder of psychoanalysis to discover the meaning of erotic transference, although at the time he believed that it was a formidable obstacle to treatment.

> Transference on to the physician takes place through a *false connection*. I must give an example of this. In one of my patients the origin of a particular hysterical symptom lay in a wish, which she had had many years earlier and had at once relegated to the unconscious, that the man she was talking to at the time might boldly take the initiative and give her a kiss. On one occasion, at the end of a session, a similar wish came up in her about me. [1895d, pp. 302–303]

Twenty years later, Freud distinguished between patients whose erotic transference could be used as a psychoanalytic tool leading to a resolution of the Oedipus conflict and those whose treatment, he believed, had to be curtailed.

> There is, it is true, one class of women with whom this attempt to preserve the erotic transference for the purposes of analytic work without satisfying it will not succeed. These are women of elemental passionateness who tolerate no surrogates. . . . One has to withdraw, unsuccessful; and all one can do is to turn the problem over in one's mind of how it is that a capacity for neurosis is joined with such intractable need for love. [1915a, pp. 166–167).

Many early analysts, for example, Bibring (1936) and Alexander (1950), concurred that such patients are unanalysable.

This chapter explores the differences between the analysable erotic transference and the more complicated psychotic erotization, for which Meltzer's (1992) concept of the Claustrum is particularly helpful. Although there is a general consensus that erotization is a defence against engagement in the psychoanalytic process, ways have been found to work with such patients despite the difficulties, mainly through closer, detailed observation of the relationship between transference and countertransference. Bolognini (1994) accurately observes that whereas erotic transference may engage the analyst's sexual awareness, the experience of erotized transference in countertransference is one of impatience and irritation. I would add anger, distaste, and even revulsion, and, when carefully internally explored, it allows the analyst to understand the patient's hate and aggression towards the object who dares to be separate and uncontrollable by the part of the self that seeks fusion.

Blitzsten (1956) was the first to coin the new terminology in a personal unpublished communication to Rappaport:

> In a[n erotic] transference the analyst is seen *as if* he were the parent, while in erotization of the transference *he is* the parent. The patient does not even acknowledge the *as if*. In the transference, therefore, something takes place between patient and analyst similar to the archaic situation, while in an erotized transference the patient insists on reinstituting the archaic situation itself and refuses to tolerate any deviation from it. [Rappaport, 1956, p. 515]

Freud knew the difference when he suggested that "They are children of nature who refuse to accept the psychical in the place of the material" (Freud, 1915a, p. 167). Those patients have no capacity for symbol formation and cannot accept the analytic situation as a metaphor for the primary relationship. Their mental functioning is often referred to as "concrete".

If a patient lacks the capacity for symbol formation, the analyst is not performing a maternal function, but she/he *is* the patient's mother. Unconsciously, the patient believes not only that the analyst is the mother, but he also has a phantasy of fusion between the infant and the mother. A separation between them would face the patient with the suffering of envy and/or loss, and both are strongly resisted. Separateness is experienced as "a dread of imminent annihilation" (Bion, 1957). In order to avoid the terror of abandonment and therefore disintegration (a consequence of the disappearance of the container), the infant uses the mechanism of massive projective identification. Klein (1946) stresses that the main motive is intrusion to become one with the object to avoid separateness, with evacuation and omnipotence playing a role. Bion (1962) develops the concept further to include the motive of communication. Excessive (or massive) projective identification denies the differentiation between the self and the object (thus resulting in a denial of external and psychic reality) and further interferes with the development of the capacity for symbol formation. Instead, the concrete mental functioning operates on the basis of symbolic equation (Segal, 1957, 1996).

Rosenfeld (1971a) re-emphasizes the use of projective identification for purposes of evacuation used for the denial of psychic reality. Driven mainly by envy, projective identification is the main vehicle of the destructive narcissistic personality highly organized like a "gang" in order to wage war on the analyst and protect the patient from the attachment-seeking and life-enhancing parts of the self. Any attempt at emotional contact with an object tantalizes the "gang" with further evidence of separateness that in turn intensifies the envy. Erotization of the aggression increases its power and violence. This type of projective identification is at the core of Meltzer's claustrum. Rosenfeld (1971b) proceeds to identify a third use that he terms "parasitical projective identification". This type of projective identification plays a fundamental part in the model of Steiner's *Psychic Retreats* (1993), though it is also present in the claustrum. Its aim is that of omnipotent control of the object's body and mind, which involves a phantasy of concretely entering inside the internalized analyst/mother. This type of intrusion, motivated by a desire to avoid envy, dependency, and separation anxiety, is accomplished silently and passively. The patient creates a parasitic existence experienced as a state of paradise, reaping the benefits of the labours of the host. It is, however, a passive, mindless state, and if and when the patient feels trapped, it becomes persecutory. The perception of imprisonment induces the terror of losing the self due to excessive evacuation into the object; hence, it produces violent rage and a "self-preservative" attack on the object. Glasser (1979) refers to this phenomenon as the "core complex", and Rey (1994) as the "claustro-agoraphobic" dilemma.

Meltzer's "The relation of anal masturbation to projective identification" (1966) focuses on the intrusive aspect of projective identification with internal objects, which can promote a narcissistic organization. He describes how, as a result of the dread of abandonment or overwhelming greed and envy, an infant may "comfort" itself with anal masturbation; this results in over-idealization of the rectum and its contents. In adulthood, such "anal character types" (as described by Freud) are obsessive, stubborn, stingy, shallow, and pseudo-mature. It is hard for the analyst to gather the infantile transference of the patient against these defences, which can include self-idealization and the delusion of self-sufficiency.

Psychic retreats and the claustrum

Steiner (1993) proposes the term "psychic retreats" for states of mind created by a powerful system of defences in which the patients are unavailable for contact with the analyst. An emotional contact with the analyst is, by definition, accompanied by anxiety and pain of separateness and the "psychic retreat" is experienced as a refuge. The retreat is most often an idealized haven, but even when it is experienced as cruel and persecutory it is clung to, believed to be preferable to a dreaded unknown alternative. The patient feels free from anxiety generated by contact with external reality (which includes the analyst) at the price of developmental stagnation. Some patients cling to a retreat to "protect" themselves from the terror of fragmentation and persecution, while others seek refuge from depressive pain. Steiner sees the retreat as a "borderline position" (not to be confused with the diagnosis of a borderline personality), out of reach from either of the two basic positions (paranoid–schizoid or depressive). In this "borderline position" the patient can, perversely, simultaneously pseudo-accept and deny reality.

> It is clear that a psychic retreat can be conceptualized in a variety of different ways. First, it can be viewed spatially as an area of safety to which the patient withdraws, and second, this area can be seen to depend on the operation of a pathological organization of the personality. The organization itself can be seen as a structured system of defences and also as a tightly organized network of object relations. The retreat may also be usefully related to the paranoid–schizoid and depressive positions and can then be seen to function as a third position to which the patient can withdraw from the anxieties of either of the former. Finally, the perverse nature of the retreat can be viewed from the point of view of the patient's relationship with reality on the one hand and in terms of the sado-masochistic type of object relationships found, on the other. [*ibid.*, p. 13]

The fundamental difference between Steiner's concept of psychic retreats and Meltzer's (1992) claustrum lies in the quality of projective identification. Steiner's retreats are primarily understood as an almost benign sanctuary and safe haven, places of refuge from a threat of intimacy. They ". . . appear as spaces inside objects or part-objects. There may be phantasies of retreating to the mother's womb, anus or breast, sometimes experienced as a desirable but forbidden place" (*ibid.*, p. 8). They are, however, metaphorical, even though described in concrete terms above. Meltzer's concept of intrusive projective identification into internal objects highlights the omnipotent–identificatory and projective–claustrophobic aspects, and the concreteness of psychic reality. It has an overwhelming quality: visceral and powerful in its primitive totality. I believe that the difference between Steiner's and Meltzer's concepts lies in the extent to which the personality engages in the retreat into projective identification. Reading the texts, it appears as if Steiner's patients retreat to protect an aspect of their experience that they value, such as freedom from an emotional contact, whereas the impulse of Meltzer's patients to intrude is predominantly one of envy and hate and a compulsion to control the object. Meltzer's understanding is more closely linked with the observation of pathologically destructive and perverse narcissistic organizations and is firmly rooted in Klein's concept of the concreteness of the unconscious (e.g., Klein, 1930). There is no capacity for symbol formation in the claustrum and it is firmly ensconced in the paranoid–schizoid position.

Meltzer (1992) proposes in *The Claustrum* that when the epistemophilic instinct is motivated by envy and jealousy, coupled with a trauma of abandonment, the infantile part of the personality can masturbate its way unconsciously into any portal of entry into the maternal object (anus, genitals, eyes, ears, nose, mouth, skin). When projected into the analyst, such unconscious phantasy is powerful and can be experienced by the analyst as accomplished by more or less violent means. This is a device of intrusive projective identification (conscious masturbation serves only as an "exciting" camouflage). The sense of identity then becomes a fixed infantile part of the personality, entrenched in the maternal (internal) object; its character depends on the portal of entry, which hints at the nature of the compartment.

Meltzer defines three main compartments: the head–breast, the genitals, and the rectum. The people residing in the *head–breast* are: ". . . the self-styled genius, the critic, the connoisseur, the aesthete, the professional beauty, the know it all . . . intolerant of criticism and deeply uneducable, in that they cannot bear teachers . . ." (1992, p. 73). This is an intellectualized, superior, arrogant, "Proustian" world. However, it can also present on the couch as an indolent, mindless, vacuous, parasitic, "Oblomovian" world. These two states of mind are characterized by an omniscience termed by Meltzer the "delusion of clarity of insight". The *genital* compartment is a brothel of endless orgiastic, priapic worship with no generational or gender boundaries. They all revel in Oedipal triumph. Patients seen in the "Oblomovian" head–breast and the genital compartments seem to be mainly sensuous, unthinking, sometimes presenting almost as a "body-ego". The compartment of the *rectum* is described by Meltzer at its best as a boarding school, and at its worst as a concentration camp, where dog eats dog, and all relationships are of a calculating and mercantile, sado-masochistic nature. Physical survival is the ultimate aim and the culture is one of sado-masochism. It is a world where

> Truth is transformed into anything that cannot be disproved; justice becomes talion plus an increment; all the acts of intimacy change their meaning into techniques of manipulation or dissimulation; loyalty replaces devotion; obedience substitutes for trust; emotion is simulated by excitement; guilt and the yearning for punishment takes the place of regret. [*ibid.*, p. 92]

Patients in all three compartments seem to lack the concept of time. Time is perceived as circular (masturbatory), like a computer game.

The claustrum and its compartments serve the defensive function of retreat. Each compartment has its own "social system" controlling the threat of expulsion—up or down—and the most terrifying is the phantasy of the expulsion from the rectum into a void of the unknown. The state of mind is one of claustrophobia and persecution. These patients unconsciously know that they are interlopers; they often experience themselves as living precariously. As they tenaciously cling to the claustrum, they are very difficult to reach, though the analyst can observe the movement from one compartment to another. Located in the head–breast the patient appears mindlessly grandiose; in the genital compartment he/she displays perverse erotization, and in the rectum there is predominantly sado-masochism and paranoia. All are dedicated to an attack on truth and are characterized by −L, −H, and −K (in the Ψ column of the grid, Bion, 1963), producing a claustrophobic sense of being closed in and presenting a particular challenge to the psychoanalytic method due to a remarkable lack of ordinary infantile transference (which requires at least a minimal sense of separation and emotional relatedness).

Meltzer and Steiner agree that these (psychic retreats and the claustrum) patients are barely available for contact, in a state of isolation, withdrawal, or paranoia. They are also in agreement about these patients' compulsion to persevere in the world of conviction of entitlement, grievance, and resentment in order to torture the object of grievance. They concur in the belief that the only way to recovery and to regain the parts of the self (lost in the process of projective identification) lies in the relinquishment of the delusion of fusion and in mourning its loss. When pain of separation is allowed, the mourning process is set in motion, modifying the pathological organization.

Case study

Mr A as a claustrum dweller

The following case study illustrates how the concept of the claustrum can be employed to understand in greater depth the primitive concreteness of certain patients. Mr A was in four analytic sessions per week with me for thirteen years; a lost boy, though chronologically adult and married. He was a good-looking young man, one of many siblings, born and brought up in a very deprived area of an Irish city. His mother left when Mr A was under four years old, and all the children were sent together to an unenlightened, grim, and punitive children's home. They came back two years later to live with their father and his then partner. Mr A's father was a burglar by occupation, and my patient had an "Oliver Twist" role: he was inserted through small windows of houses in order to open the front door from inside. Unusually for patients in private practice, Mr A had had an actual, concrete experience of violent intrusion into a house as a metaphor for a mother's body. He remembers one occasion when he was punished for being attracted to a ball rather than to a more valuable item in a burgled house. He was about thirteen when his father chose to "improve" their relationship by making my patient a drinking partner. The boy used to go to school either drunk or with a hangover after sharing a bottle of whiskey through the night, and he left school semi-literate at about fifteen.

The assessment highlighted a borderline personality organized in the paranoid–schizoid position, whose sexuality was polymorphously perverse. His gaze was disturbingly intrusive. He had a penchant for smelling women's used underwear. He had olfactory hallucinations, a clear attempt to (k)no(w)se me. He imagined smelling sewage, chocolate, bacon and eggs, perfume, sweat, vomit, semen, etc. He experienced them upon his entrance to the consulting room, or during a session, and those hallucinations were a concrete manifestation of his projective identification at any given moment, an unwanted, disgusting part of himself, as well as his wish to find good food in the analysis. He was a claustrum dweller, mainly in the anal and genital compartments. In his own words, Mr A felt "imprisoned" and he was afraid to allow himself to think; he was convinced that thinking and feeling "would swamp his head".

Although it was obvious that emotionally Mr A was a little boy with no established sexuality, his graphic descriptions of genital and anal excitation during the session made it hard for me to hold on to the damaged child. Mr A described crude and vulgar sexual fantasies, full of murderous violence, rape, prurience, confusion, and self-stupefaction. A few examples of his dream imagery: he was fondling a cut off breast; an African tribe murdered babies by putting them alive through a machine. Babies came out from a sewer—some still partly alive. He was offered a job to examine women's genitals; he was slitting the throat of a dirty prostitute; cutting a man's eyes with a razor. His mouth was open so wide that he was able to bite my whole head off; he pushed me into an alligator-filled lake and watched me being devoured; he was stepping over decomposed bodies that became alive and chased him, and then he became one of them. The most unsavoury perverse fantasies were used as a means to stop him from thinking. They were as addictive and anaesthetizing as his alcoholism, before he dried out.

A powerful, most unpleasant erotic transference (as I thought then) emerged early, in the first few weeks of his analysis, with demands to be loved and physically held. A few months on, the following exchange made me reassess the situation and face his erotization. Mr A was complaining that I would not touch him because I considered him to be dirty and repulsive. I suggested that we think of continence rather than incontinence: he was able to wipe his own bottom rather than fantasize of having it rubbed by me. His answer was that he would throw himself down the stairs on the way out and then I would have to minister to him. This showed me the degree of his concrete thinking and the mindlessness of his perverse preoccupations that prevented him from acquiring the capacity to understand a metaphor. I realized that, despite the existence of parts of his personality that were genuinely life- and attachment-seeking, I was not faced with a normal infantile transference, but with massive projective identification. To quote Rosenfeld (1983), "In the symbiotic phantasies of oneness, the analyst is believed not only to satisfy all the patient's desires but he is also experienced as approaching the patient with equal demands and desires." (p. 263). I had a reasonably clear picture of a borderline psychotic structure of the personality, whose perversity allowed him to be blinded to his fragmentation and kept him safe from the experience of emotional pain.

He was like quicksilver: his projections turned into projective identification in a split second, as, for instance, when his murderousness was almost immediately perceived as mine, and then his, when he felt he had to attack me in self defence. Equally fast were the movements of the different parts of his personality. For years I could not relax; I never knew with whom I would be dealing on the couch from one moment to the next. For example: he had a strange thought that he was drinking my words. Then he demanded to be touched like a normal baby would. His frustration gave vent to rage and confusion between breast and bottom: "I can see you now shitting in my mouth." The desired object was instantly turned into a hated one.

My countertransference experience depended on the part of his personality that was available to me at any given moment, since he was defended against real emotional contact by being in the claustrum. The pervert disgusted me; the violent bully frightened me. The deprived, deserted, neglected, and abused child was desperately painful to bear, and I was aware of a wish to hold him. Paradoxically, what allowed me to cling to those rarely manifested libidinal aspects of his narcissism was the fact that he sometimes literally called me "mum", thus helping me to remember how young he felt.

For the first four years I concentrated on careful observation of his life in the claustrum, saying very little, more or less describing it to him using his communications to me, with the occasional fleeting contact when he appeared to be slightly more reflective. When he was mainly in the anal compartment, I focused on describing his terror and tried to depict the nature and experience of his anxiety around violence and attack. When in the genital compartment, I refrained from addressing the pornography and centred on the anxiety of loneliness and abandonment should he feel expelled from that place of erotic excitement. In the head–breast compartment, I described on the one hand his sense of stopping time in a state of mindless, static existence and, on the other, anxiety about a discovery that he might be "found out" in the consulting room (mother's body). These observations made sense to my patient. Much of my use of transference took the form of stressing that what we were talking about was happening right then with the two of us in the room, emphasizing that I was an *invited visitor* into his internal world. Otherwise, my comments were treated as agreeing with his perception of the world, because he could not conceive of another perspective, and my attempts at analyst-centred interpretations were taken as confirming my inadequacies or alleged misdemeanours. Interestingly, Mr A mostly claimed to be concerned only with the "here and now", insisting "everything is only about us". The "us", however, allowed me no independent existence. I had to wait for isolated moments in order to glimpse normal infantile transference when he was desperate for contact, and seize those. Slowly, those moments became more frequent and more prolonged.

One such moment was in a session when he blamed me for infecting him with a cold (I had one the previous week) and then reported an image of me in intercourse with my husband. He believed that it was a healthy fantasy, proving that he did not hate me any more for "not giving it to him". He thought that I would be pleased. I decided to focus on the infantile nature of the material and emphasized that he refused to stay in his cot. After an initial sulky silence, he began to cry, his first tears, as he relayed a conversation with his father, at the age of fourteen. The father had told him that he had attempted to abort my patient using a screwdriver. At first, I was shocked and enraged on his behalf, then I knew that I needed to think. I did not know whether it was a fact or a phantasy of either Mr A's or his father's. Was it about a primitive attempt at abortion; was the phantasy one of murder or self- murder; or was it a phantasy of "screwing" (destroying) parental intercourse (my internal thinking, cf. Britton, 1989) in the here and now? I had no idea, but I knew that the session was coming to a close and I had to say something. I said, "You feel damaged and unwanted and those are hard feelings to bear. It is hard for you to see sexual intercourse not as an act of violence that pollutes, damages, and kills, but as an act of love." He said that he needed to be physically held. I said that when I hold him in mind, he fears that I might infect him. His response was that he was sure that he got his cold at work. Thus, we managed for a fleeting moment to recruit the services of an observing ego through the withdrawal of projective identification.

Following that session, I felt occasionally that the intrusion into me with his eyes was also a search for his "I"s, as if he was somehow trying desperately to find his own identity. Sometimes, it also had a quality of desperately hanging on to my gaze.

The first shift into the threshold of the depressive position and the emergence of the Oedipus conflict

Six years into the analysis, Mr A showed the first inkling of the possibility of leaving the claustrum. He dreamt that there was a bird locked in a room, very frightened and flapping about. He was in the next room with other people who were drinking something from a shared cup. Mr A did not want to share the cup, so he cupped his hands and drank from them. Then someone was about to attack him. He rushed to the room with the bird and saw it flying out through the little window in the ceiling. I interpreted that when he did not want to share my breast with my other analytic children and pretended that his own hands were a breast/cup, he believed that he was I, and, lo and behold, found himself stuck inside me and open to an attack by daddy's penis. Yet, there was a part of him that knew he did not need to be stuck inside; he could use his mind (the ceiling) to find a window to really being in the world, bearing its pains and delights.

After this, things started moving. He had a dream in which a yew tree came down from the sky—the right way up. Mr A and another man were looking for a place in a well-tended garden to plant this tree. A middle-aged gardener woman said that they would have to book a planting place and there was a waiting list of many years. This was a change from his usual undifferentiated sexuality, where everything was back to front or upside down. He also connected "yew" with "you", and I think that he knew that we still had many years of work and dreaming ahead. That same week, he saw some children playing when on his way to my consulting room. Then he had a thought of falling down my stairs and cutting himself, after which I would comfort him and bandage his cuts. This was a change from his frequent fantasies of throwing himself down the stairs and watching me broken-hearted at his funeral. He was able to imagine being a child with a containing (bandaging and comforting) parent. He became a committed analytic baby, but a new storm cloud was gathering.

Mr A's wife was longing to have a child. He was stunned, shattered, confused, and frightened. He kept asking, "How can a baby sign his own death warrant?!" He was terrified of losing his wife if he did not agree to give her a baby. He was able to treat her longing seriously (even though it was incomprehensible to him) and felt that he cared for her enough to want her to be happy. He agreed, and the baby was conceived quite quickly.

Although there was a significant shift, Mr A was still fragile. He was in a terrible state during the pregnancy: paranoid, confused, and his nights were nightmarish. His driving became more dangerous: he could not judge distances as well as before or decide when he could pull out to overtake. I was very concerned about his dicing with danger; his car as a "container" had become dangerous under the stress of a three-way relationship. He found himself withholding things from his wife. Like Little Hans, he became a constipated child expecting a sibling. He had frequent dreams of imminent explosions and earthquakes. Yet, he made an effort to be kind and supportive to his wife. After seeing the first scan he came in beaming. He could not understand how on earth he could ever have thought of not wanting that live little thing. Yet, upon entering the consulting room, he smelt something bad, like a cat. So, it seemed that his conflict and bad feelings were avoided here and replaced by splitting and projective identification: he had the beautiful baby and I had only a smelly cat.

Still, we trudged on. In the next dream

> Mr A was a little girl, who got a lift from two women driving a lorry. He asked to drive and they let him. He drove on confidently, but soon got into trouble and had to slam hard on the brakes. He arrived at a toll bridge and handed over a bag of crisps, but it was no good, the toll man wanted money, which Mr A didn't have.

I interpreted this dream as a concrete picture of the envy of his wife's pregnancy (the two breasts propelling a large womb–lorry). Although he "obtained" permission to drive this pregnant womb, he was unsure and gender-confused (a girl) and could not get past the potent daddy (being only little, with crisps instead of money). This was the first emergence of a potent paternal object as opposed to the cruel, frightening, and drunk men in past dreams. The admiration involved in the envy was clear; he did not want to abort the baby any more; he just wanted to have it himself—since he could not be it. And we both understood that he had a long bridge to cross.

A healthy baby, John, was born and Mr A attempted to resolve his unbearable conflict by asking me to be named as the baby's legal guardian in a will. In a way, it was a brilliant unconscious solution: on the one hand, in his identification with the baby, he would have me guaranteed for life. On the other hand, it would make me his legal "wife" and he would not need to abandon his erotization. It was a perfect "deal" (Feldman, 2008), in which he would withdraw his grievance in exchange for my acquiescence to his demand. Although part of him understood this interpretation, he was incandescent with outrage at my refusal to be the baby's legal guardian, which lasted for at least a year.

Regression to the claustrum followed by re-emergence into the threshold of the depressive position

Following the birth, he regressed back to the claustrum, trapped in a state of mindlessness, confusion, polymorphous perversity, paranoia, and violence. His fragmentation and identification with the aggressor/victim is obvious in the following dream:

> A man is being chased and shot by another man. They are running up and down various levels of a four-storey house (my consulting room was in a four-storey house). Each time the man gets shot, the assailant fragments and disintegrates, but then the shot man is integrated into the shooter, and they both come alive again.

Mr A was again a hostage to the narcissistic gang, and in its brutality and mindlessness he lost the concept of time and space and identity. Yet, this state was not uniform, and, at times, Mr A was desperately willing to work. On those occasions I was moved, watching him struggle. Consider the following Monday session, starting with a dream.

> I had such a disturbed busy night. I dreamt that a Rottweiler bit Rover on the nose. I laughed—it looked very funny. But then I thought that

> he was going to bite off Rover's leg. So I asked the owner whether I could beat him with a stick on his genitals. He agreed . . . (silence) . . . I am thinking that you will say that I am again competing with John, and that I want to attack his penis not to grow bigger than mine. But I don't want him to be disabled and lame . . ."

This was said haltingly. (Rover was a dog from his childhood—a needy and defenceless part of him.) There was a projective identification with his defenceless baby, followed by an attack on this dependency. There was also the curious fact that he had asked the owner's permission. I wondered whether it related to an unconscious phantasy of a homosexual sado-masochistic affair. I sensed him becoming angry, but he contained himself in silence. He continued: "I am sure that I could be happy with you for ever, just you and me." I said, "You seem to be using this obsessive fantasy like a drug to allow you some kind of a thoughtless oblivion." He became overtly angry and shouted, "Why shouldn't I, it is so unfair. John can. All he wants is to snuggle up to a breast, and Mary lets him do it forever . . . All you want of me is work, work, work! Why can't I have what John has?!" I said, mindful of his concrete thinking, "So, now you seem to be angry not because John might develop a bigger penis and perhaps Mary might prefer him to you, but you actually feel hurt that Mary gives John what she does not give to you . . . you feel displaced by somebody much smaller rather than bigger." The projective identification was both with the baby and the mother. Mr A said in a grown-up voice, "I know this is nonsense, I couldn't wish for a better wife."

There was another snippet of a dream, he continued, but he wanted to get to a second, "big one". (I felt he was skipping over something and I asked for that snippet.) "Oh, it isn't important; it is just that

> *I took an old man out for a treat, and he was ungrateful and wasn't enjoying it . . . I can't even remember what the treat was . . .*

I responded, "You are right that Daddy, the old man, my husband, wishes to be given treats by me, not by you . . ." Tears of rage appeared and angry shouting: "No, this is all I get, I have to be a good father and a husband, and I get nothing in return! I can't understand why you insist on no physical contact. I need a hug, at least you could shake my hand; how can I go on developing when I have been so deprived. I never had a proper mother . . ." I felt uneasy, as if I should be sympathetic towards him, but I was not. I noticed that his right arm moved in the direction of my chair; I knew that he could not reach it or me, nevertheless I swivelled away and felt angry and intruded upon. He continued, "You are just mocking me; why won't you let me do both? I might be more inclined to work if I could have an occasional hug". His arm drew back; now he was sad and despondent, ". . . I think that in my dream I believed that if I am nice to your husband and don't hate him, like I always do, you will soften . . ."; he started sobbing. At this point, I felt somewhat warm and maternal towards him, but at the same time I thought that there was a ploy there, to force me concretely into a maternal role. I was also thinking that this must have been a communication as to how he was affected by the baby at this moment. He carried on with his "big dream":

> There was a powerful house which would do nasty things to people inside it, unless they did their tasks right. If they did well, the house would reward them by flying them out to New York. There was some anxiety whether it would squash the people on the ground, but it was clear that there would be enough warning for everybody to leave and not get hurt. There was a couple in the house and the husband noticed that the wife wanted to buy more ornaments like the one she had, to distribute them everywhere. The husband wanted her to have just one—it would be more attractive in its specialness . . .

He associated to *The Wizard of Oz*. I remembered that his father used to say that New York had its streets "paved with gold" (like the "yellow brick road'). I was thinking about the magic and the deceptive appearances, about all the characters in *The Wizard of Oz* as parts of his personality. The orphaned Dorothy was stormily transported into exile, and all her travelling companions believed that they were lacking something: The lion wanted courage; the tin man, emotionality; the straw man, a thinking mind. Yet, they were all helpful to each other and they all wanted altruistically to help Dorothy. Their love for her enabled them to rediscover in themselves the attributes that they believed to be lacking in themselves.

I was thinking about the patient's sentimental belief in the circularity of time and mindless happiness ever after, about his intrusiveness and possessiveness and the wish to be the only special one. And I wondered whether he had moved on from his chaotic gender confusion to an unconscious awareness of the need to bring the aspects of his bisexuality together in order to be a really good husband and a father to his son, which he consciously dearly wished. To have an idea of gratitude was an enormous leap for Mr A. I heard him say, "This is a long silence. I don't like to think that you don't understand the dream either."

I said, "You have experienced me as a bad house in the past few weeks." He said grinning, "With knobs on. Funny, that was my dad's expression." I added, ". . . and if you cannot *be* John you will *have* him by being mummy yourself . . ." My thoughts about this dream were that it presented a picture of his narcissistic organization. He is in the house (through intrusive projective identification), and he *is* the house. He is the husband, the house / mother / wife, the couple, and the special child / ornament. Through the oscillation of projective identification with the baby, with the mother, and with the couple, he succeeds single-handedly in being the whole family in one. Mr A left deep in thought and able, I felt, to consider the interpretation.

There followed a long period of time in which we oscillated between regressive and progressive trends, at times frightening and painful to both of us. Each time he got in touch with his neediness and vulnerability, the gang part of him attacked it with polymorphous perversity and murderousness and suicidal despair. The way he expressed it was that each time he put out his arms to be picked up, his penis took over. He felt that it was "stupidly unbearable". Mindless, mechanical sexuality was displacing emotionality. Yet, he was desperately trying to be a good father. He was frightened of what he might have been projecting into his son, but he was also learning from him. He said to me, "I want you and only you, but when I think that I cannot have what I want, I feel enraged and also frightened . . . do you think that it is possible for a child to feel that if he doesn't get what he needs, he might die?" I answered that it was possible, but the problem was that he could not differentiate between need and want. After a while he responded, "I know what you mean . . . I was with John in a shop and he screamed that he wanted sweets . . ." (and then in a small voice) ". . . oh, this is how *I* am . . . I can't understand where you get your patience from."

The insight of loss and the onset of mourning and work towards a resolution of the Oedipus complex

The turning point came when we were discussing a dream in which he was hiding inside armoured cars or climbing up ladders—anything but being ordinary and keeping his feet on the ground. He became aware of feeling that he had to wait endlessly to change, because, as he put it, "If I stop waiting, it would mean that my mother is dead." He was desperately clinging to the belief that his need could be met if his mother were alive. He had been keeping himself stagnant in order not to mourn his lost object, as well as not to lose the notion that he was an acceptable child who could be mothered.

Slowly, during the next three years, Mr A was able to mourn the loss of his mother and along with this came a troubling question: how could he possibly manage both to accept that his mother would not come back to him, to let go of her, and at the same time to trust me not to abandon him during weekend and holiday breaks? What slowly began to unfold was the pain of longing for the lost childhood that not only could never be, but which was never containing. "I thought that my whole dream was to get my childhood back with you, and if this is impossible because I can't live with you, and you will never kiss me and sleep with me and tuck me up for the night . . . if I cannot have the childhood I never had, then everything is lost . . . but then it becomes sort of unimportant because I have this huge feeling of something good and nothing matters any more . . . Is this what you call love?" The psychic turmoil abated and the experience in the consulting room became one of normal erotic transference of a child who was discovering a sincere emotional attachment.

Mr A became ever more passionately and kindly attached to his son, and started growing up with him. In his own naïve way, he said, "I think that I'm beginning to understand what love is; it is bigger than anything else in the world." This semi-literate man started reading to his son and for himself. He genuinely began educating himself. He found pleasure in his work; his marriage became much more solid.

The termination stage over a period of almost three years saw an ever-increasing sadness with growing stability. Two dreams were most significant. In the first dream

> he and I returned together from a trip and I invited him home. He thought to himself that in the past he would have given his right arm for this, but now it felt like a normal thing. I had things to do, so we arranged to meet by the cake shop. But I didn't come for a long time and then he was waiting for me with his son. Then I came back changed into his wife, who said that she had spotted a cake that he would like. He was pleased, because although his wife was late, she clearly had been thinking about him.

Mr A finally got the idea that he could be held in mind and that the marital relationship was with his wife.

In the second dream

> Mr A was observing a child who was hugging someone desperately—he didn't want the person to leave. Then his son was big and wearing a suit. Mr A was upset about him being grown up and leaving home. But then Mr A had to go to "a very responsible job" and he had to walk past a wild beast. Someone said that the beast was asleep, but Mr A could see it was awake. He wanted to shoot the beast, but was stopped by a warrior woman who told him that she had put the beast on a very strong leash and Mr A had to hold the leash and trust her to keep him safe . . .

The significance of the dream was that I had to let him go, trusting him to be safe. The erotization of the claustrum was long gone; the Oedipal erotic transference that replaced it was translated into a genuine affection, which, in turn, slowly gave way to sadness over the inevitability of separation. His external life had become more enriched, more adult.

Discussion

When I first assessed Mr A, I had no illusion about the hard work ahead. I was encouraged by the fact that he had given up alcohol a couple of years beforehand and was teetotal. The main reason I was prepared to take on the challenge was a certain unmistakable naïve child aspect of him. Although I was very aware of the massive projective identification of infant parts of himself from the beginning, I held on to what I believed might have been its communicative aspects. Thus, I was prepared to consider that, apart from the intrusiveness, he was also attempting to make me feel his own early experiences of holding his arms up to an absent mother or a drunken father.

According to Etchegoyen (1991, Chapter Twelve), erotic transference develops slowly and unevenly in an attempt to delay the resolution of the Oedipus conflict (the conflict reaches its crescendo at the threshold of the depressive position), whereas erotization (psychotic transference) aims at the preservation of the narcissistic organization and becomes evident already in the early stage of analysis. Both may serve the purpose of resistance to psychoanalysis, but are also useful analytic tools.

I wish I had read Etchegoyen's paper when I started working with Mr A, but I had not. Although I was right to hang on to the damaged, infantile, and desperately needy parts of his personality in order to survive the perverse onslaughts, it had taken me a few months to realize that I was not dealing with erotic transference, but with its psychotic counterpart. I had to face the full impact of his erotization, and that forced me to think about its nature. What I was observing was autoerotism, devoid of any capacity for recognition of the separate existence of an object. I was helped by Rosenfeld's concept of "symbiotic projective identification" (1983), which appeared as transference and as a powerful weapon of the narcissistic gang that kept the vulnerable and needy parts of his personality hostage. In the countertransference, I was remorselessly faced with various bits of a person in a fragmented internal world, and this fragmentation was rigidly adhered to for some time. In a very strange way, these projections were often distastefully painful, baffling, and sometimes boring, and I had to remain in a state of not knowing, waiting to understand.

There was a first glimpse of the possibility of Mr A's leaving the claustrum in the sixth year of analysis, in the dream about the bird flying out through the window. During the following years, a confused child emerged, and the psychotic erotization slowly gave way to a more neurotic erotic transference. All those years of interpretations and my attempts to remain steadfast against the constant barrage, and perhaps a residue of some archaic memory of a possible experience of care and intimacy, allowed some voice to the normal infantile parts of his personality. I had a sense of the possibility of analytic work in the transference of the here and now as the tyrannical grip of the gang steadily loosened, allowing other parts of the personality some say.

In that psychic shift, Mr A was able to have enough sense of the needs of his wife that he agreed to conceive a child. Something soft and humane within him was struggling with his egotism. His internal turmoil around the pregnancy and birth propelled him back into the claustrum, but he kept emerging from it more and more frequently and for ever-increasing periods of time. As Spillius (2007) states,

> I believe that continuous experiences of fluctuation between the anxieties, defences and object relations of the paranoid schizoid and depressive positions involve further developments of awareness of separateness of others together with awareness of the "otherness of others". [p. 201]

I was also able to observe the twisting and turning between exhibitions of psychotic erotization and erotic transference, where he was painfully struggling with normal Oedipal longings, rivalry, and guilt. When Mr A started slowly and painstakingly to read to his son, it began with a degree of projective identification with him. But then I noticed a genuine effort to become literate and to educate himself. He started using the epistemophilic instinct in the service of exploring his relationship with his son, developing an interest in reading, a curiosity about the world, and a desire for his own intellectual development, rather than in order to intrude into his objects, as had been the case throughout most of his life.

The final shift came with his internal recognition of the loss of his mother. Steiner (1993) states,

> in order to regain parts of the self lost through projective identification it is necessary to relinquish the object and mourn it. It is in the process of mourning that projective identification is reversed and the ego is enriched and integrated. [p. 59]

Mr A was finally able to mourn, and in the process he also discovered a zest for life. At a later stage, he was also able to mourn the loss of his analysis, of which I learnt through letters and occasional follow-up sessions. He grew to be happy at work and in his marriage, one that produced more children. Despite severe deprivation and early damage, there was an eventual resolution of the Oedipal transference, and Mr A became able to "love and work".

References

Alexander, F. (1950). Analysis of the therapeutic factors in psychoanalytic treatment. *Psychoanalytic Quarterly, 19*: 482–500.

Bibring, G. (1936). A contribution to the subject of transference resistance. *International Journal of Psychoanalysis, 17*: 181–189.

Bion, W. R. (1957). The differentiation of the psychotic from the non psychotic personalities. *International Journal of Psychoanalysis, 38*: 266–275 [reprinted in: *Second Thoughts. Selected Papers on Psycho-Analysis* (1967). London: Heinemann Medical Books; reprinted London: Karnac, 1984].

Bion, W. R. (1962). A theory of thinking. *International Journal of Psychoanalysis, 43* [reprinted in: *Second Thoughts. Selected Papers on Psycho-Analysis* (1967). London: Heinemann Medical Books; reprinted London: Karnac, 1984].

Bion, W. R. (1963). *Elements of Psychoanalysis.* London: Heinemann Medical Books [reprinted London: Karnac, 1984].

Blitzsten, N. L. (1956). Personal unpublished communication. In: Rappaport, 1956, p. 515.

Bolognini, S. (1994). Transference: erotised, erotic, loving, affectionate. *International Journal of Psychoanalysis, 75*: 73–86.

Britton, R. (1989). The missing link: parental sexuality in the Oedipus complex. In: R. Britton, M. Feldman, & E. O'Shaughnessy (Eds.), *The Oedipus Complex Today* (pp. 83–101). London: Karnac.

Etchegoyen, H. R. (1991). *Fundamentals of Psychoanalytic Technique.* London: Karnac.

Feldman, M. (2008). Grievance: the underlying oedipal configuration. *International Journal of* Psychoanalysis, *89*: 743–758.

Freud, S. (1895d). *Studies on Hysteria. S.E., 2*: 1–306. London: Hogarth.

Freud, S. (1915a). Observations on transference-love. *S.E., 12*: 159–171. London: Hogarth.

Glasser, M. (1979). Some aspects of the role of aggression in the perversions. In: I. Rosen (Ed.), *Sexual Deviation* (pp. 278–305). Oxford: Oxford University Press.

Klein, M. (1930). The importance of symbol-formation in the development of the ego. In: *The Writings of Melanie Klein: Love, Guilt and Reparation and Other Works*. London: Hogarth Press, 1975.

Klein, M. (1946). Notes on some schizoid mechanisms. *International Journal of Psychoanalysis, 27*: 99–110 [reprinted in: *The Writings of Melanie Klein, Vol. 3: Envy and Gratitude*. London: Hogarth, 1975].

Meltzer, D. (1966). The relation of anal masturbation to projective identification. *International Journal of Psychoanalysis, 47*: 335–342 [reprinted in: D. Meltzer, *The Claustrum*. Strathtay, Perthshire: Clunie Press, 1995].

Meltzer, D. (1992). *The Claustrum*. Strathtay, Perthshire: Clunie Press.

Rappaport, E. A. (1956). The management of an erotized transference. *Psychoanalytical Quarterly, 25*: 515–529.

Rey, H. (1994). *Universals of Psychoanalysis in the Treatment of Psychotic and Borderline States*. London: Free Association Books.

Rosenfeld, H. (1971a). A clinical approach to the psychoanalytic theory of the life and death instincts: an investigation into the aggressive aspects of narcissism. *International Journal of Psychoanalysis, 52*: 169–178 [reprinted in: J. Steiner (Ed.), *Rosenfeld in Retrospect*. London: Routledge, 2008; and in: E. Bott Spillius (Ed.), *Melanie Klein Today, Vol. 1*. London: Routledge, 1988].

Rosenfeld, H. (1971b). Contribution to the psychopathology of psychotic states: the importance of projective identification in the ego structure and the object relations of the psychotic patient. In: P. Doucet & C. Laurin (Eds.), *Problems of Psychosis*. The Hague: Exerpta Medica [reprinted in: J. Steiner (Ed.), *Rosenfeld in Retrospect* (pp. 131–149). London, Routledge, 2008].

Rosenfeld, H. (1983). Primitive object relations and mechanisms. *International Journal of Psychoanalysis, 64*: 261–267.

Segal, H. (1957). Notes on symbol formation. *International Journal of Psychoanalysis*, 38: 391–397 [reprinted in: *The Work of Hanna Segal* (pp. 49–64). London: Free Associations Books, 1986; and in: E. Bott Spillius (Ed.), *Melanie Klein Today: Volume 1, Mainly Theory* (pp. 87–101) (with the 1979 postscript). London: Routledge, 1988].

Segal, H. (1996). Symbolic equation and symbols. In: N. Abel-Hirsch (Ed.), *Hannah Segal: Yesterday, Today and Tomorrow* (pp. 111–113). London: Routledge, 2007.

Steiner, J. (1993). *Psychic Retreats*. London: Routledge.

CHAPTER FIVE

A five-bar gate: love and hate in the structure of the mind

Jan Harvie-Clark

> "I hate and I love. Why do I do it, perchance you might ask? I don't know, but I feel it happening to me and I'm burning up."
>
> (Catullus, *ca.* 50bc)

> "Without contraries is no progression. Attraction and Repulsion, Reason and Energy, love and hate, are necessary to human Existence."
>
> (Blake, *ca.* 1790–1793)

At the end of a long break, two patients returned for their first session. The first, whom I shall refer to as Ms C, a young woman in her twenties, has been in analysis with me for almost a year. This is her first long break.

Starting analysis has had a very considerable impact on her, or, rather, on her body. Now she arrives on the dot of her appointed hour. On greeting me she looks at me with suspicion. I immediately feel vaguely uncomfortable. She indicates that she wants to sit in the chair, and she stares at me. She asks if I have had a good holiday. Then, with politeness over, she tells me she has been terrible. I ask her to tell me about it. For the next half an hour she tells me of her terrifying somatic symptoms. These reached a crescendo two days ago, when she felt that there was a tightening band around her chest. She is sure that I cannot appreciate how awful she feels; no one can understand, no one else can feel like she does, otherwise people would not walk around and get on with their lives in the way that they do.

As she describes the dreadful feelings she had over the holidays, I find myself breaking out in a sweat. I note this and think about it while I listen. I think of the rage and the frustration that she has projected and which cannot yet be verbalized, which is as yet unconscious, but which binds her round and squeezes her as though she is being tortured.

Later, another patient, Ms A, comes. She is rather older than my first patient, and considerably older in terms of her psychological understanding. She has been in intensive treatment with me for six years, and we have done a considerable amount of work together. Before the holiday, she spoke of her wish to reduce the number of her sessions with a view to working towards an end. We agreed to see how the holidays went. Previous holiday breaks had been very painful for her. They had been dreaded and experienced as a most painful loss. We had come to understand this as the loss of a secure place in my mind. This holiday and reunion were strikingly different, and she looked different, more attractive and somehow more structured. She sat rather gingerly on the side of the couch, smiled knowingly and warmly at me, and said it felt funny to be back. She lay down and said so much had happened she did not know where to start. She spoke, however, fluently and without hesitation, and I said very little during this session, only remarking at the end that she seemed to have had a lot of fun these holidays. In contrast to my reaction to the first patient, a reaction that included hate in my countertransference (Winnicott, 1947), with this patient I sat smiling, enjoying her stories and rejoicing with her that she could now get so much more out of life. My countertransference, thus, included something that might be called love. Perhaps I could suggest, along with William Blake, that I had an experience of both heaven and hell on the first day after the holidays.

In this chapter, my focus will be on the role of love and hate in the consulting room, on the affects that I feel are at the heart of the psychoanalysis that I practise, affects that are of particular importance in the analysis of some patients. Freud (1940a [1938]) wrote that "After long hesitancies and vacillations we have decided to assume the existence of only two basic instincts, *Eros and the destructive instinct*". Eros is the instinct that binds together, "to establish ever greater unities", that brings the various dissenting internal voices together into some sort of compromise, so that something, some action, thought, or idea can come to pass. The "aim of the second is, on the contrary, to undo connections and so to destroy things" (p. 148)). The force of these two instincts can be called, for simplicity and clarity, love and hate. The poets, such as the two I have quoted in the epigraphs to the chapter, have specialized down through the ages in describing these moving forces in the human being. Freud called them components of the sexual instinct. Freud, at the start of his writing (1905a), said the aim of psychoanalysis was to make the unconscious conscious, to bring to light what had been repressed and was defended against. Then, when the patient was acquainted with the workings of his mind, he would be cured, and this cure would be effected by love. Later, in *An Outline of Psycho-Analysis* (1940a [1938]), he suggests that "love has its origin in attachment to the satisfied need for nourishment" (p. 188), and that from the beginning of life "the act of eating is a destruction of the object with the final aim of incorporating it" (p. 149). In Piontelli's grim observation of little "Martin" (1985), she notes from her earliest observations how he uses his tongue to try to comfort himself, and then how, as he grows, he grabs food and stuffs it into his mouth as soon as he can, seeming to swallow it without any apparent enjoyment. Martin grows into a very disturbed child, who seems to illustrate Freud's point about the fantasied destruction and incorporation of the object, which, in his case, was a totally frustrating, self-obsessed mother on whom he was, none the less, utterly dependent.

Although Freud developed his ideas on the structure of the mind, he maintained his dual instinct theory. Thus, love and hate, he felt, are both involved at every stage of development and at every level of activity; both have to be available to be used. Freud (1940a [1938]) warned that internal conflict weakens the ego, and that "Holding back aggressiveness is in general unhealthy and leads to illness" (p. 150). This is the theoretical starting point for my contention that the conflict between love and hate is at the heart of analytic work. With the integration of love and hate, there can be room to develop new dimensions: within the personality, in object relationships, and in regard to the experience of life.

Just as love might be said to be the feeling force of Eros, stemming, as Freud claimed, from an experience of satisfaction, hate can be said to be the feeling force of the destructive instinct, stemming from an experience of frustration. Perhaps, at the start, love and hate are barely object related (Balint, 1952). Certainly, they are not integrated. Winnicott (1945) writes that the infant needs a period of holding and containing so that some basic integration of satisfaction and frustration, of love and hate, can be achieved. This basic integration can be seen as the beginning of a structure in an infant's mind. Psychoanalysts have continued to add their own theoretical and clinical experience to early theories of the development of psychic structure, and the neuroscientists have now contributed with "evidence based" claims about the early structuring of the brain. As psychoanalysts, we examine how our method reaches and treats the mental distress and confusion in the minds of those who come to seek our help, and how we try to effect changes in primitive psychic structure.

Essentially, I believe I am trying to help through a special kind of listening and understanding. In order to facilitate change in psychic structure, psychoanalysis, with whichever theories we as individual practitioners embrace, has truly to become our own. The following makes sense to me:

> Psychoanalysis is about both knowing and being. An analyst serves truth not only by trying to see it and point it out to his patient, but by embodying it in his relationship to his patient and to his theory. . . . In this way he may help the patient to become the embodiment of his own truth. [Parsons, 2000, pp. 67–68]

Psychoanalysis is the complex set of theories about the human psyche that we use when we sit and listen, when we listen to another, and, at the same time, to ourselves. Helping someone, however, can seem far away as we sit for hours, to earn or augment our living in this most difficult way. Something has to sustain us through the awkward and uncomfortable moments; the often difficult and mind-bending hours; the painful and sometimes heart-rending experiences; through the complaints and accusations of patients; through the rigorous training and endless presentations and assessments; through the exposure to one's fellow students, to one's colleagues, to one's supervisors; to "others", the world outside the consulting room.

I wonder if it is ultimately love that enables us to put ourselves forward as another's companion–helper in the therapeutic enterprise? I wonder if it is love for the object, or perhaps love of psychoanalysis? It seems to me that having been enabled to free myself (or at least feel freer) through my experience of my own personal analysis, exploring my thoughts and feelings and thinking about them, I now use this ability to listen to another, to try to enable another to come into his or her own self. I would add it makes me feel better to use myself in this way, and, thus, there is an element of self-love that I am employing in my professional life. This is perhaps one of the many narcissistic aspects of the profession that needs carefully to be monitored within the countertransference. Yet, as Winnicott (1947) writes, the loving—and I am including self-loving—aspects of the work are tempered by the hating aspects: the session ends after fifty minutes regardless of whether or not the patient wants it to; there are weekend and holiday breaks; there are bills to be paid. As Dimen (1994) writes,

> . . . the curative power of psychoanalysis . . . is regularly undercut by the money that permeates it. As analysts we all know how rapidly our narcissism or, as Freud put it, our self-preservative instinct, leads us to equate the loss of an hour with a bill we'll have to find some other way to pay; how disjunctive, that is, contradictory, this thought is to the personal relation that we are about to lose, with the feeling of loss that looms . . . [pp. 89–90]

I suggest that the love expressed in the practice of psychoanalysis is so bound up with hate that perhaps it cannot be called love. Even before I get into the consulting room, I am caught between my love and my hate for what I am doing. From the start of the session I look towards the end of it; from the first session of the day I look towards the last session of the day; I enjoy being paid and I enjoy the holiday breaks in my work. It can be no surprise that this conundrum is what I meet when I eventually arrive in the room to be faced with the love and hate of another. The title of this paper is meant as a metaphor to help focus attention on the structure, importance, and function of these affects, affects which can be considered to be the "bookends" of all other affects. All affects fall between the two opposites of love and hate, affects often seen in terms of "good" and "bad": shame, guilt, arrogance, envy, fury, resentment, would be in the "bad", uncomfortable, painful category; pleasure, pride, anticipation, generosity, gratitude, forgiveness (Symington, 2008), in the "good".

The construction of a gate comes to my mind in order to visualize the range, structure, and function of affect. Unpleasurable, painful affects are at one end of a spectrum of gradations of the same basic affect, at the bottom of my gate, and come to an equilibrium as they rest more easily within us, along the middle bars. Exciting and passionate affects are at the other—top—end of the gate. Both ends of the spectrum / gate are felt to be disturbing to the stasis—the comfortable middle ground—in which we try to live and love and work. Intensity of feeling removes us from the ordinariness of life, transports us to another world, and, however captivating that is, it is always somewhat disturbing, dangerous, and even addictive. It distances us from the usualness of life, and, thus, affect needs to be bound to prevent us from going mad in one direction or another: mad with passion, mad with grief, mad with fury. The structure of my gate is, thus, a metaphor for this binding of affect.

A gate with which I am familiar is a field gate. The drystone walls of my beloved Cumbrian fields are broken by such gates. The gates have to be sturdy, as they will be opened and shut in all weathers. The gates may be wooden or metal, but the structure is always similar. They usually have five, but may have six or seven, horizontal bars. These are held together by two vertical bars at each end and two crossbars secured diagonally across the horizontals. The premise of this chapter is that for a well-operating mind (or a well-operating analytic treatment), the structure of love and hate have to be held in such a robust and sturdy way as to allow the in and out flowing of feeling from the field of our mind (and body) into the world beyond.

> And lest he [the patient] should fall into a state in which he is inaccessible to all evidence, the analyst takes care that neither the love nor the hostility reach an extreme height . . . If we succeed . . . in enlightening the patient on the true nature of . . . transference, we shall have struck a powerful weapon out of . . . his resistance and . . . converted dangers into gains. [Freud, 1940a [1938], p. 177]

It is the task of the analyst to manage as best she can her own affects, and to allow for the in and out flowing of feeling in such a way as to permit the reconstruction, or, in more benign cases, the repair, of another's mind, in order to allow for psychic change. The analyst needs a good enough, well-structured gate to her own mind in order to be able to bear the exigencies that this method of treatment will inevitably throw up. The treatment needs both parties to the analytic enterprise to be able to work together up and down the emotional register, to allow the patient to come to know himself. The analyst has to tolerate intense feelings, maintaining the psychic structure of her own mind, and, thinking through the transference–countertransference interplay in the treatment, allow her patient to discover that intense feelings can be allowed and tolerated, can be felt, and, at some point, can be thought about. In 1940 Freud wrote that "There can be no question but that the libido has somatic sources, and that it streams to the ego from various organs and parts of the body" (1940a [1938], p. 151), so that it becomes a whole body experience in the consulting room that will persuade the patient of the truthfulness of the experience he shares with his analyst. Similarly, in my opening vignette, it was a projected somatic experience that persuaded the analyst of the patient's unconscious rage.

The hinges of any gate are vital to its operation. If it does not open and close it is not a gate, even if it looks like one. How often, when one is out walking, is it that one sees what looks from a distance like a gate, only to find after tramping over a muddy field that it is a fixed gap in the boundary! The hinges of our affects, in my metaphoric gate, are our childhood experiences, which should, ideally, equip us for a full affective adult life, rather than provide inflexible, unmoving gaps in the boundary structure that defends our psyche. Gates, however, are easier to control and operate than are our minds. To quote from Kohon's "Love in a time of madness", in Green and Kohon's book *Love and its Vicissitudes* (2005):

> From the beginning of life it takes at least two to tango: what is on offer is not just milk: it also includes the mother's own instinctual desires and unconscious fantasies. In this encounter between the unconscious of the mother and baby, the breast is a libidinal object for both participants; the dynamics of give and take are multidimensional and overdetermined. The baby is confronted with the task of metabolising something which never arrives as always the same; he will never quite know what he is getting next time round. Warm milk, cold milk, milk that tasted sour, poisonous milk, milk too rich to be comfortably digested, milk received from an eroticised breast. Milk that gives pleasure; the same milk, inaugurating a life of unpleasure. Not just milk then, not just simple nourishment to help him survive; it is rather a complex emotional package to be unwrapped and metabolised. So, here it is: the first mouthful of meaning that the baby will receive. Love and hate. [p. 64]

Thus, right from the start of life (and, of course, from the start of psychoanalytic treatment), the crossbar operates, the bar which strikes through the whole range of emotions available, in the quote above imagined as the mind of the mother who offers "not just milk". Perhaps we shall discover that, from the moment of conception, the foetus is immersed in an amniotic fluid, and fed through a placenta, with a similarly "complex emotional package". We do, however, know that after birth an infant has to draw his or her own breath, and, as he or she starts to interact with the outside world, the hinges begin to be formed. How the infant is received, welcomed into life, and subsequently related to, is crucial for the development of the hinges. Of fundamental importance is the first and pivotal experience of another, usually of the mother. The helpless infant depends entirely on his environment, not only for his physical survival, but also, and of equal importance, for his psychic survival. Before birth, all he needed was continuously available to him; now he is dependent on what the adults around him choose to offer, and what is offered is, as Kohon so beautifully describes, highly complex.

I am imagining the structure of the infantile mind to develop so that it becomes similar to the structure of my gate: the vertical posts and the top and bottom must gradually become a firm structure to which the other bars can be attached. In a reflection of this early situation, the mind of the analyst, like that of the mother, needs to be firmly constructed, with all the parts of the gate of her mind held robustly in place. Through the mind of the analyst, the patient meets a framework on which he can learn to depend. Like hefty cattle and wayward tractors, patients will lean up against the gate of their analyst's mind; they will test the structure, the containment, and the timely ability to allow them in and out of the psychic space of the other. Like the infant described above, patients will never quite know what kind of milk/interpretations they are going to receive. I am not exactly the same in every session, as I am a human being and not a mechanical device. I am inevitably affected by all kinds of events, both internal and external to me, and often quite separate from my patient, however well analysed I might be, and however much I try to leave my own matters outside the consulting room. The more "thin skinned" (Rosenfeld, 1987) the patient, the more he or she picks up on my differing feelings, particularly my unconscious feelings. After a recent rather sharp response and a harsh interpretation to a patient who has been in treatment with me for a number of years, she complained about my unusual cruelty on this occasion. I think she was right, and undoubtedly I hurt her. On another occasion I would have heard her material in a more benign way, and allowed her to come to her own interpretation of it, instead of forcing my own hateful response on her.

We know that what patients bring into the consulting room is crucially determined by their infantile experience, as well as by their recent experience both outside and inside the consulting room. I knew that the patient I have just referred to was insensitively treated early in her life by objects who did not have her in mind as a vulnerable, little, separate person from themselves and their concerns. I repeated that in my harsh interpretation. We also know that transference situations when the patient lies on the couch will replay the early infantile dynamics, and that in our countertransference we will relive something of this early situation with our patient. That someone comes to ask for help is already a tribute to the experience of a helpful "other", even if engaging with the help, once in the consulting room, sometimes feels more like a battle engagement than a therapeutic one, sometimes more poisonous than nourishing.

A patient, Ms B, came to see me some years ago, having been referred for psychoanalytic treatment after a suicide attempt. Her story, as it unfolded over the four years of her four-times-weekly analysis, was of an inconsistent and narcissistic mother, neglectful of this, her eldest child, as she struggled to manage successive pregnancies and a large family. This neglect was experienced by this child/patient as hostile. The patient felt she was mostly unwanted as the person she was, and experienced herself as a thorn in her mother's flesh. I discovered this mother through my countertransference: as I sat through the hours in the consulting room I found myself unable to concentrate on Ms B's words. My mind wandered all over the place through her sessions, and, as I became concerned about what was happening, I turned to my peer group. As we discussed the material and considered the transference outside the consulting room, I began to find I could overcome my irritation and dislike of her and to hear her story.

Ms B had been cared for by her maternal grandparents for a good part of her first year of life. There had grown up a family myth to explain this, but, through reconstruction, Ms B and I were able to wonder if, in the face of the mother's difficulties, the grandparents had come to the rescue of their first grandchild, and that for the rest of her life grandmother had kept a watching brief, a role I was now required to take over. Ms B had retained a great love for her grandmother, and, in fact, her suicide attempt occurred soon after her grandmother's death. As I began to think that, once on the couch, Ms B had demanded a continuation of the grandmotherly care, but instead discovered initially a repetition of the maternal neglect, I was able to overcome my negativity to her complaints. Together, we were able to reconstruct her early childhood, and the desperate situation in which she found herself when she lost her grandmother, first in the distant and then in the recent past. Until we had worked through to this point, my holiday breaks were very difficult for her to bear, but, soon after, once (in line with the metaphor I have chosen) I had regained the middle bar of the gate of my mind, she felt ready to work towards an end.

Only when I became able to listen to a "babbling baby", who had gradually but steadily in my presence found words to convey the intensity of her experience, could I share with her the awful inconsistency of her maternal environment. We could see it together from near and afar. I could then listen to her pouring out the stories of what she and her siblings had suffered, of how she had struggled to reach out to help her siblings. I was astonished by her speedy recovery as she became able to use the analytic space to lean up against the gate of my mind, and to integrate her affects; how she was able to use me as a developmental object, a continuation of the one she lost too early in her life, but from whom she now demanded separation in order to continue on her own. It was as if I was privileged to watch a beautiful butterfly emerge from an imprisoning chrysalis. She could then proceed on her own. Indeed, she is one of a few patients who have remained in touch with me, allowing a certain continuity of the benevolent and, I would say, loving interaction that was so vital to her. I was vital to counteract the hate. Although, until the start of her analysis, she was barely conscious of the poisonous maternal atmosphere of her childhood, her early experience certainly had poisoned her enjoyment of her life and creativity. In analysis, she found a space in which she could pour out the craziness and hateful actions and atmosphere which had all but overwhelmed her internal world, and from which she had tried to escape by killing herself. She found a non-judgemental space where she could be heard, and she could then reorganize her internal world through feeling whole and of value within herself, and live on with pleasure and creativity instead of unpleasure and destructiveness. In this case, it seemed that when the analyst could find a way of managing her own hatred (in this instance, outside the consulting room in her peer group), the patient became able to tolerate hers, and find space for her capacity to love and to become creative.

Perhaps this is an illustration of the working of the crossbar of my metaphorical gate. The analysis provided a benign space (when I had sorted out my own hate) where the hatred, confusion, and distress could be reassessed until a more benevolent equilibrium could be found, and the gate of her mind could swing more easily to let me in or to keep me out. The horizontal bars of love and hate could be separated and seen for what they were, while they could be held in place by the vertical bars of the analytic structure (here, the analyst's mind as well as the treatment structure she provided). The crossbar, allowing movement in the psychic space between the horizontals, firmed up the structure, and as soon as she felt this was firmly enough inside herself, that she had internalized both the structure and the mind of her analyst (both the love and the hate), she could use this for herself. When she told me she wanted to work towards an end, I was surprised and uncertain that enough could have been securely achieved in so short a time, barely four years. Her continuing communications in the form of long letters detailing family and personal news have reassured me, and indicated that the structure of the gate of her mind is more secure.

The spectrum illustrated by the bars of a gate seems an especially useful metaphor for particular pathologies. Where there is a gate, but the affects are overwhelming, perhaps due to unfused aggression, it can be said that the bars of the gate are not properly secured. For some very disturbed and damaged patients, there can seem to be hardly any construction, and analytic work is long and arduous for both parties. In these cases, both patient and analyst struggle to work together so that the frame of a mind can be established: and only then can the affective bars be fixed in place. For some patients, their minds seem to swing freely on childhood-determined hinges, only to discover that the bottom bars of the gate have remained hidden. For other, more neurotic patients, a gate can be in place, but the hinges in need of attention even if the bars may be fixed, as the gate cannot swing freely to allow psychic contents in and out appropriately. We more often conceptualize this as rigid defences than as an unmoving gate. Sometimes, part of the love–hate structure of mind is disintegrating, or has been inadequately constructed. As you walk around the Cumbrian countryside, you find gates in all states of decrepitude, and gates which look like gates but do not act like gates.

The second patient, Ms A, whom I presented at the start of this chapter, the one who came in after the break to give me a wonderful description of her lovely holidays, did not continue in the same vein in subsequent sessions. She and I have struggled through the years, as, indeed, I understand she struggled through her early years and her life before she started analysis. At the start, and for a long period of this five-times-weekly, eight-year treatment, Ms A felt extremely dependent on my continuing availability. She was in a training that threatened to become derailed by her overwhelming rage, frustration, and neediness. She began to test my ability to contain her furies and her desires by claiming the couch was too soft. She lay on the floor beside the couch. I interpreted that my arrangements did not suit her. At the start of the next session and thereafter, she used the couch. All through her sessions she used copious amounts of tissues from the box that I provided, evacuating her tears and "snot", and leaving the used tissues in the bin in my room before she left. After a time, I interpreted her need to show me how blocked up with misery she was, and how she wanted to get rid of all this into my bin so that I could see what discomfort I was causing her and contain her after she had left.

Ms A was able to complete her training while in treatment, and developed an increasingly successful professional life. She began to establish herself as an independent young woman, although I often felt that I had a screaming, distressed child on my couch. Gradually, over the years, she became more able to integrate her wild loves and hates. She became more able to tolerate the extremes of her intense feelings as she was able to find, time and again, her place on my couch, and more able to contain these feelings as she found a container in her analyst. She became able to accept my interpretations that she had been so anxious about her rage with me for abandoning her over a weekend or holiday break that she was terrified that I would not come back, or not want her in my room. Eventually, she reached the stage described at the start of this chapter, when she had been able truly to enjoy a holiday of her own. By allowing her to find a safe place, by supporting the analytic frame and our shared space, and by speaking with her about her love and hate, she came to be a more integrated, contained human being.

That is, until we agreed after the holidays to work to an end. Thereafter, a torrent of intense negativity was unleashed, now directed squarely at the analyst and the analysis. It was as though none of the gains of the past few years counted for anything in the face of her intense fury with me for agreeing to work to an end of the treatment. For many months of this last year we did not have a termination date. I felt that she should set the date, that it should be her decision, in contrast to many decisions about her care in her childhood, when she was passed across the world from one parent to the other. I was, thus, forced to bear the uncertainty, as well as the torrents of rage, which often left me feeling wrung out like an old dishcloth, and exhausted at the end of a session. I was sustained by my knowledge and experience of the process of the last part of an analysis, when the work of the previous years returns like a kaleidoscope to be worked through once again before the work is finished. But I did find it difficult to bear the intensity of her feelings, her furious jealousy and envy: jealousy of what I had and envy of what I was. She cited every aspect of what she could see I had—a large house—and what she thought I probably had—a husband and children. She wanted all these things. Then there were all the more intangible aspects of my person and my life that in her fantasies she imagined I had: but mostly what she cried about was what I had not given her. She faced me with her accusations that I had, over the years, taken all her money and all her resources, and deprived her of the adventures she might have had if she had not been bound up in a relationship to me.

It was often difficult to maintain my analytic composure in the face of this storm, to maintain my thinking and put back to her, time and again, that which was hers, the gains she had made and the fruits of her labours. She was now in a very different psychic space from where she had been when we had started work. But it was true that she had not yet found a satisfying partner, nor had she a child, both of which she wanted badly, both of which she imagined that I had. She felt she needed to be apart from the analysis to find her own partner. I understood and interpreted this as her fear that I would spoil any relationship of her own with an envious attack, as each of her parents had attacked the other all her life and as her mother had unconsciously and enviously tried to destroy every enterprise she had attempted. I had now to take a back seat to allow Ms A to go forward on her own in her life, and consolidate the good work we had done together.

Ms A herself knew she needed to see her analysis through to the end, but it was so painful to keep going, to keep going at this time in her life, to work slowly and painfully towards saying goodbye. It felt like an achievement on both our parts when a termination date was agreed for the end of the year, and when we reached it.

I could consider that the bars of love and hate in the gate-like structure of her mind, for this patient, had become jumbled up, unattached to vertical posts, and so she was unable to sort out and manage her affects. Through the transference and countertransference, we experienced the passions and furies that previously had disrupted an ongoing development of her life. She had been unable to develop her relationships, career, and creative talents. Every endeavour had crashed on the jagged rocks of her intense and overwhelming feelings, and the ensuing disappointment was experienced as an earthquake of considerable magnitude. I hope that through the analytic experience, and through the ongoing nature of my ability to survive as a thinking, reflective, and understanding analyst, she can maintain a survival of her own thinking, reflective mind. I hope that the bars of love and hate are more firmly fixed in the structure of her mind, and that she can use the crossbars to experience the different emotions without becoming stuck at some extreme point; that she can think about how she feels, as I have tried to think with her, to put in place a thinking structure that can mediate and place the terrible feelings in both a historical and a present, comprehensible narrative.

Sometimes, during a break in analytic work, I wonder why do I, again and again, set out on this difficult path to meet the loves and hates of patients, when it is so very difficult to meet and manage them within myself? But then I think the pleasure in my work comes from seeing someone being able to move on in life, with affects available for exploring and experiencing life in a different way. With the more bounded structure of the metaphorical gate, having worked through love and hate in the transference, patients change and move forward, each in his or her singular way; this gives me deep pleasure.

With the integration of love and hate, the structure of the gate is in place, and there is a freer flowing both in and out of the mind, a greater capacity to experience life with its joys and disappointments, its pleasures and frustrations, and its relationships. We need a structure to our minds, boundaries to the self, and an internal representative of the original "protective shield", so that we can open and close this metaphorical gate to the world beyond ourselves. These structures serve ego strength and stability, and preserve emotional authenticity. When the gate is in place, and when it swings freely on its hinges, the analysis can end with the hope that our patients can discover further structures to add to those we have been able to create together.

References

Balint, M. (1952). Love and Hate. In: *Primary Love and Psychoanalytic Technique.* London: Karnac [reprinted 1985].

Blake, W. (*ca.* 1790–1793). *The Marriage of Heaven and Hell*, G. Keynes (Ed.) (2nd edn). London: Oxford University Press, 1966, p. 149.

Catullus (*ca.* 50 bc). In: *The Oxford Dictionary of Quotations* (p. 133). Oxford: Oxford University Press, 1978.

Dimen, M. (1994). Money, love and hate: contradiction and paradox in psychoanalysis. *Psychoanalytic Dialogues, 4*: 69–100.

Freud, S. (1905a). On psychotherapy. *S.E., 7*: 257–268. London: Hogarth.

Freud, S. (1940a [1938]). *An Outline of Psycho-Analysis. S.E., 23*: 139–207. London: Hogarth.

Kohon, G. (2005). Love in a time of madness. In: A. Green & G. Kohon (Eds.), *Love and its Vicissitudes* (pp. 62–83). London: Routledge.

Piontelli, A. (1985). *Backwards in Time*. Strathtay, Perthshire: Clunie Press for the Roland Harris Trust Library, Monograph No. 1.

Rosenfeld, H. (1987). *Impasse and Interpretation*. London: Routledge.

Symington, N. (2008). Generosity of heart: source of sanity. *British Journal of Psychotherapy, 24*: 488–500.

Winnicott, D. W. (1945). Primitive emotional development. In: *Through Paediatrics to Psycho-Analysis* (pp. 145–156). London: Hogarth, 1975.

Winnicott, D. W. (1947). Hate in the countertransference. In: *Collected Papers: Through Paediatrics to Psycho-Analysis* (pp. 194–203). London: Tavistock, 1958.

CHAPTER SIX

Terror, impasse, hope: fragmentation as resistance

Jessica Sacret Hering

Introduction

In this chapter, I want to describe a psychic position, arrived at in the analyses of certain patients after some years of intensive work, which presented difficulties in analysis and working through and which seemed to contain a strong risk of falling into impasse. The features of these analyses at a particular point in the work were similar enough to make it worthwhile to identify the dynamics as I understood them and to elaborate them further. This psychic position—in essence a series of fluctuating defences against an experience of fragmentation—in turn depended on relatively stable defensive positions established early on in life. The analysis and working through of this phase appeared to me to represent a crucial turning point in the analysis of these patients, the negotiation of which would mean the difference between a result for the patient that allows progress into something more psychically healthy, or, alternatively, a relapse into the familiarity of old defences.

These patients appeared to have had an experience of psychic fragmentation at a very early point in development. The frustration of primitive and intense wishes and desires, overwhelming to the early, fragile ego, had led to the defensive strategy of disintegration or fragmentation, either directly of the ego, or indirectly by the launching of a disintegrating attack on the object and then re-introjecting that disintegrated object. Some (Klein, 1957) would say that envy of the goodness of the breast could play an important part, too, in this early rage. This ongoing tendency to fragment the ego leads to instability at its core. If severe, the individual can be vulnerable to schizophrenic illness. If not so severe, an unstable ego can develop, leading to the difficulties of the schizoid pattern of development (see, for example, Fairbairn, 1952; Guntrip, 1968; Rey, 1994). In analysis, these latter patients whom I discuss here then come to wish to avoid the recognition of their fundamental, libidinal wishes at all costs, in order to avoid the anticipated frustration and the anticipated experience of severe disintegration, which had previously been a consequence. All of this is, of course, unconscious.

This set of circumstances then presents a real challenge to the progress of the analysis, as crucial steps, particularly the internalization and establishing of a good enough internal object, linked with good experiences in the analysis, are impeded at the deepest level if the underlying reasons for the fragmentation cannot be addressed. Melanie Klein repeatedly emphasized that a strong ego is founded on the internalizing and maintenance of a good internal object, the coalescing of good experiences into a stable good object in the early months of life. With the patients discussed here, a good internal object was not established with enough stability to withstand the onslaughts of persecutory anxiety resulting from bad object experiences, whether constituted from primarily internal or external sources. The love and longing and desperate dependency associated with recognition of a good object is, for these patients, linked with the phantasy of the inevitability of frustration and ensuing fragmentation. If, in time, these difficulties can be worked through and there can be a shift towards depressive level functioning, the guilt that arises as a result of the earlier aggression and hatred directed towards the now recognized good aspects of the analyst can be so overwhelming as to be unbearable.

At this point, the analysis is vulnerable to impasse. The predominance of bad experiences in the early months means that the normal splitting between good and bad objects cannot be diminished, so that the possibility of ambivalence cannot be established. The patient may resort time and time again to angry attacks as a way of defending against awareness of guilt, which is felt to be extremely persecutory. It is at this point particularly that the analysis of the dynamics has to be thoroughly understood and interpreted, helping to lessen the guilt and to pave the way towards helping the patient to bear the responsibility and the pain of reality. Recognizing the dynamics as described can allow an understanding of the hatred and aggression as being linked with the survival of the ego, albeit at a primitive level, and, thus, having an important defensive function which needs to be understood. This situation does not rule out that there may also be primary murderous hatred that can amplify and reinforce the defensive rage.

The epigraph from T. S. Eliot, thus, refers to the psychic situation where the past unconsciously holds a sense of catastrophe, and there are profound fears in contemplating a future that unconsciously is expected to resemble the past. The patients find themselves in a position where nothing feels safe, where threats to their psychic integrity, experienced as possible annihilation, can be felt to menace both their inner and their outer worlds. In the analytic work, it can be hard to see how these patients can leave their analyses with the realistic hope of taking something substantial away with them, unless the fear of fragmentation, its aetiology and the defences against it, can be thoroughly analysed and worked through in the context of a contemporary containing object.

Around 1946, Klein was emphasizing the importance of the early introjections of the good and loved object as a primary activity in the creation of a good internal object, which comes to form the focus of the fragile ego and around which it can integrate: "The first good object acts as a focal point in the ego. It counteracts the splitting and dispersal, makes for cohesiveness and integration, and is instrumental in building up the ego" (Klein, 1946, p. 6). The patients to whom I refer had too little early good experience to enable them to form a stable, good, internal object. They all suffered circumstances that led them to extremes of frustration.

For reasons of confidentiality, I do not give detailed background and histories of these patients, but instead present a composite of their clinical material. Because the psychic experiences with which I am concerned belong to the deep unconscious, the actual reality circumstances of their early and current environments are not inherently relevant to understanding the issues that I wish to describe, except for the crucial circumstance that the patients shared a significant experience of loss of their primary carer in the earliest period, from birth and during the first year of life. This loss would have been due to situations arising such as periods of prolonged neglect, separation, serious post-natal depression of the mother, or death of the mother or primary carer. The experience of loss varied in length and intensity in each case, but the psychic experience, the loss, frustration, and ensuing fragmentation, and the defences against these experiences, were essentially the same for all. I use the letter P to stand for a composite picture of these patients.

Of its nature, the phantasy of severe disintegration cannot be known as such, only feared. What is encountered in the countertransference is the tremendous resistance on the part of the patient to allowing contact with primitive wishes and desires, whose frustration has, in the past, led to the disaster. If this resistance is not understood for what it is, it can be a very difficult experience for the analyst, both because of the reality of the blocking defences (Schafer, 1997), which can in themselves be extremely frustrating if not understood, but also because there is a projective identification into the analyst of the massive frustration originally experienced by the patient, often accompanied by a projection of the experience of fragmentation as well.

Here, there is a risk of impasse. To defend against contact with what is felt to be a terrifying experience of impending psychic disintegration, the patient will resort, on the one hand, to blocking defences, that is, denial, rigid splitting, and projective identification. On the other hand, under the sway of a more extreme sense of threat, he may turn to more perverse defences, for example, to identifications with "bad" internal objects which, at that point, are felt to offer protection (Meltzer, 1968; Rosenfeld, 1971a).

Splitting, fragmentation, disintegration

Henri Rey (1994), in his groundbreaking book *Universals of Psychoanalysis in the Treatment of Psychotic and Borderline States*, speaking of the schizophrenic aetiology, says,

> Under the sway of persecutory anxiety and the fear of catastrophic dissolution of the ego—primitive and elemental anxieties which arise from the beginning of life—he proceeds to use splitting repetitively and intensively to get rid of bad parts of himself, which leads to a fragmentation of the object and of the fragmented parts of the ego, as well as fragmented parts of internal objects. [p. 11]

The patients I am describing in this chapter are not splitting or split to the degree that Rey is describing here; but there is a significant degree of abnormal splitting, sometimes not so severe as to stop the patient from functioning apparently fairly normally, or even well, but which, nevertheless, in analysis reveals serious problems in identity, in functioning in intimate relationships, coping with stressful situations, and situations involving responsibility. For it is in these situations that the inherent weaknesses in the ego manifest themselves and create anxieties about breakdown, which are, in essence, fears, as Rey describes, of "the dissolution of the ego".

In the literature, it is mainly Melanie Klein (e.g., 1935) and those analysts in her tradition who refer to the phenomenon of fragmentation. Hinshelwood (1989), in his invaluable *Dictionary of Kleinian Thought*, defines it as, "The severe splitting of the ego, typically in relation to the difficulties encountered in the paranoid–schizoid position. This gives rise to a sense of fragmentation [or disintegration], of going to pieces". The *chronic tendency to fragment the ego*, linked with massive frustration (Bion, 1957), already weak from a number of pre-existing circumstances, is characteristic of the borderline condition. Bion speaks of the "nameless dread" linked with this experience.

Thus, the term "fragmentation" is used in this context to refer to the extreme states of disintegration that can be caused by splitting of the ego. The phenomenon of splitting itself is ubiquitous, and, for Klein at least, part of normal development. Problems arise when the normal splitting of the earliest, primary object into "bad" and "good", kept separate in order to protect the good object, cannot be worked through as development progresses because the bad object is felt to be overwhelming to the good object. This generally is the underlying aetiology of a manic depressive mode of functioning.

Pathological splitting, on the other hand, occurs under situations of extreme threat, fundamentally inhibits normal development, and, at its most severe, may lead to a later schizophrenic mode of functioning. In the patients under discussion, the "bad" and "good" aspects of the object cannot be integrated because the "bad" object experiences are unconsciously felt to lead to the fragmented state. However, there have been enough good object experiences, or the individual has a strong enough libidinal drive, for the process of idealization and identification with the idealized object to occur.

Freud (1894a) recognized the phenomenon of splitting and, acknowledging the work of Janet and Breuer, said,

> . . . it may be taken as generally recognised that the syndrome of hysteria, so far as it is yet intelligible, justifies the assumption of there being a splitting of consciousness, accompanied by the formation of separate psychical groups. [p. 45]

For Freud, splitting is the result of conflict, but this was a descriptive term only, having no explanatory value (Laplanche & Pontalis, 1973, pp. 428–429). However, Bleuler (1911) used the term *spaltung* to denote what he thought of as the fundamental symptom of schizophrenia.

In the UK, Fairbairn (1952) developed and emphasized his understanding of the importance of schizoid (splitting) mechanisms which underlay the symptoms of hysteria and schizophrenia. This view was taken up by Melanie Klein in her complex formulation of the "paranoid–schizoid" position (Klein, 1932, 1935, 1946). Crucially, Klein extended the explanatory relevance given to splitting mechanisms, understanding them as being the consequence of the operation of the death instinct within the early primitive ego. This was her explanation of the severely disintegrated states encountered in the most disturbed schizophrenics.

For Klein's theory of development, the ego is present in very rudimentary form right from the beginnings of life. It is also relatively unintegrated. She writes (1946), ". . . the early ego largely lacks cohesion, and a tendency towards integration alternates with a tendency towards disintegration, a falling to bits" (p. 6).

Many non-Kleinians, notably Winnicott (1960), dispute the existence of an ego, however primitive and unintegrated, from the beginnings of life. However, it is worth noting that the postulation of an early, undifferentiated, non-ego state of existence, is not incompatible with Klein's formulations of the vicissitudes of the early ego when it does begin to emerge.

A consequence of this early ego's tendency to fall into bits (Bick, 1968) is that the infant is highly dependent on the holding (Winnicott) and the containing (Bion) functions of the primary caretaker, usually the mother, for a crucial sense of integrity of body and mind and the possibility of the formation of a strong ego. In the absence of this function being performed satisfactorily, such as with my maternally deprived patients, the developing infant will always be vulnerable to later states of disintegration and the tendency to fragment. The early ego would, in normal circumstances, be vulnerable to being overwhelmed by its own powerful primitive wishes or id impulses; equally, a perceived threat from the outside can be experienced as overwhelming.

Here, it is worth making the distinction between the usage of the term "disintegration" and that of "fragmentation". Generally, the notion of fragmentation, particularly in Klein, is linked with the idea of an active process, in a case where, for example, the wish of the self is to fragment the ego or the object in order to avoid the experience of rage or pain felt to be unbearable. This defensive use of fragmentation is clearly more likely to be used when the earlier experience of holding and containment has not been good. The term disintegration carries a more passive implication, and is associatively linked with the idea of early unintegration.

The task of psychoanalytic work inherently involves the stirring up of the most primitive wishes. To recapitulate: the patients in this paper have an experience of unbearable early loss and frustration, which has led to a terror and dread of dependency, the source of which is unconscious. In them, this is a symptom of early, encapsulated, split off, or simply unprocessed (Schore, 1994) traumatic experiences. Their difficulties are not as severe as in the disintegrated schizophrenic, in whom the disaster is lived out and is evident in overt behaviour.

"At one" phantasies

The need to avoid the experience of disintegration or fragmentation produces a characteristic defence where the patient's phantasy is sometimes described as if being "at one" with the analyst. This phantasy, in patient P, discussed below, is by no means a complete loss of the recognition of separateness and difference, but operates quite specifically at the more primitive level of the personality, where the idealized object, split off from the highly persecutory object, is projected on to the analyst and identified with, specifically to avoid the experience of separation, which elicits the fragmenting rage which has to be defended against.

The "at one" phantasy—where patient and analyst are implicitly felt to be ideal together—serves as an important defence against the infant's early rage and hatred and the consequent sense of persecution and fear of fragmentation. Along with this defence, a false self develops, marked by compliance and fear of conflict. Experiences that could possibly lead to negativity are phobically avoided, and there is a denial of separation with its dangers of conflict and frustration, which are, to some extent, averted by means of the idealization of the self and object "at one".

Rey (1994) illustrates the "at one" phantasy of merging or fusion with the object:

> The fear of separation from the object and the desire to penetrate into it and fuse with it into a primal unity can be so intense that it surpasses human understanding. Thus a paranoid and persecuted patient complained ceaselessly . . . full of rage and despair because I did not love her, after having seduced her by my interpretations and having led her to believe she was loved. She found proof of my wish to torture her in the fact that I did not let her penetrate into me physically and fuse with me. On this subject she lost all contact with reality and insisted that such a fusion was possible. [p. 13]

Projective identification

At times when the fact of physical separation can be contemplated, projective identification is utilized to preserve in the patient the illusion that they have no need for the analyst. Their capacity for thinking is preserved, but feelings linked with primitive phantasies are split off and projected into the analyst, so that the patient's awareness of dependency becomes, in phantasy, the analyst's need for the patient. For example, I was startled one day when P, during the period when he often dreamt of me as a lavatory, informed me that he knew I was unhappy not to be seeing him over the forthcoming break. Equally, vulnerability and awareness of difficulties are denied in favour of superiority, arrogance, and perfection. Klein (1935) states that "the desire for perfection is rooted in the depressive anxiety of disintegration"; and again, "the idea of perfection is so compelling because it disproves the idea of disintegration" (p. 270).

The projective identifications of these patients are described as excessive (Klein, 1946) and pathological (Bion, 1962), and they certainly possess these qualities. The word "rigid" also conveys their relentlessness and the way in which consistent interpretation has little impact. The patient is likely to pay lip service to the interpretations, while really thinking that the analyst is simply denying their true feelings and projecting into the patient.

Hatred of reality is profound, as is often said, but reality is hated because it brings with it awareness of overwhelming need, linked with a newly acknowledged good object, and consequent intense frustration originating with the infant left without its mother for far too long. The contributing factor of primary envy also cannot, in some patients, be discounted.

Recognizing the original trauma can help us to understand the relentlessness and power of the primitive projections. Projection of need is inevitable in the protection of the early ego if deprivation has been strong. In this context, Klein (1935) speaks about the avoidance of frustration as being linked with a terror that the distinction between the good and bad object will be abolished. It is only when projective identification becomes less intense, when projections are taken back and depressive thinking begins to take hold, that introjection of good object experience can be possible.

The vicissitudes of introjection

Successful development depends on the formation and maintenance of a good internal object formed by positive, helpful experiences that have been introjected. Implicit here is the notion that good experiences can, indeed, be taken in. It is a central thesis of this chapter that, when there is a core area of fragmentation, internalizations of good experience cannot occur. The "at one" defence, projective identification, primary envy, and omnipotent defences erected against dependency, are all obstacles to taking something in from an object. In this context, Hanna Segal (1981) refers to "blocked introjection".

Schafer (1997) examines the notion of blocked introjection, or blocked incorporation, as he would rather put it, in some detail. He says, ". . . the phantasy of blocked incorporation may be primarily defensive of the self: for example, in the exclusion from the self of bad objects or substances and their less concrete manifestations in bad ideas or feelings" (p. 141). He also suggests that blocked incorporation may be protective of the object, either from orally damaging cannibalistic phantasies, or, more generally, from the subject's phantasied internal destructiveness. The subject may also be blocking incorporation in order to maintain the status quo of a defensive system controlling the internal world.

Hanna Segal (1981) writes of the deleterious effects of envy on the introjective processes:

> The importance of envy lies in the fact that it interferes with the normal operation of schizoid mechanisms. Splitting into an ideal and a bad object cannot be established since it is the ideal object that is the object of envy, and therefore hostility. Thus the introjection of the ideal object, which could become the core of the ego, is disturbed at its very roots. Defences against envy may be equally detrimental to growth . . . [p. 22]

I would include in the category of inhibited introjection the possibility of the infant's blocking of projections from the mother when these are experienced as bad, intrusive, or violent. There may also be the blocking of the reintrojection of violent projections from a mother unable to contain them.

Thus, without the internalization of good experience, the personality may develop apparently normally, but can have a crucial weakness at the core, where the deepest, primary libidinal wishes are denied or attacked. Rey (1994) also speaks of this problem for the developing ego and its difficulties in analysis. He says,

"... the question of his or her identity is a major problem for the schizoid", and suggests this is the result of faulty introjective identification. He links this to feelings of persecution and fear of the object experienced, through projection, as highly destructive, envious, and insatiable.

In my work with P, it gradually dawned on me how tense he was as he lay on the couch. His body was tense, but so was his mind. It was as if he had to respond to my interpretations almost before I had finished speaking. He could not let my words penetrate, and his verbal responses at this time, which seemed to come just from his mind, split off from any affect, had the quality of pushing away my communications. I had the sense that he was protecting an inner world which was in bits, with expulsive words and a bodily armour of muscles (Ogden, 1989) which he cultivated by means of obsessive visits to the gym. It seemed that he did not want to take in even the kindest of words.

André Green and the central phobic position

André Green (2002), in describing a configuration similar to that of my patients, speaks of an area of functioning in borderline patients that he calls "the central phobic position". He arrives at this understanding via his appreciation of "a particular quality of associative behaviour ... its role in maintaining a central defensive position . . . and a particular functioning of the mind that the author terms phobic" (p. 45). In particular, Green found these patients avoiding a central area of functioning that he attributed to "a flight from taking cognisance of a prohibited desire" (p. 46).

For Green,

> What the analyst is mainly faced with in the transference with "borderline" patients is destructivity that is directed predominantly *first and foremost at the subject's own psychic functioning*. Destructivity is made use of by negativistic defences of which Freudian splitting is the subtlest form. [*ibid.*, p. 47]

In this paper, Green elaborates in his inimitably elegant style his understanding of an area of psychic functioning, which is not dissimilar to what I have described in terms of splitting, projective identification, omnipotence, introjective refusals, and the rejection of reality. His central point is also to do with the phobic avoidance of a central, core area of psychic functioning. He says of his patient, ". . . what stopped him from associating . . . was *the anticipation* of where it might lead him, which he desperately tried to avoid". Later, he continues, ". . . the patient is revealing a state of threat caused by the consequences of establishing meaningful links between a number of themes in the patient's mind . . .". Later still, he says that the meaningful insight being avoided is felt to lead to a "catastrophic outcome" (*ibid*., p. 56).

So far, Green is describing similar mechanisms from the viewpoint of his understanding of gaps in the patients' free associations. His paper describes something more disturbed and disintegrated than the phenomena I am identifying, but it seems clear that we are in similar psychical territory, viewed from differing theoretical and technical standpoints.

The patient "P"

I will now turn to the composite patient, P, whose analysis traversed the emotional and conceptual terrain described above. Immediately following his birth, P's mother had a serious accident, which meant she was hospitalized for nearly two years, and remained somewhat disabled thereafter. Father, not coping very well with this catastrophe, got various assorted helpers to look after his infant, while carrying on with his demanding job. There was little or no consistency in the care of the infant, who only just survived. When mother returned home disabled, she was a broken figure in the patient's mind. At the age of about three, a nanny was engaged, who then became a consistent and helpful figure to P until he was six years old. By this time, Mother had recovered quite well and seemed to show her guilt at her abandonment of her child by allowing herself to be totally controlled by his wishes and demands. P, however, became relentlessly bitter and resentful until his mother died, which occurred before he came into therapy. Father, it appeared, was capable of love and kindness and could show care towards P, but could be violently angry when P did not do as wanted. P's hatred went underground, and he developed a personality of compliance towards authority figures, but relentless defiance towards his parents, while living in a highly developed phantasy world in which he was a famous artist, internationally acclaimed, whose work was greeted with constant adulation.

P came into analysis in his thirties, when his career was not going the way he had imagined it. While good and reasonably successful in his field, he was not the lauded figure of international fame that he had fantasized about. The transference quickly became one of thinly disguised denigration, with a veneer of co-operation and intellectual agreement. Meanwhile, he complained bitterly and with furious contempt about the shortcomings of his parents and others in his present life, especially those supposed to be helping him. These complaints had an expulsive quality, by which means he tried to evacuate into me his bad and despised internal object. His first years in analysis were remarkable for the consistency with which he found pressing reasons to leave the country, often for weeks, whenever a break was pending. By these manoeuvres, he showed how unmanageable were his feelings of loss.

After a few years he became an artistic consultant, and, to some extent, reconciled himself to this more modest role in life. P was able to work quite effectively in his structured work environment, his difficulties mainly expressed in his lack of intimate relationships and in his analysis, which was soon to reveal the ego weaknesses and rigid defences against true intimacy and interdependency. I began to see in him a split between his thinking, reality-orientated processes and his primitive emotional chaos.

P struggled in the early years, in a way characteristic for these patients, with a confused sense of himself, and the need to project both the idealized and despised aspects of himself into me in order to feel "at one" with me and in control of me at a phantasy level. In his early dreams, he had no object to evacuate into; he regularly dreamt of being in formal situations such as a dinner party in which he could not stop himself from peeing uncontrollably under the table. Later, he dreamt about looking for a lavatory. Later still, I was the lavatory that could at least hold his deeply despised dependent wishes. I was made very much aware of his early lack of care and how his phantasies and dreams reflected this lack of containment and chaos in such a concrete way.

The struggle against dependency needs

After a few years of the analysis, there were changes. P appeared on the surface to be extremely dependent. He became anxious to get to his sessions on time, and implacably intolerant of any impediment to getting to see me, full of rage and anxiety if he was made late by something beyond his control. He expressed fear and anxiety before weekends and breaks. It became clear, however, that this was not true dependency, which involves the recognition of the object as being separate and able to help.

At this point, P was having sessions four times weekly. When, mindful of his apparently desperate and uncontainably difficult feelings during the three day break from Thursday to Monday, I offered a session on the Friday, I was met with a vehement refusal. He had too much to do, he could not afford it, his wife would be furious, and so on. None of these explanations seemed to reflect the reality of his situation. The suggestion of the extra session had put him in touch with fears of a hated, despised, and terrifying dependency, normally located in me or his wife. His fury at the suggestion that he needed anything from me was put into his wife.

During this time, he had a frightening habit of having a serious accident just before I was due back from a break. On one occasion, he managed to poison himself "accidentally" the day before his first session back with me. The time just before the analyst's return is the most dangerous, because the analyst becomes again linked with an early good object whose absence cannot be denied, when the patient is closest to an awareness of dependency on a desperately desired object; I saw the poisoning and "accidents" as a concretization of the fragmentation created by frustration and rage.

The "at one" phantasy means the refusal to take in anything from an object except at a superficial, intellectual level. Taking in the emotional meaning of interpretations, symbolic of taking nourishment from the mother, is partially or completely blocked. In order to take something in from an object, separation and difference has to be accepted.

In his longed-for need to be "at one" with me, P would feel very disturbed when I said things he had not thought of himself, but he also hastened to find ways to agree with me. This did involve him thinking genuinely about himself, but the pressure and motivation was to see it the same way as I did in order to regain a sense of being of one mind. Rey (1994) also illustrates this problem: he speaks of how the patient reproached him constantly that he was not in agreement with what she was saying. "This produced two people which she hated."

P could experience an interpretation indicating that our minds were different as if it made him into a helpless victim of an inexorable process, persecuting him unbearably once he left a session. The experience of separation put him in touch with his envy, which roused hatred of my idealized capacities. He would launch a disintegrating attack on me in his mind, but then have only a disintegrated, fragmented object with which to identify. He would describe the awful and unbearable state of mind on his return. He dealt with this by finding ways to persuade himself that I was being cruel and sadistic, so he could feel justified in hating me. Klein (1935) describes the way that the distinction can be blurred or abolished between the good and bad object. The good object is desired, but when frustration is great, it becomes a bad, terrifying object.

It is of importance to understand the source of the panic at separation that can be mistaken for dependency. The phantasy of the patient of being "at one" with the analyst can appear to be remarkably similar in its manifestations to the usual indications of extreme dependency. The patient displays great anxiety at times of breaks and separations. On analysis, however, it becomes apparent that the anxiety is linked with the threat felt by the patient that is posed by the recognition that the phantasy of being of one mind does not coincide with reality. P was schizoid, but not schizophrenic: his sense of reality was not completely occluded. When he came to consider that I was going on a break without him, he did not, for example, on the whole, believe that I was going away because of trying to cure myself of my passionate love for him, as does Ian McEwan's (2000) erotomanic character Jed in his novel *Enduring Love*. Instead, he simply switched his allegiance and "at one" phantasy to his wife, and I was the one to be left outside of the phantasy couple who could give each other everything. Typically, at least in the early stages of this phase, once the separation happened, problems and anxieties disappeared as P abolished (annihilated) me as object, or projected into me the dread of loss. Thus, he would return from breaks, about which he had previously been terribly anxious, having had a wonderful time.

Some of the consequences of projective identification can be puzzling, as the patient may act on the basis of the phantasy while speaking as if aware of the reality. Before reaching a point where more realistic wishes can be entertained by the patient, a long period of work can be necessary, mainly focusing on the interpreting and working through of the projective identification.

P, for example, did not believe at a cognitive level that physical fusion was possible. On exploration as to what such oneness might actually mean in reality, P did recognize the impossibility of such a phantasy being realized in the real world. But, although this could be acknowledged at an intellectual level, it persisted at the phantasy and emotional level, until, in time, the phantasy developed into a more realistically simple wish fulfilment that I could always be there when he wanted. This eventually could be worked through in the normal way, when the reality was no longer felt to be catastrophic.

However, P had felt at one level, for many years, that I was in a state of being in love with him. He suffered from anxiety about what he believed was my rage and envy during breaks. This was closer to the true erotomania of Jed in *Enduring Love*. In the novel, Jed has the delusion that the central character is in love with him and that his rejecting behaviour is because of an unwillingness to admit to his true feelings. P was sometimes deluded to that extent. He often genuinely feared my displeasure when he had been away, and I saw this as the rigid projective identification of his own primitive love and need and his defence against his own hatred and annihilating rage. In *Enduring Love*, Jed's murderousness finally emerges, and illustrates how the "love", if thwarted, reveals the enormous hatred against which the "at one" defence is erected. This projective identification resists interpretation with the greatest tenacity, and for P the process of disillusionment was extremely painful and slow.

Thus, P would feel that I had to be looked after before he could go out in the evenings, otherwise I would totally reject him the next day for abandoning me. He would construct phantasies about my whereabouts, which he then believed, and which relieved his anxiety that I was not left alone. In the fullness of time, however, he was able to see more clearly the true nature of our relative positions in terms of dependency, and recognize the solidity of the reality of our actual relationship.

The manic defence

Along with projective identification of unwanted parts of the self comes a manic state. P began to speak as if he were perfect and vehemently hated his imperfections, feeling that my interpretations were bringing them to his attention.

For Klein, the manic state defends against the anxieties of disintegration and of schizoid persecution on the one hand, and utilizes the defences of omnipotence and control and devaluation of the object on the other. These are in order to defend against depressive anxieties of pain and guilt. After much analysis of the primitive persecutory anxieties, P came to see his phantasy of his own perfection and the allied sense of superiority and contempt for others. He began to feel profound guilt; however, this awareness could not be maintained.

The core experience in the transference and countertransference

After work in the analysis had proceeded for some years on the omnipotent defences, the blocking of introjections of good experiences, and the projective identifications, P came to recognize more and more his idealization of himself, his sense of superiority over others, and his phantasy of his own perfection which had accompanied the projection of his own faults and weaknesses into others. This included especially his intense dependency, which he had utterly disdained and still bitterly despised.

At this point in his analysis, his love and longing for the goodness of his objects had been aroused, and P's splitting of the good and bad became more obvious. During this period, he became intensely engaged with me and those close to him in his life. At this time, he could feel guilt and the need for reparation in the shape of feeling shame and wanting to apologize for his past angry outbursts and intense condemnations of others. He wanted to do better by them, including myself. At other times, these feelings were completely absent and split off, and he would revert time and again to this cycle where he could not bear the guilt his angry behaviour had aroused. Sometimes, he became very withdrawn and rejecting of contact when his hatred was stirring up a wish to launch an annihilating attack on me, which, in his phantasy, would make me fall into bits or defensively retaliate.

A particular pattern of interactions developed which continued on and off over a period of some years, needing a long period of working through. On these occasions, P would come into the session suffused with rage and condemnation at unforgivable behaviour visited on him, as he felt, by his wife or other members of his family. When I analysed this in the transference in terms of my unforgivable behaviour in being separate and not controlled by him, I was met with furious denials, violent condemnation, and assertions of hatred. He attempted to divert attention from my interpretations with contemptuous and mocking rejoinders, with a degree of abusiveness in tone and content that was hitherto unknown. The next session would be filled with guilt, and genuine expressions of regret for this behaviour. At times, he showed some insight into the original source of the problem: his longing for an absent mother. This depressive position functioning could last for one or two sessions following the outburst, then would be split off again, as if the guilt and remorse had never been. The expressions of ordinary affection and gratitude towards his family and towards me became transmuted into the old idealizations, where we were all felt to be collectively wonderful, and the rage was once more split off. At these times, interpretations along these lines produced only intellectual understanding.

When the episodes of violent attack began, I was aware that P's reaction to my interpretations meant that the rage that was stirred up was literally unbearable for him and he was evacuating his fragmenting self into me and then feeling I had evacuated it straight back into him when I interpreted. I understood this also as indicating that P was showing me how it had felt to be a child with a parent who was violently attacking him, as I knew that P's father had been violent, both verbally and physically.

These interpretations did help, and enabled us to more fully explore the terror and dread that P had experienced in his childhood.

This included the reality of his father's aggression towards him for no apparent reason, experienced by P as an attack on his very existence. At times, P identified himself as victim of that violent aggression which, at other times, he expressed towards me, then became sadistic, enjoying inflicting on me what he felt had been inflicted on him. Because of his childhood experience of having a parent who often seemed to hate him, the fragmentation of his ego in avoidance of that pain was projected into his object.

This fragmented part of his self, projected violently into me, was extremely hard to contain, and I felt I experienced directly the unbearableness that P had experienced as a child. In those moments, I wanted to get rid of the experience and get rid of P, and had to wait to recover my capacity to think and reflect on what was going on. The experience with P's father had been in addition to an experience with a mother felt to be part of the early split between ideal and persecutory. She had been adored, and P's hatred toward his father contained early Oedipal hatreds, which I interpreted, in general trying to facilitate Oedipal developments, including the triangular space for thinking that Britton (1989) refers to.

Turning to bad objects for protection

Klein (1935) points out how annihilating attacks can be aimed at good objects as well as bad. She also stresses the terror at the loss of good objects, and, at such moments, the threat of primitive persecution can be extreme. At the same time, as the analysis has enabled an acknowledgement of something good enough in the analyst, the guilt at annihilating wishes can also be powerful. This anger with the analyst may or may not be suffused with envy and sadism, but, at the same time, the libidinal part of the self is terrified at the destructiveness towards the analyst as good object. At this point, if an attack is mounted, there is also a terror of the imminent loss of this good object. It is at this moment that the patient can turn to the bad objects for protection, for the protection that is required is against the persecuting guilt of the attack on the good object, and terror at its loss, which can feel unsurvivable. The bad objects are linked only with hatred and murderousness; love is split off and denied, avoiding guilt and enabling the attack to be freely pursued.

The identification with bad objects entails the denial of love and of any good object experience. If there is no love (of the patient to the analyst in the form of gratitude for help, or, in the mind of the patient, of the analyst to the patient in terms of *caritas* and staying with the patient through thick and thin), then the analyst can be viewed as solely bad, and attacked without guilt.

To differing degrees, P and the patients in this discussion moved into this position at crucial moments, when the destructive parts of the self, as described by Rosenfeld (1971), become defensively idealized. The internal objects may be tightly organized, as he and Steiner (1993) describe, as a "gang" or "Mafia gang". This conceptualization can also be linked with the recognition of the existence of a narcissistic organization (Meltzer, 1968; Sohn, 1985). The function of the gang is to hold hostage the dependent, vulnerable parts of the personality that are capable of relating to a good object. It is generally felt to offer protection from pain, anxiety, and guilt, and this ensures powerful defences against depressive position functioning.

In a dream,

> P was bidding farewell to some friends who were leaving his house. When he went to find them, they were trapped, with armed guards surrounding them. These armed guards reminded P of the Egyptian gods standing at the entrance to a temple that he had seen on recent travels. This was interpreted as parts of the self, idealized and organized so as to keep under guard some "good"—that is, libidinal—parts of the self.

Here, I think an important point can be made about Rosenfeld's original conception (1971) of the parts of the self being divided into healthy "good" parts and destructive "bad" parts. This is also where those of Kleinian orientation can be misunderstood. While there is indubitably a gang-like organization that can be discerned in some patients, and the majority of the patients who form a basis for this paper have reported dreams in which a gang or gang-like group features explicitly, the exact reason for the emergence of such a structure needs to be carefully considered.

If it is the case that the libidinal parts of the self are trapped and guarded by "bad" parts that are idealized, is this because the "bad" parts are primarily destructive—that is, issuing from death instinct impulses? Or may it be that the libidinal parts of the personality are being kept in check and guarded by angry, negatively toned parts because the libidinal parts, if unchecked, lead to just such a psychic disaster as is being suggested in this chapter? That is, that the gang-like structure may be organized for defensive reasons to protect the libidinal parts of the ego from disintegration. This idea links more closely with Steiner's (1993) suggestion of a psychic "retreat", and Eric Brenman (1985) goes further in suggesting that his patient's narcissistic organization has the function of hijacking the patient's goodness and perverting it to the side of cruelty in order to avoid a psychic catastrophe. We can never prove or disprove the presence of primary destructiveness, but when we know about profoundly inadequate early provision, and understand the implications of Bion's descriptions of the function of containment, it makes sense to keep an open mind.

In another dream,

> P was captured by a gang of thugs. He then made overtures to the leader, and later found himself chatting in a friendly way with them all. A woman was standing nearby who was injured in some way.

Both dreams show the wish to turn to something negative. But, in the second dream, there is an awareness of guilt and a reference to the knowledge of damage done to a good object.

Because I could not sense P wanted to exercise control over his attacks on me, I was made to understand the violence of his internal world, and the way in which he turned to bad objects for protection and enjoyed being sadistic. When, subsequently, all elements of the situation were repeatedly analysed, he was able to feel a more enduring guilt and sadness for his sadistic attacks. Meanwhile, his guilt lessened with the diminution of his omnipotence, and my recognition of how difficult and traumatic his childhood had been.

The threat of impasse

At some points in this part of the analysis there was a real threat that impasse could develop. Even if I understood and interpreted correctly, and in a non-persecutory style, P's guilt could make him cling more desperately to his grievances and hatred, escalating into a vicious circle. I was concerned that there would come a time when

P would feel he had caused too much damage and the guilt would remain unbearable and irreparable.

For prolonged periods, P oscillated between the familiar primitive defences, which could end in violent rage, and his attempts to stay with something more loving in himself. He still tended to move into the familiar defences of blocking, denial, projective identification, or the manic defences where he devalued the whole experience of the analysis and wanted to leave. But the detailed interpretation of the meaning and feared consequences of dependency, in terms of inevitable frustration and the terrors of disintegration, brought him in time to a more realistic appreciation of himself, his past, the reality of his experience, his internal world, and the realities of what I could offer. But his guilt, exacerbated by omnipotence, tended to make him withdraw back into rage, victimhood, and the blaming of others for his difficulties.

I found, in time, that central to the process of change was my repeated interpretation of his terror of destroying and, thereby, losing his good enough internal figures, linked with myself in the transference. Equally important was his recognition, finally, that he had not in reality harmed me. I also understood how he felt his aggression towards his mother had caused her disabilities. His profound guilt, based on primitive omnipotent phantasies, diminished and allowed some hope into what had often felt like a hopeless situation. Increasingly, he managed to draw back from the familiar path of annihilating rage as I was able to interpret why he had felt this to be the only way open to him, and why he believed it would end in the disaster which he had experienced so many times and which caused such desperate feelings of helplessness and despair. When this was understood sufficiently by both of us, P began to feel safe enough to allow the beginnings of a benign change in the cycle.

A technical issue

An important aspect of this process was a technical one. P needed to be familiar with his rage, hatred, and murderousness, the extent of which had always been split off and denied, so that he could recognize and learn to bear the consequences of giving in to these feelings which would end in the greatly feared fragmented state. Of crucial relevance to this process was the exploration I tried to initiate with him on an ongoing basis, concerning his sense of the reality of the capacities of his object, myself. Had I actually been damaged by his attacks? Could I understand, and, more importantly, could I bear his hatred? In his paper "The importance of being hated as a prerequisite for love", David Morgan (2002) shows how very important it is that the patient be allowed to explore his phantasies about the analyst's mind and capacities. Morgan suggests an extension of John Steiner's (1993) "analyst centred" interpretation to help a patient move away from the stuckness of their projective identifications. He says, "The investigation as to the accuracy of their perceptions is extremely important" (p. 162).

Morgan's technique is to invite the patient to explore the reality of the phantasy that emerges in the projective identification into the analyst. Working with a perverse patient, he says,

> [my] interest is to explore how these issues arise in the transference and how the accompanying fear of a descent into psychosis, and the disintegration that accompanies their treatment, can be managed with interpretative work that invites the patient to explore my reality so as to discover an object that might be able to think rather than aggressively act upon him. This is important because it is often difficult for patients to distinguish between interpretation and aggressive intrusion . . . [p. 154]

Implicit in this stance of the analyst is a willingness to be questioned and to risk being found wanting, fairly or unfairly. This is particularly relevant where a parent has in reality had difficulty in allowing criticism. Also implicit in this technique is the recognition that patients are often exquisitely sensitive to, and on the alert about, the analyst's true feelings at any given moment. However regularly one may interpret the patient's anxiety that one cannot bear his hatred and contempt (the "analyst centred" interpretation of Steiner, 1993), this can still leave a patient fearful that his anxiety may be realistic. P could also, of course, be anxious that it might *not* be realistic, which would remove his defensive alliance with bad objects and usher in the onset of guilt.

With P, I found that in the earlier stages of his rages I had to stay silent in order to bear the very unpleasant feelings within me. When I could think, I had to discern what was transference, what was being projected, and what was my own response to this. Later, I learnt that my silence was experienced by the patient as indicating he had damaged me.

The thrust of Morgan's paper (*ibid.*) is to argue that the patient needs to know the analyst can bear his hatred before he can feel safe to allow himself to love, and that this needs to be genuine. I found this was borne out in my work with P. In time, and helped by my having to think through time and again the sources of these attacks from P, I had processed adequately enough to interpret with some equanimity. In spite of having felt I had been containing his annihilating rage quite well and for some while, it was only at the point at which I had genuinely integrated this often hateful aspect of P in my own mind with my knowledge of his good and loving aspects that he said to me on one of these previously fraught occasions: "I can think about this now, as I can hear you're not condemning me."

P had somehow become aware of my being able genuinely to understand him as a whole person, capable of both loving and hating during his attacks on me, and this made all the difference, allowing a more benign process to develop. So, while it is perhaps inevitable that at first I sometimes could not bear the intense and prolonged attacks, when I finally genuinely *suffered* them, as Bion (1970) puts it, the patient will know it, perhaps only unconsciously. Inadequacies in the function of containment consequent on an absent or unavailable mother is, of course, the most common source of fears of destructiveness.

In the course of this process, P learnt gradually to let me contain his most difficult annihilating feelings and, finally, to try to contain them himself. In time, a fragile foothold in the depressive position was achieved, which was to be strengthened gradually over very many months. This finally made it possible for P to leave his analysis with a sense of hope for the future, recognizing, for the most part, that life did not have to be as devastating or hopeless as he often had experienced it, but nor was it either as exciting as when the idealizing, narcissistic, sadistic, "at one" phantasies had reigned supreme. In spite of his propensity to fragmentation and core introjective weakness, P's negativity was worked through in the analysis sufficiently for him to internalize some good object experience, leaving me with a reasonable hope that he would be able to sustain something that would help him manage his life and relationships better.

References

Bick, E. (1968). The experience of the skin in early object relations. *International Journal of Psychoanalysis, 49*: 484–486 [reprinted in E. Bott Spillius (Ed.), *Melanie Klein Today: Developments in Theory and Practice,* Vol. 1, 1988].

Bion, W. R. (1957). The differentiation of the psychotic from the non psychotic personalities. *International Journal of Psychoanalysis, 38*: 266–275 [reprinted in: *Second Thoughts. Selected Papers on Psycho-Analysis* (1967). London: Heinemann Medical Books; reprinted London: Karnac, 1984].

Bion, W. R. (1962). *Learning From Experience.* London: Maresfield Reprints, Karnac, 1984.

Bion, W. R. (1970). *Attention and Interpretation.* London: Tavistock.

Bleuler, E. (1911). *Dementia Praecox or the Group of Schizophrenias.* New York: International Universities Press.

Brenman, E. (1985). Cruelty and narrow mindedness. *International Journal of Psychoanalysis, 66*: 273–281 [reprinted in: E. Bott Spillius (Ed.), *Melanie Klein Today: Developments in Theory and Practice, Vol 1.* London: Routledge, 1988].

Britton, R. (1989). The missing link: parental sexuality in the Oedipus complex. In: R. Britton, M. Feldman & E. O'Shaughnessy (Eds.), *The Oedipus Complex Today* (pp. 83–101). London: Karnac.

Eliot, T. S. (1963). *The Family Reunion.* London: Faber.

Fairbairn, W. (1952). *Psychoanalytic Studies of the Personality.* London: Routledge and Kegan Paul.

Freud, S. (1894a). The neuro-psychosis of defence. *S.E., 3*: 41–46.

Freud, S. (1895d). *Studies on Hysteria. S.E., 2*: 1–306. London: Hogarth.

Green, A. (2002). The central phobic position: a new formulation of the free association method. In: P. Williams (Ed.), *Key Papers on the Borderline* (pp. 45–82). London: Karnac.

Guntrip, H. (1968). *Schizoid Phenomena, Object Relations and the Self.* London: Hogarth.

Hinshelwood, R. D. (1989). *A Dictionary of Kleinian Thought.* London: Free Association Books.

Klein, M. (1932). *The Psychoanalysis of Children.* London: Hogarth.

Klein, M. (1935). A contribution to the psychogenesis of manic depressive states. *International Journal of Psychoanalysis, 16*: 145–174 [reprinted in: *The Writings of Melanie Klein, Vol. 2.* London: Hogarth, 1975].

Klein, M. (1946). Notes on some schizoid mechanisms. *International Journal of Psychoanalysis, 27*: 99–110 [reprinted in: *The Writings of Melanie Klein, Vol. 3: Envy and Gratitude*. London: Hogarth, 1975].

Laplanche, J., & Pontalis, J.-B. (1985). *The Language of Psycho-Analysis.* London: Hogarth [republished London: Karnac, 1988].

Meltzer, D. (1968). Terror, persecution, dread—a dissection of paranoid states. *International Journal of Psychoanalysis, 49*: 396–400 [reprinted in: D. Meltzer, *Sexual States of Mind* (pp. 99–106). Strathtay, Perthshire: Clunie Press, 1978].

McEwan, I. (2000). *Enduring Love*. New York: Vintage Books.

Morgan, D. (2002). The importance of being able to be hated as a prerequisite for love. In: D. Mann (Ed.), *Love and Hate* (pp. 137–146). London: Brunner-Routledge.

Ogden, T. (1989). *The Primitive Edge of Experience.* Northvale, NJ: Aronson.

Rey, H. (1994). *Universals of Psychoanalysis in the Treatment of Psychotic and Borderline States.* London: Free Association Books.

Rosenfeld, H. (1971). A clinical approach to the psychoanalytic theory of the life and death instincts: an investigation into the aggressive aspects of narcissism. *International Journal of Psycho-Analysis, 52*: 169–178 [reprinted in E. Bott Spillius (Ed.), *Melanie Klein Today, Vol. 1*. London: Routledge, 1988].

Schafer, R. (1997). Blocked introjection/blocked incorporation. In: D. Bell (Ed.), *Reason and Passion: A Celebration of the Work of Hannah Segal* (pp. 139–146). London: Duckworth.

Schore, A. (1994). *Affect Regulation and the Origin of the Self.* Hillsdale, NJ: Erlbaum.

Segal, H. (1981). *The Work of Hanna Segal*. New York: Aronson.

Sohn, L. (1985). Narcissistic organisation, projective identification and the formation of the identificate. *International Journal of Psychoanalysis, 66*: 201–213 [reprinted in: E. Bott Spillius (Ed.), *Melanie Klein Today, Vol. 1*. London: Routledge, 1988].

Steiner, J. (1993). *Psychic Retreats.* London: Routledge.

Winnicott, D. W. (1960). Ego distortion in terms of true and false self. In: *Maturational Processes and the Facilitating Environment*. London: Hogarth Press.

CHAPTER SEVEN

Phobic attachments: internal impediments to change

Michael Halton

Introduction

This chapter is concerned with a group of patients who suffer from entrenched narcissistic and phobic defences. Because of this, they find establishing deep emotional contact with other people to be very problematic. It would be misleading to say they are suffering from a narcissistic personality structure, as the term is usually understood, with its connotations of omnipotent self-sufficiency and self-regard. These patients are well aware of an emotional need for other people, and consciously they desire and seek out closeness. However, when they move towards their object or their object makes too close a move towards them, they become anxious and are often overwhelmed with phobic panic and fears. The nature of these fears is often mysterious and confusing to themselves, and they find it difficult to make sense of their own reactions, which seem to be at such odds with the closeness and intimacy they most consciously desire. At best, these patients feel uneasy and awkward when confined in emotional closeness to another person, and at worst, this can deteriorate into a full-blown state of claustrophobic entrapment, accompanied by experiences of a loss of self and depersonalization. They often seek help because these difficulties have led to a marked impoverishment in their social and emotional lives, whether they are consciously aware of this or not. It is important to stress that while some of these patients may be on the borderline end of the spectrum in terms of mental functioning, others may be operating with a considerably more mature level of psychic organization and do not, at first acquaintance, present as especially ill. However, they are all generally unhappy and discontented with their lot and find the ordinary ups and downs of life an ordeal.

Once these patients enter analysis they are often committed to the process, attend regularly, and are deeply reliant on the consistency that daily analytic sessions provide. The problem seems to be when it comes to using the analysis as a transformative experience to open up their internal world and deepen the contact with their own mind (Bion, 1965; Bollas, 1979). Any attempt to locate and name split off relational experiences and parts of the self, and internal objects in the transference–countertransference dynamic, meets with more than the normal resistance. Typically, they cannot learn from the experience of a close and deep transference relationship with their analyst, as this is precisely the thing that they are phobically allergic to. In other words *having* analysis rather than being *in* analysis becomes *the* central difficulty. Both the analyst and patient sooner or later come to realize this fact, and they are then both faced with the prospect of a treatment that looks stuck and interminable, and which seems to show no hope of ever resolving into an acceptable and satisfactory conclusion.

It is important to mention that this group of patients are not particularly cold, neither are they distant in the way they relate to people, nor do they depend excessively on forms of hyper rationality, as one might expect from the descriptions of schizoid or "thick skinned" narcissistic patients described by Rosenfeld (1987) and Britton (1998). If perverse elements are prominent, they are nearly always ego dystonic and a source of discomfort and guilt. The patients I am thinking of have much in common with Britton's descriptions of "thin skinned" patients, in that they make tenacious emotional attachments. However, they also differ, in that they do not display the clamorous, controlling, demands for exclusive intersubjective understanding that seem to be so characteristic of the "thin skinned" group. They seem to have established in some area of their ego sufficient integration to function in a fairly stable manner; however, they do demand to be "of one mind" with their objects, and oscillate between this and the wish for genuine independent thought of their own.

Essentially, the patients I will describe seem to have had an early phobic response to their primary object, which they experienced as malign. This early difficulty with accepting maternal care appears to have played a significant part in distorting and preventing internalization of a good object and the ego integration one would hope for in normal development.

Theoretical background

A history of early infantile trauma due to a failure of maternal containment and / or maternal impingement is probably implicated, to some extent, in the phobic structuring of the personality. Rosenfeld (1987), Winnicott (1960c), and Kohut (1971), among many others, have all emphasized the centrality of adverse infantile experiences of impingement in the aetiology of these conditions. Winnicott puts it thus:

> If maternal care is not "good enough" then the infant does not really come into existence, since there is no continuity of being; instead the personality becomes built on the basis of reactions to environmental impingement. [1960c, p. 54]

Rosenfeld's evocative description of these patients as having an emotional "thin skin" is that they are easily wounded, quick to feel misunderstood, and so on. These "thin skinned" patients also resemble, in some ways, what attachment theorists describe in their studies of infants who have had an "insecure attachment" in early infancy; they are noted for being very clinging, yet feel neither secure nor properly trusting of the object they desire and depend on (Ainsworth, Blehar, Waters, & Wall, 1978; Bowlby, 1969).

Britton (1998), while agreeing with the importance of early maternal experience and environmental trauma in severe cases, suggests that in milder cases there is reason to believe there is also something in the temperament of the individual that predisposes them to be hypersensitive to impingements, leading to a complex interaction between early experience and temperament. Britton has tentatively suggested an innate factor that opposes maternal containment in early infancy, which may be the developmental precursor to Klein's (1957) discoveries about envy. He calls this factor "psychic atopia", (Britton, 1998, p. 58.) a sort of allergy to other people's minds and their thinking, an aversion to the awareness of otherness and difference. In analysis these patients react to the analyst's interpretations with the response, "But those are your thoughts, that's not what I was thinking", and they find it difficult to interact creatively.

Klein (1957, 1959) often stated that the internalization of a mother who is capable of both love and understanding is essentially the basis of the developing ego and a *sine qua non* for the development of healthy ego functions. Klein believed love (affect) and understanding (cognition) to be the two maternal functions that constitute the necessary conditions for an adequate integration and working through of the problems of the paranoid–schizoid position. Though an internalized helpful object may be present in some form in the patients in question, it also has a powerful counterpart in a malignant internal object whose prime motive is not to love and understand, but to hatefully destroy and spread mental confusion.

With Bion's series of publications (1959, 1962a,b), cognition (the capacity to think and make sense of things) was given a central place in psychoanalysis. He introduced a radically new idea in his 1959 paper, "Attacks on linking": his clinical and conceptual leap was to observe that if the infant's early preverbal projection of experiences are felt to be unacknowledged and, therefore, "uncontained" by the mother, an object is established in the infant's internal world that is not merely a representation of this uncontaining figure, which is unreceptive, impenetrable, or absent. An object is instituted that has an *active* internal *presence* and whose purpose is to attack any attempt by the infant to establish meaning or understanding. Thus, the infant's efforts to make links with the external object world, together with making links with their own experience, are seriously compromised. While there may also be an internal object that is absent, deadened, or dead, this is experienced differently as the *passive* presence of something that is lifeless and/or missing. Bion postulates an internal object that has an *active* presence, intending to invert the process of containment and integration, and ensure that emotional/sensory experiences do not acquire any rudimentary shape or meaning. This "something" in the mind is felt to stop experiences developing into what he terms "proto thoughts': they have much in common with Freud's (1915e) notion of "thing representations" and what Klein (1957) refers to as "memories in feeling". They are experiences that can be felt but not recollected or mentally represented in words or images. In Bion's model of the "container and contained" (1962b), this internal object is malevolently intent on keeping raw sensory experiences from being transformed into something that can be named and thought about. Furthermore, this malevolent object is felt to destroy whatever rudimentary order and sense has already been established, and turn this sense back into incomprehension and non-sense. Bion has named this mental phenomenon −K (minus K), where K represents the epistemophilic desire for knowledge: the infants natural desire to "reach out", to understand, and to be understood.

In this profoundly disturbing state of affairs, there is something akin to a perverse inversion of the epistemophilic instinct. The internal object, instead of lovingly providing knowledge and understanding in response to the infant's searches for meaning, is felt malevolently to impose confusion and misunderstanding. This experience cements the phobic belief that any truly close proximity of another mind to one's own mind constitutes a profound challenge to the self's psychic integrity.

Britton (1998) has expanded and developed Bion's ideas to show their far-reaching clinical implications. He writes of malignant object experience:

> From the transference the basic fear is of malignant misunderstanding. By this I mean an experience of being so misunderstood in such a fundamental and powerful way that one's experience of oneself would be eliminated and thus the possibility of the self establishing meaning would be eliminated. [p. 54]

In the transference, the internalized primary maternal experience, which was in some way deeply aversive and a threat to psychic integrity, is revived. When the external analyst is constituted from such an internal object, he is felt to be so detrimental to life that intimate relations with him have to be controlled and regulated in an extreme manner. Analysis cannot, therefore, provide real comfort or conviction that the relationship could provide a benign place of rest. There is no real belief in a relationship of deep intimacy that could be the basis for emotional growth. Thus, accommodation and manipulation are believed to be the only real *modus operandi* for survival. The task, as the patient sees it, is how to secure *some form* of emotional contact with the analyst, felt to be essential to everyday existence, while avoiding the life-threatening area of infantile disturbance from ever being touched.

In the transference–countertransference, this can be seen when any direct emotional contact is sought by either patient or analyst. What starts off as a benign attempt to communicate by either party rapidly turns into a −K experience; both patient and analyst feel profoundly misunderstood by the other, and a sense of dread and a state of horrible confusion fills the consulting room. When this ominous "bad experience" persistently occurs, or threatens to occur, sometimes with great force, it sets limits to the pace at which any analysis can proceed and inevitably makes for a difficult, lengthy, and painful process for both parties. Transformative experiences are infrequent and hard won.

These patients, therefore, present a number of technical difficulties and challenges for any analyst once they come into treatment. The in-depth and detailed working through in the transference of early infantile conflicts, which is the key to psychic change, constantly threatens to revive a full-scale repetition of the early catastrophes that seem to reside at the core of their internal psychic world. Analysis is deeply desired and felt to be indispensable to life, yet, equally, it is intensely mistrusted, feared, and hated. If they "surrender" to the experience of being the "infant"/"patient", they believe their adult ego functions will be completely lost to them. Confusion and panic will then have dominion over their mind and they will be left with no means of making sense of what is going on. Unknown to themselves in any clear way, the deep intimacy they so desperately seek is also felt to be overwhelming and destabilizing. Klein (1958) wrote,

> In neurotic and still more in psychotic individuals, the struggle against such dangers threatening from the deepest layers of the unconscious is to some extent constant and part of their instability or their illness. [p. 243]

It appears that, to resolve this problem, these patients resorted in early infancy to splitting off malevolent object experiences and parts of the self so that another part of their personality could establish object links and develop along less conflicted lines. Freud first explored this mechanism to accommodate to reality in his paper, "The splitting of the ego in the process of defence" (1940e [1938]). The infant acquires a stability and normality of sorts through the careful selection and control of their object choices. This precarious stability depends on the regulation and management of emotional distance and contact with their chosen objects. In the internal world, the split is then institutionalized between a life affirming and a life denying internal object, one keenly sought, the other phobically avoided. Maternal functions such as physical care and emotional understanding are sought without fully recognizing the *relationship* to the person who performs these functions. What they seem to be saying is "feed me, love me, hold me, understand me, but do not expect acknowledgement that it is *you* who is doing these things for me". Object relatedness and its troublesome feelings of gratitude and envy are, therefore, obviated, and no real psychic development can occur.

Yet, in spite of these early difficulties, these patients have managed to forge an identity for themselves that has stability and which gives them the capability for tenacious self-reliance. In the case of less ill individuals, they have established an area of functioning that can demonstrate an impressive capacity for warmth and insight, and they can appear socially successful without being obviously compliant or conveying the elaborate contrivances of a "false self" (Reisenberg-Malcolm, 1992; Winnicott, 1960b), or a blatant, self-absorbed, narcissistic personality. To those who know them as friends or close work colleagues, they can seem, through developmental splitting, to be well adjusted, personable, and emotionally convincing. Hints of something not quite right often only appear as a reticence to realize ambitions in the spheres of love and work, for which they seem amply equipped and more than capable of achieving. It appears, then, that some parts of the personality have managed a certain amount of depressive working through and integration of internal conflicts, while leaving other significant parts of the personality firmly corralled off and untouched by the influence of reality.

The cases I want to describe vary from one another in their level of disturbance and personality characteristics, yet they have a common phobic core complex towards their primary object. At the base of their psyche is a malignant maternal object, real or imagined, that functions in a manner that is the reverse of what we would expect in normal maternal functioning. In studying this group, I intend to focus primarily on the phenomenology of the transference–countertransference and try to draw out some common characteristics. I will discuss three patients who illustrate these difficulties. They differ from one another in the degree to which they have neurotic, borderline, or schizoid features; however, diagnostic distinctions do not have great relevance when one is in the midst of working with deeply disturbed levels of psychic experience.

Mrs A

Mrs A was in analysis four times a week for nine years. She was forty-four years old when she began, an only child who had come half way round the world to get away from her parents. She was married, but neither she nor her husband wanted children. She was a painter and worked part time in a variety of jobs in the field of publishing. Her husband worked away in another city during the week, so she would only share a physical space with him at weekends; he was also a distant and emotionally undemanding figure. She frequently changed jobs, as her work relationships often terminated in acrimony because of conflicts with her employers. The issues were pretty much the same every time: after a rather idealized start, during which time everybody was enamoured with her, she would come to feel controlled and exploited. In common with many "thin skinned" patients, she felt persecuted by other people and other people felt persecuted by her. She also found living with herself a difficult undertaking.

I want to concentrate on the period during which analysis had lessened some splits and a much more psychotic picture emerged in the transference of a relationship to an internally dreaded mother who controlled her and blocked the development of her identity. I think it is very significant that this patient's mother was said by relatives to have had a breakdown at her birth and was unable to put her feeding infant down. Mother clasped her baby daughter in her arms, carrying her around like a vital organ of her own body. So, this patient probably had an early experience of a maternal figure who was so profoundly anxious that no degree of separation was allowed to exist between them. I think this patient experienced her maternal object's need for her not just as a suffocating encroachment by a desperate and disturbed figure, but also, at a deep unconscious level, as a malignant maternal desire to obliterate her fledgling identity as a separate person.

From time to time, her mother would write to her; however, when these letters arrived she was overcome with panic, and, on a few occasions, she had to go to the postbox to post them back to herself. This was a bid for more time in order to prepare for the colonization of her mind that would follow should she dare to open them. In extreme states of anxiety, leaving them unopened on the hall table was not an option, because their concrete physical presence was sufficient to induce insomnia and dizziness. The maternal transference to the analyst, however, was of a different quality: I was revered and clung to for certain properties she claimed I possessed. However, I often had difficulty in recognizing anything of myself in her descriptions. She would tell me about my politics, literary tastes, attitudes, and habits, but they rarely showed any observation of my real attitudes and attributes, hints of which inevitably emerge in any long treatment, however rigorous the analyst's technique. During this period she would place my bills under her pillow at night and treat them as holy relics to be preserved, in a similar fashion to her mother's jewellery, which she kept stored and looked at from time to time as part of a secret ritual. She never wore the jewellery, as this would have triggered the sensation that her mother was concretely taking possession of her body.

My countertransference was one of feeling helplessly controlled by the patient's version of reality, and depersonalized into something akin to mother's jewellery or the monthly analytic bills, while the patient insistently told me who I was and what I thought, which had no bearing on my objective or subjective reality. In the transference, I think we can see that, through projective identification, I was put into the position of the helpless, depersonalized part of the patient, whose identity and experience was blocked and annihilated, while the patient unconsciously identified with the malevolent maternal object that enforced and controlled what should pass for reality.

In this calmer phase of the analysis, the patient *lived out* the phantasy of being conjoined with her analyst. She had an agreeable dream in which we were Siamese twins joined at the head. She also had a fleeting thought of nominating me as the sole beneficiary in her will. After much detailed interpretative work and clarification, something seemed to slowly shift as this phantasy became more conscious and understood by both parties. Following this, a deep, hateful bitterness emerged. The analysis was transformed from a highly controlled situation where the patient orchestrated everything, into a very stormy and disturbed affair, dominated by a protracted and intense paranoid transference. In calmer moments, the patient complained that sessions were an impediment to getting on with her life, but they would rapidly turn into heated arguments and explosions of hate. Increasingly, each session became the scene of threatened madness and mayhem. She protested that her analyst was a seductive "Svengali figure", getting rich and aggrandizing himself at her expense, intruding to mess with her mind, or sucking her life blood like a vampire.

Once the narcissistic phantasy of fusion lessened its grip, the realization dawned that I was not simply an extension of herself. She began to see that she often had a pretty poor judgement of what I was thinking or feeling, and at these moments all hell broke loose. She sometimes leapt off the couch in a rage, slamming doors, or kicking the tyres of my car when it was parked in the driveway of my consulting room. The car seemed to stand concretely for my separate identity and my mobility to move towards and away from her. In this patient, the emerging awareness of separateness that followed when the narcissistic defences lost some of their power unleashed psychotic persecutory forces that had hitherto been deeply split off from awareness.

The process of emerging out of a narcissistic mode of functioning into a paranoid–schizoid state has been described particularly well by Steiner (1987, 1993). In Mrs A's case, it led to a ricocheting between intense hatred and intense fears of fragmentation. Whether the narcissistic aspect of the transference was idealized or paranoid, it was marked by a delusional state in which the analyst was concretely felt to be an internal phantasy object, and −K was in the ascendancy.

However, when there was evidence that I could detach myself from this role and have analytic thoughts of my own, it caused havoc, as she felt profoundly abandoned. Conversely, the patient also had a deeply felt conviction that my attempt to "know" her mind was an attempt to drive her insane and to rob her of her own thinking capacity. The predominant feeling at these moments for both patient and analyst was "this shouldn't be happening", and it helped for me to verbalize to myself that the analytic couple was now in the thick of a hitherto split-off, infantile catastrophe "that shouldn't have happened". Patient and analyst in the grip of this kind of experience often become alarmed that they are trapped in a sado-masochistic nightmare from which neither can extricate themselves. The patient feels this especially acutely, as they believe they cannot separate from the source of their destruction because of the fervent belief that the analyst is also the source of their continued survival and salvation. Of course, it behoves the analyst to carefully scrutinize his countertransference and technique, and question if he is misunderstanding or failing to sensitively contain projections. But I think no matter how carefully the analytic work is carried out, the experience of malignancy is unavoidable, if it is a central core of psychic reality.

Mr B

The second patient, Mr B, came to analysis five times a week for thirteen years. When he began, he was a forty-year-old man who lived alone, and found it extremely difficult to share physical or mental space with anyone other than his dizygotic twin brother. Yet, he craved the presence and comfort of others and was a workaholic, work providing the dosage of social contact he required for his mental stability.

His mother was twenty years younger than father. Accounts from family friends and relatives suggest that mother was emotionally cut off, at times paranoid, and dramatically hysterical, particularly in the patient's early formative years. She was also treated for puerperal depression following the birth of a third child, a daughter, some eight years later. Father seems to have been more emotionally available, but controlling and unstable. Mr B felt his father flooded him with worries to the point that both of them would almost tremble with anxiety. Both he and his brother seem to have developed a particular aversion to mother, and compensated for this with a troubled attachment to father and each other. Rather like Rome's mythic founders, the twins Romulus and Remus, who were raised by a she-wolf, the brothers would fantasize together about grandiose projects, and feed each other's inflated ideas about fame and fortune.

Mr B sought help because of a partial breakdown in his capacity to function at work and an ego dystonic sexual perversion involving domination and submission. His attempts at sexual relationships were handicapped because he could not stay overnight with a woman without suffering acute depersonalization or derealization; sometimes, he had fleeting out-of-body experiences. Before he started analysis, he found a workable solution to these problems by exclusively frequenting prostitutes for sexual gratification of a mild sado-masochistic kind.

Like Mrs A, Mr B also felt that unless he rigidly controlled his emotional distance to his external objects, he was in danger of feeling compelled to adjust his identity to whomever he was with. This would result in his losing his own experience of himself, and he felt exhausted after being with others for any length of time. He often experienced eye contact as penetrative, and had to self-consciously limit it to protect either the other person or himself from invasion.

One of Mr B's recurring masturbatory phantasies was to have a woman stand naked while he stood behind her. He imagined that she faced a blank wall, so she could not see him, although all the time he had her in his view. The woman had to solve a riddle or problem, but she can have no clue about its nature and, therefore, no means of solving it, as he is the only one who knows the riddle and the answer, but will not reveal it. The woman can only escape and stay alive by solving the riddle.

I think this Kafkaesque set-up perfectly captures Mr B's internal psychic reality, if we understand that he projects into the female figure the naked, defenceless, and terrified part of himself who cannot make any sense of his experience, nor can find anyone who can help him make sense of things. In the place of a receptive, helpful object is a cruel, life-threatening, and brick-walling object that will not let itself be known, seeks to sadistically create terror, and fosters a situation of confusion and incomprehension. The infant's original incomprehension and terror is projected back into the primary object and the trauma is converted into a sadistic triumph (Stoller, 1976). The infant/patient is back in control and the whole business is glued together by a sexualized, hateful excitement.

This arrangement was a familiar feature of Mr A's sessions and often enacted in the transference–countertransference interaction. Mr A would bring very complicated associations and speak in a quiet, slow, elliptical manner that was highly controlled. He mumbled or stopped in mid-sentence or gave minimal information on a subject, and then asked what I thought. I was confronted with seemingly unintelligible material, where context or motives were missing and linking connections were left unsaid. Mr A would talk in a highly abstracted manner, so that I could never be certain of his meaning and had to continually make a guess at what he meant, or constantly seek clarification, and by these means he pulled me into his sphere of control. I found that if I did have a go at offering my thoughts, they usually missed the mark, and asking Mr A for clarification on issues rarely clarified anything. During this phase of analysis, the patient was rarely confused, while it was I who was at sea and expected to make sense of the senseless. Mr B, meanwhile, secretly watched from the wings at my helpless struggle! When interpretations did get through, the reverse dynamic took hold; the patient felt that my interpretations confused and disordered his mind; he felt very vulnerable and frightened. He could not find meaning in my ideas and was unable to mentally metabolize his own experience, which felt like somatic sensations in his throat or chest.

However, Mr B was not exclusively locked in a cruel way of relating and, like all the patients I am trying to describe, he was also capable of moments of sincere tenderness and affection. As his analysis moved along and he partially worked through some of the underlying fear, he sometimes found me to be receptive and sympathetic. As both he and I began to get some understanding of what was repeatedly enacted, Mr B felt cared for, and an area of concern and love would open up, only to disappear again as the strain of the closeness moved to fusion and became too much.

Towards the end of his analysis he brought the following dream, which I think movingly captures his horrific dilemma in tolerating affection and the anxieties of separateness. This dream came in the session following the day after he and I had agreed to set a date to end one year hence:

> In the dream the patient is slowly walking alongside a narrow, shallow canal with barely any water left in it. A large fish struggles to follow him. It has a human face but there is a huge gash where part of the mouth and one side of the face should be. A separate glob of round, bleeding flesh also floats along behind the fish's tail. The sight is horrific and unbearable to the patient because the fish still has one eye, as if conscious and having to watch its own agonised death throes. He finds the salmon pink, exposed flesh particularly disgusting.

Mr B's associations at first linked his brother to the face of the fish. Mr B feels his brother drags him down with his repeated phone calls to talk endlessly about work problems, but later he acknowledges that this is really his problem, as he cannot resist getting caught up with his brother's worries.

I first interpreted the fish as Mr B, and said he feels he will soon be a fish out of water—the supportive, life-sustaining medium that analysis provides and which he feels keeps him alive. Now we have fixed a date to stop, there is a belief that life will come to a final tragic end. Other associations the patient provided suggested that the glob of round flesh was linked with the patient's internally damaged mother/internal analyst, both of whom, he feared, also would not survive the bloody rupture of termination.

I think the dream gives a privileged glimpse into Mr B's deepest early relationships. The sight he could not bear to see was his half-dead, mutilated, infantile self, forced to watch and experience the agony of having no intact mouth or eyes that could form a comforting link with his object, and there being no undamaged maternal object or part objects, such as the nipple and breast, that could feed and nourish him. Try as he might to get away from this infantile catastrophe, it follows him like a ghost, and reminds him he will soon die a painful death as a fish out of water. I think his unconscious psychic reality was a fear that he would be left at the end of treatment with a pink wound where a mouth should have been, haunted by a persecuting mutilated pink breast/vagina where a mother/analyst should be (the pink glob of flesh). The session was profoundly painful and moving, and one of a number of significant turning points that enabled the patient to envisage and give shape to his internal experiences that had hitherto been insoluble riddles and senseless dreads.

Mr B's emergence from the narcissistic state is not into a paranoid–schizoid fragmentation, as with the earlier material from Mrs A (taken from a much earlier point in her treatment). Mr B's material, I think, shows the move from the sadistic, narcissistic control and isolation exemplified by the masturbatory fantasy (enacted in the transference) towards the "depressive position" nearer the end of his analysis, where he is able to envisage and depict in the dream his irreparably damaged objects and parts of the self. Here, the feeling is one of great psychic pain, felt almost physically (Joseph, 1981) and represented as damage to the physical self and its objects. This calls to mind Freud's statement in *The Ego and the Id* (1923b), " The ego is first and foremost a bodily ego" (p. 23).

Dr C

My third case is Dr C. She came to analysis five times a week for fourteen years, rarely missing a session. I will present some material which suggests that, although a part of this patient's ego had developed healthily, another part of the ego was inextricably bound up in a sado-masochistic way with a punitive superego. I will try to show that this noisy and hysterical sado-masochistic arrangement, in turn, provided a barrier against a psychotic area containing a malignant maternal object that was believed to want to annihilate the infantile self.

The patient was a forty-three-year-old married woman, with two children. She came from a middle-class family and spent the greater part of her childhood in the Far East. She had a brother seven years older, who was married, and a single younger sister. Her mother appears to have been a somewhat brittle woman, who found closeness with her children difficult. Mother's career in politics meant she was frequently absent for short periods from the family home. The patient became pseudo mature, politely independent, and emotionally avoidant of her mother from an early age. Dr C "made her own arrangements", mothering herself and seeking a maternal presence in a series of nannies. There was an overriding sense of bleakness to her childhood years, but in spite of this she possessed a certain liveliness. From as early as Dr C could remember, mother was written off altogether in her mind as little more than another useless sister, and kept at a polite distance. With the advent of her own children, the picture of her mother has modified a little, but has not appreciably changed.

Father comes across as a warmer and more loving figure, who played an important maternal role in the patient's childhood. However, father was also felt to be ineffectual and distracted. Dr C had a deep sense of love and devotion to her father, which sometimes surfaced in the transference and was evident in the way she would defend psychoanalysis from any external criticism. But, for a long time, when she was with her analyst it was another matter; she was my fiercest critic and if anyone was jealously suspected of being one of my valued colleagues or someone she thought I might admire, like Freud, I was sure to hear something bad about them.

Partly to reassure me and partly to avoid guilt over a constant stream of jealous and provocative criticisms, she would say, in a rather superior manner, that she never trusted me in the early years of analysis until she could be openly denigrating without fear of retaliation, and she admitted that she sometimes feared she might lose control of herself and physically attack me or smash up the consulting room. As a child, the patient was agreeable and well behaved, and little of her provocative rage and jealousy was apparent to herself or anyone else. So, it seems the capacity to openly express anger brought its own solace and sense of reassuring contact after a childhood of so much good behaviour.

In adulthood, Dr C. was professionally successful, attractive, and well liked by friends and colleagues. After considerable analytic work she managed to make progress with some of her claustrophobic anxieties, and, with much procrastination, married. Little time elapsed before sex became problematic. Although she could enjoy sex, she felt disinclined to be physically close and wondered if she just had a low libido. She often hinted that she wished her husband and her analyst had the confidence or desire to persist in the face of her repeated rejections and coldness. But what I wish to stress were the occasions when she seemed quite terrified at the prospect of sex, either because she felt her desires were insatiable and too much for her husband, or because she was afraid of being drawn into a physical contact that threatened to unbalance the boundaries of her mind, as well as the fragile hold over her bodily integrity.

In spite of these areas of deep disturbance, she could at times be perceptive, warm, and down to earth, conveying a convincing sense that a part of her personality possessed a good grasp on reality. She had a capacity to experience things with depth of feeling and conviction. She seems to have done a good job in the early years as a mother, and derived great comfort from the physical intimacy with her son and daughter. However, like the other two patients, Mrs A and Mr B, Dr C's analysis revealed deep fissures in her personality, and, at deeper levels, there were islands of fragmentation which created obstacles to her taking in interpretations. As the analysis proceeded, these islands of fragmentation threatened to enlarge into continents. Periods of idealization and erotization came and went, until the transference–countertransference dynamic emerged in an organized way around two alternating arrangements that had a certain stability.

The maternal transference was characterized by a silent suspiciousness: Dr C was distant and self-reliant; the analyst's assigned transference role was to listen and concur with her self-analysis. When I deviated from this role and had an idea of my own, I quickly became the "crow mother" of her dreams. This "crow mother" was a critical, penetrative, and narcissistic figure who was malignant in intent. In the countertransference, I had to bear being seen as critical and cruel, no matter what I said or did. I was not allowed to extricate myself from this position and would be accused of evading my own guilt and responsibility should I try to do so.

In the paternal transference, by contrast, she could have moments of love and affection, but she still needed to maintain a defensive pseudo-reasonableness, and I, as analyst, needed to be warmly guided and supervised. My countertransference feelings were mostly around being ineffectual and/or an admiring onlooker. I was required to function only in receptive mode, not to make much real emotional contact. If I did, it was to be orchestrated along predetermined lines. I was expected to have nothing to say that she had not already thought about herself. Thus, there was no "sex", no "penetration", and no "liveliness", in her most intimate relationships, with the exception of her children. In this powerful position, she felt protected from any anxiety and guilt, but also from an awareness of the analyst possessing any knowledge or understanding that was different from her own and which she might not be able to predict or control (Feldman, 2009).

My countertransference was often a feeling of being an impotent, depressed father or a disregarded non-mother, while "She who knows best" runs the therapy and analyses herself, feeding herself with her own interpretations. From her point of view, this was essential, as she had to protect herself from "He who knows best" (the analyst/crow mother disguised as someone benign) dominating her mind and the whole analysis. In this situation, the patient and I seemed to travel along parallel lines where nothing I said got any emotional purchase on her mind and my interpretations just disappeared into the ether. If I became insistent in my attempts to get through to her, this simply gave her unequivocal evidence that I *was* the cruel, "crowing" object she insistently maintained I was. If she sensed or imagined that I felt defeated by her insistent claims of my "badness", she would revive me with some reference to one of my good qualities. I think these "tonics" for the analyst's flagging spirits served two purposes. First, to make sure I did not give up and withdraw from her, as she desperately wanted and relied on my efforts to make contact with her. Second, to deny any real sense of my human frailty, so that she could deny any awareness of the possibility of her own guilt. If the analyst could take anything, analysis was just an "as if" Tom and Jerry cartoon, and every hateful, deforming attack simply repaired itself in an instant. No action had any real consequences, and there was no need for her to feel any concern or remorse towards me, as there was no real damage done to the analyst, herself, or the joint work.

When these two defensive systems eventually wore thin and interpretations occasionally got through to her, she would suddenly go blank and be unable to focus or remember what either she or I had just said, and we would suddenly enter an area of confusion that had psychotic dimensions, where words failed to make any sense. Some of this was also captured rather poignantly in her physical movement. She could be very poised and composed at the start of a session, well organized physically and intellectually, but if I managed to get through to a deeper layer of anxiety, this would upset her equilibrium and she would get off the couch at the end of the session all arms and legs, as if disassembled. At times, I thought her legs might buckle and fail to carry her to the door as she attempted to leave the room. I understand this to reflect some very early failure in the patient's sense of being physically as well as emotionally held and contained. It was striking how, for long periods in the early part of her analysis (and presumably in infancy), she used her considerable native strengths to provide some rudimentary holding for herself. I think of this as a kind of mental equivalent to the holding of breath and movement in order to keep still, preserve life, and keep out of harm's way.

In the early years of analysis, she seemed able to talk superficially and to wait indefinitely in sessions (as well as during breaks) without much visible frustration, while I would be pacing up and down in my mind, hoping for something, anything, alive and real to happen! When this eventually shifted, she could not bear to wait for anything; weekends and holiday breaks were an agony and she had spasms of insatiable hunger. She rarely spoke spontaneously at the beginning of sessions and there was usually a 2–3 minute delay before she voiced her thoughts with guarded deliberation. In contrast, the ends of sessions were always a minor trauma, irrespective of whether, by her reckoning, it had been a good or bad session. Separations then became indistinguishable from a malevolent attack on her well-being.

The balance between control and chaos shifted in the direction of chaos as the analysis proceeded and as she acquired greater insight into her omnipotent projections. She would rant at herself for being "mad"; the more shocking the expletives she used to attack herself, the better they served to expiate her guilt and panic. What seemed so difficult for her to bear was an increasing insight into her phobic and sometimes envious reactions to good analytic understanding.

Analysis became overwhelmingly threatening in a way that she could not understand. In these situations, the only way she felt able to create a boundary between herself and the analyst was to assert herself by provocative and vigorous disagreement, or to come late to her sessions and generally not agree with any analytic interpretation that was offered. In this impenitent, argumentative state, she was identified with an omniscient, all-powerful figure, totally confident in her ideas, arguing with an analyst who was *always* wrong *all* of the time. Unlike phantasies and thoughts, which can be experienced as hypothetical, her beliefs at these moments were more like delusions, felt to be concretely real and more akin to dogma. If she *felt* something, she saw no need for a reality check. When her quasi-delusional assertions encountered any reality that disconfirmed her feelings, her assertions would be fiercely clung to, as if her life depended on not letting them go. Reality was incorporated, refashioned, and folded into her existing beliefs and it seemed unimportant whether her reasoning convinced herself or her analyst, only that she had something to continue to fight and argue with mattered. The patient would openly or silently refashion the meaning of any interpretation into her own existing ideas in order that the fresh meaning the analyst provided could be evaded. When she recovered some observing part of herself and could view more clearly her own explosive and paranoid behaviour, she felt deeply ashamed and frightened for her sanity. Interspersed between these very difficult periods there were moments of deeply felt love and gratitude. However, these positive feelings were only a momentary relief, since feeling need and affection rapidly became another source of anxiety that threatened to spiral out of control.

I will now present some details from a Tuesday session, which I think illustrate some of the issues I have tried to highlight. In the previous session, she felt her anxieties had been understood and she left the session deeply touched and relieved. She was on time and after the usual delay said:

> "I'm flummoxed! I gave a good talk at the conference and they all liked it because it was down to earth. Why am I professionally successful? Why do people think my work is good? In one of the surgeries today, I did two really good consultations. Though the patients were pitching up with very different requirements, funny [pauses], still I can't talk about it to you. [All this is said in an atmosphere of defensive self criticism that is not very deeply felt and that we are very familiar with.] There are some really crappy doctors out there, but I feel I'm not allowed to say this out loud, especially not to you! I expect you to say I'm arrogant, I don't

deserve the praise, that I'm shit really. I said to myself, 'if they really knew how disturbed I really am . . .'" [Stops talking.]

I said, "I think you want me to say something critical so we can be joined in the usual way and we won't then have to see that there are two patients here at the moment, one who wants an argument for defensive reasons, and another who felt understood yesterday, gave a good talk today, and feels she has moved forward."

Listening to this material, I thought that the underlying anxiety was an awareness that she had enjoyed her success, and, in a part of her mind, had acknowledged my help from the previous session. This had moved her, but, at the same time, this awareness deeply troubled her because of a fear of need and dependency and a threat to her self-reliance. This had to be avoided by means of self criticism and an attempt to draw the analyst into an argument.

The patient immediately replied, saying, "I knew you were going to say something negative, I just knew it; there you are true to form. Well done!" I decided to wait a bit before speaking and to side-step this excited response for the moment, as it was unclear how real her paranoid reaction was. I continued, saying I thought the problem was she could not enjoy her success because it meant openly acknowledging that both she and I had moved forward in her mind. It meant acknowledging that it might be possible to move on to something new and more co-operative, but that did seem very frightening.

She again replied instantly, saying, "I don't think so. Oh, that's just fucking rubbish. I do acknowledge things." I responded, "Yes and no, it may be that you acknowledge things, but you feel it is imperative to do so secretly, as it brings a feeling that you will lose control of yourself and the situation." This is followed by a long pause. I think in this pause the patient becomes anxious as she catches sight of herself being aggressively defensive and realizes she is not entirely convinced by her own statements, yet struggles with an intense anxiety about the emotional closeness between us. She eventually says, "I feel bad, maybe I feel guilty", but then instantly dismisses this and attacks again, saying, "That's what you're always telling me I should feel. That's what I should feel according to you if I was a good compliant patient like you want me to be. Come on, admit it, that's what you want from me, you want me to say *mea culpa*, you want me to leave this session feeling bad, feeling worse than when I came in. I was feeling good about myself before I got here. I feel if I listen to you I will get so muddled; you make me feel I'm going mad. This session is getting stressful. It's going all wrong." I then said I wondered if by "going all wrong", she meant that we had become a very nasty couple who just hate each other. The patient replied, "Yes, I feel you're bad, I do, I do!! It's times like this when I feel this analysis is bad for me, you're trying to drive me mad, I feel like getting up and going." This no longer feels just hysterical or simply provocative as it had done earlier, but now has an edge of genuine terror to it.

When she has calmed a little, she says, "But I mean it, what if I did lose it and attacked you? I don't think you could cope with that, but I do come pretty near to it. I can't afford to let my guard down, I have to be vigilant with you. I have to watch myself. I don't want to be left at the end of this session with my insides hanging out. Who will put me back together then, a forensic service? Where will you be when I need you? Maybe you're right. OK, I know you're right, I can feel it. If I wasn't so fucked up and bitter, I'd walk in and say, 'Hey, I gave a great talk', and I'd be able to say 'Thank you'. I don't know what's the matter with me! I just can't do it. I can't do it! It's like at the end of sessions, I can't turn round and say goodbye to you, I can't force myself to do it!" I tried to explore if she felt in her mind that I had started crowing with my own importance and taken too much credit, but this did not go anywhere. She then said, "I did think you would be proud of me but I can't bear to have these thoughts, they feel so embarrassing, and it's humiliating to have to talk like this. I'm really frightened I'm not going to be able to cope without coming here over August."

Her mood then alters to a sadder, quieter state: "Some part of me doesn't really believe you are callous, but I can't help feeling you're trying to destroy me. I know you're not, I just can't stop attacking you. When I came down this road just before the session I felt an instant sense of relief. I just feel so scared. I need to keep control of myself. I am frightened about how I'm going to cope without analysis over the summer and I feel I'm becoming very chaotic. I got confused shopping in the supermarket about what I was buying. I left the house keys at work and now I can't find my mobile. I don't want to feel like this, I can't bear it, I really can't bear it."

Later in the session she brings a dream;

She is in a building, which is on fire. The place has the feeling of the capital city of the country in the Far East where she lived as a child. Loads of people are dying, and she is desperate to escape. She is with somebody who may be her son, but in the dream he is eighteen [her real son is only eleven]. Like a combat soldier, she manages to catapult herself over a wall, and escape. "It's like I had this cartoon-like springiness." Her son seems to have some kind of policeman-type role, and he stays and tries to help save people, but dies in the chaos. "I'm with a patient standing outside the building, but I can't hold my feelings in any longer and break down and wail and sob." Then a colleague, a sympathetic older man, comes to comfort her, but some masonry falls from the building and hits him; it is not clear if he is dead or just injured, and she waits alone for an ambulance.

She links the sympathetic older man with me. The building reminds her of the place where one of her favourite nannies used to take her, and a traumatic early memory around the age of five of being collected by her mother and manhandled down the stairs to a waiting car. "I didn't want to go to my mother, she terrified me." The building also has some vague feeling about her family home. "Oh, I've just remembered another bit of the dream: when I am standing outside afterwards I look back at the burning building and I can see through one of the windows a little fat hand, sort of funny, like a hand that might belong to a Down's child. I think it links in my mind with having a third child and I'm not sure I can cope."

The dream is, of course, complex and multi-layered, but what I want to focus on is the pervasive sense of disaster. I commented on her terror and her fear of being trapped in the building and linked this with how she had spent a large part of the session enacting her escape by trying to draw me into combat with her. I went on to wonder if the burning, collapsing building was linked with her own anger and her mother's anger whenever she was manhandled out of her refuge, much as she feels her analyst is manhandling her out of self-sufficiency and the "I know best" stance.

She replied, "Well, I sort of feel there is something in that; I don't know, I just feel overwhelmed. I know that if I can't stop giving you a hard time I will be the one that will pay in the end and I will feel terrible. How much time is there left?" She looks at her watch and continues, "I was thinking about the Twin Towers, it's a miracle people survived. I can't get over the picture of those people jumping rather than staying behind to be burnt alive. They obviously felt that the terror of falling was infinitely better than staying behind to wait their fate. I heard from X [a journalist friend] that a lot of the news footage was edited to remove the really disturbing stuff; the public were protected to prevent widespread panic in Western countries."

I think there is some insight in this dream. Dr C knows she cannot be a superwoman, it is a false cartoon strength that gets her over the wall, and she cannot manically evade all this anger, grief, and disturbance.

> Avoidance is not sustainable, and she has to face the grief and the dead objects she leaves behind in the building. At critical moments, the analyst is probably experienced as too weak to survive her onslaughts, or to bear the truth of her inner world and this contributes to her resort to manic excitement. I also think there is overwhelming guilt and despair linked with the injuries to her good objects. When I interpreted the dream further by saying that she felt we were both unable to prevent these relentless attacks, she burst into tears and started sobbing, very movingly and with great pain.

In the following Wednesday session, she referred to the Queen's speech at the time of the London bombings. The Queen had said something about those who avoid love, avoid grief. I think this material movingly depicts the difficulties of working through problems in relation to depressive loss and grief, and learning to bear to see the true nature of the internal world, when, at the deepest level, there is felt to be a lack of containment by the primary object. Contact with her inner world means having to confront an internal primary object that was felt to have failed to contain infantile projections at a very basic level, what we might call a "brick wall mother". In its place, in Dr C's case, is an inflamed, engulfing terror that threatens to destroy everything. In the above material, I think we can see how Dr C's layered defences give way as the session proceeds. First we see a relatively stable "I know best" narcissistic structure enacted in the transference. As this is analytically addressed, it increases anxiety and a provocative sado-masochistic transference emerges, which in turn morphs once again into something more akin to a psychotic state, with directionless rage and terrifying confusion. Eventually the depressive awareness of loss emerges with the dream. Like Mr B's dream, Dr C's dream pictures a violently damaged internal world that feels beyond the resources of the patient or her objects to repair. The patient is left broken down and grief stricken by the remnants of her internal world, uncertain if anything has survived except a handicapped Down's syndrome baby and a half dead analyst/father.

Discussion

According to Bion's (1962b) theory of the container and contained, the effect of excessive envious attacks is to thoroughly confuse unconscious phantasy with external reality to produce an agglomeration of the two, and, therefore, there is an impediment to learning from experience. Establishing a sense of reality is being able to see the difference between what is internal and what is external experience. Truly unbearable states of mind are probably unbearable when they consist of unconscious delusions coupled with fragmentation of ego functions, occurring in the presence of an ego destructive −K superego. Properly speaking, they are not states of mind at all, but concrete experiences that cannot be thought about or encompassed, since there is no available part of the ego to contain and reflect on the emotional experiences, and no sense of an external object that can afford any assistance. The experiences are felt to be so extreme and concrete that they are felt to overwhelm and destroy the mind's capacity to think about or bear them, initiating a primitive psychic fight/flight reaction or withdrawal. I think all three of the patients I have described illustrate this state of affairs. Only when sufficient psychic integration has been accomplished and some mental representation takes place do we then begin to see depictions of the situation. For example, it was only well into her analysis that Mrs A was able to describe her state of mind as watching herself in a car crash in slow motion. Mr B in his dream had to watch his "fish-self" die a slow, agonizing death. Dr C dreamed of the collapsing building and the horror of the Twin Towers. In all the three cases I have mentioned, analysis awakened this −K monster from the depths, embodying it in the transference relationship in a sustained and unequivocal way, giving rise to the conviction that any close contact or separation between patient and analyst spelt disaster. Sanity and order were felt to be coterminous with being *in* analysis without being intimately *analysed*. Complex phobic defences and unconscious phantasies structure this split, and a relatively stable balance establishes itself between omnipotent self-reliance and claustrophobic dependence in what I have termed phobic attachment.

What I have tried to show in the three case examples in this chapter is that these patients all have a common object at the base of their psyches, a −K monster. When they come into analysis and a deep relationship with their analyst becomes available as a transference experience, they all report having startling terrors and confusions. As can be seen, sometimes this is between self and object and at other times, it is an internal confusion about their own subjective experience. As the transference experience unfolds and the defences lessen, the malevolence of this internal object surfaces more clearly and dominates the transference–countertransference interaction. These experiences seem frighteningly raw and unfamiliar for the patient and are, almost certainly, difficult for the analyst as well. Having analysis becomes a very puzzling and incomprehensibly difficult undertaking, and then gets worse as the transference–countertransference interaction, together with the setting, is felt as exceedingly dangerous. Later, as the patient becomes more familiar with these experiences and has more insight into them, anger alternates with despair and hopelessness. The patients then have an internal struggle with their own intolerance of interpretations and direct emotional contact with the analyst, and they often feel cheated and deeply upset as they become more aware of the contact they are missing but cannot tolerate. Coupled with this is an increasing sense of guilt about not letting their analyst function properly. As contact with deep emotions is so threatening, it means that analysis proceeds by a series of tiny quantum moves, often interspersed with long periods of stuckness and repetition. When these difficulties are at their height, the patient can hardly bear to be in the consulting room with the analyst (it has to be said, that sometimes this can be vice versa!), but neither can they bear to be without their sessions. They dread separations and breaks, and the idea of analysis ever ending is unthinkable.

The patient's capacity to learn from the experience of analysis (assuming the analyst's skills and sensitivity are "good enough") can be taken as a true measure of their contact with reality. After many years of interpretative work and struggle has lessened the tendency toward splitting and projection, and a degree of insight has been gained, a significant shift occurs, as the patient no longer fears the analyst's malign influence so much as fears *the experience of being analysed*. They are then more consciously fearful and hate their own mind, both what it contains and what it is capable of doing. This is because when an interpretation (experienced as more or less correct and essentially benign) does manage to touch them, it could as easily unleash terrors and confusions as bring relief. Under these circumstances, the patient is no longer convinced that the analyst is bad, but cannot make sense of how horrible analysis has become; it stirs up the phobic reaction, which is acknowledged as coming from himself. When contact is felt to be good and helpful, there seems to be an interim arrangement where the analyst is no longer accused of making the wrong interpretations, but he is not able to be thanked, either. The old formula for resolving the problem by projection, by believing they have an analyst who is doing something bad to them, is not quite believable any more. Being in analysis rather than being analysed, the compromise solution sought for so long, now feels emptier and does not satisfy. The patient, from time to time, still feels that he is part of a malevolent couple, but this is less fixed, the projections are more fluid, and can be taken back more readily. Alongside this, a crucial development seems to occur in tandem, as if quite independently, which is the capacity for a calmer love towards their analyst and their external objects. Slowly, a state of mind emerges in the patient which reveals a more open valuing of analysis for the *understanding* it affords, a movement towards K.

In conclusion, one might pose the question of whether the intense level of mistrust seen in these patients in their reactions against analytic work is a narcissistic response of self-preservation, or whether the "mistrust" is an envious spoiling used to disguise and justify a concealed desire to keep analytic work sterile. My clinical experience leads me to think that it is impossible to resolve this issue. One needs, technically, to hold both models in mind to enable analytic work to proceed. What is certain in these cases is that great desire goes hand in hand with great fear.

References

Ainsworth, M., Blehar, M. C., Waters, E., & Wall, S. (1978). *Patterns of Attachment: A Psychological Study of the Strange Situation*. New York: Erlbaum Press.

Bion, W. R. (1959). Attacks on linking. *International Journal of Psycho-analysis, 40*: 308–315 [reprinted in: *Second Thoughts*. London: Maresfield Reprints, Karnac, 1984].

Bion, W. R. (1962a). A theory of thinking. *International Journal of Psychoanalysis, 43*. Reprinted in: *Second Thoughts. Selected Papers on Psycho-Analysis* (1967). London: Heinemann Medical Books [reprinted London: Karnac, 1984].

Bion, W. R. (1962b). *Learning From Experience*. London: Maresfield Reprints, Karnac, 1984.

Bion, W. R. (1965). *Transformations*. London: Maresfield Reprints, Karnac, 1984.

Bollas, C. (1979). The transformational object. *International Journal of Psychoanalysis, 60*: 97–107.

Bowlby, J. (1969). *Attachment and Loss, Volume 1: Attachment*. London: Hogarth.

Britton, R. (1998). *Belief and Imagination*. London: Routledge.

Feldman, M. (2009). *Doubt Conviction and the Analytic Process, Selected Papers of Michael Feldman*. London and New York: Routledge.

Freud, S. (1915e). The unconscious. *S.E., 14*: 159–204. London: Hogarth.

Freud, S. (1923b). *The Ego and the Id. S.E., 19*: 3–49. London: Hogarth.

Freud, S. (1940e [1938]). Splitting of the ego in the process of defence. *S.E., 23*: 273–278. London: Hogarth.

Joseph, B. (1981). Towards the experiencing of psychic pain. In: *Psychic Equilibrium and Psychic Change, Selected Papers of Betty Joseph*. London: Routledge, 1989.

Klein, M. (1957). Envy and gratitude. In: *The Writings of Melanie Klein, Vol. 3, Envy and Gratitude and Other Works*. London: Hogarth, 1975.

Klein, M. (1958). On the development of mental functioning. In: *The Writings of Melanie Klein, Vol. 3, Envy and Gratitude and Other Works*. London: Hogarth Press, 1975.

Klein, M. (1959). Our adult world and its roots in infancy. In: *The Writings of Melanie Klein, Vol. 3, Envy and Gratitude and Other Works*. London: Hogarth Press, 1975.

Kohut, H. (1971). *The Analysis of the Self*. New York: International Universities Press.

Reisenberg-Malcolm, R. (1992). 'As-if': the experience of not learning. In: R. Anderson (Ed.), *Clinical Lectures on Klein and Bion*. London: Routledge.

Rosenfeld, H. (1987). *Impasse and Interpretation*. London: Routledge.

Steiner, J. (1987). The interplay between pathological organisations and the paranoid–schizoid and depressive positions. *International Journal of Psychoanalysis, 68*: 69–80.

Steiner, J. (1993). *Psychic Retreats*. London: Routledge.

Stoller, R. J. (1976). *Perversion: the Erotic Form of Hatred*. New York: Harvester Press.

Winnicott, D. W. (1960b). Ego distortions in terms of true and false self. In: *The Maturational Processes and the Facilitating Environment*. London: Hogarth Press, 1965.

Winnicott, D. W. (1960c). The theory of the parent infant relationship. In: *The Maturational Process and the Facilitating Environment*. London: Hogarth Press, 1965.

CHAPTER EIGHT

Two impulses to end an analysis: exploring the transference and countertransference

Philip Roys

Introduction

During the course of an analysis, it is not uncommon for patients to suggest or demand an end to the work. The topic of ending may be introduced explicitly or may be referred to indirectly or unconsciously. This chapter is concerned with the question of how the analyst might make sense of, and respond to, such developments.

The ending of analysis can, on the one hand, promote a recognition of separateness and the possibility of fuller involvement with the external world, allowing analytic achievements to be consolidated and further developed. Alternatively, ending can permit an escape from the possibility of facing painful conflicts and dilemmas. The impulse to end, therefore, contains both developmental and defensive possibilities.

In forming a view as to whether, in a particular case, it is the developmental or the defensive aspects which predominate, the literature concerning the criteria for analytic termination may be consulted. This literature refers to *external* functioning (e.g., Klein, 1950) or *symptomatic* relief (Freud, 1937c), but, as one would expect, most authors place greater emphasis on the achievement of *analytic* and *internal* goals. These are considered in terms such as the predominant defensive constellation or level of psychic development (Klein, 1950, the balance towards depressive rather than paranoid–schizoid functioning being regarded as developmentally more advanced), or the internalization of an analytic capacity. Pedder (1988) and Schacter (1992), for example, both stress the importance of this latter achievement to enable the patient to negotiate future life challenges.

Whatever the criteria favoured, the analyst will need to consider their application to the particular patient in question. Reference may be made to reports of the external world, and some light may be thrown on these questions by dreams. However, I think it is primarily via the transference and countertransference that a sound conclusion will be reached. Indeed, it can be argued that there is, in fact, nothing else to rely on; as I hope to demonstrate, even the reports of external activities and dreams pass through the transference–countertransference "filter".

Matters are further complicated, however, by the fact that the *subject* of ending comes to have crucial meaning in its own right within the transference–countertransference matrix. The issue of ending cannot be considered independently of this. As soon as it emerges, and no matter who raises it, the subject of ending (independently of any external criteria) will have meaning for, and carry the potential to be used by, both patient and analyst: for example, the patient may wish to escape the analyst's oppressive "yoke"; the analyst may feel rejected by the patient; or a sado-masochistic enactment may be created. Understanding such meaning or meanings can be seen as crucial in reaching a conclusion as to whether defensive or developmental possibilities predominate in any conscious or unconscious reference to ending.

Clinical material: history

I would like to consider these questions in relation to the analysis of Mrs Z. She was born in a war-torn country where her father had been held as a political prisoner. When she was eighteen months old, the family was forced to escape from this country in rather dramatic circumstances and then led an unsettled life in another dangerous environment.

When the patient was aged six, she came to the UK with her mother and two siblings, leaving father in the foreign land; the family were virtually destitute on their arrival in the UK. Initially, they were "taken in" by a part of the family who were already established in London, and, after a number of moves between relatives, mother and the children obtained social housing.

The patient describes her mother as having been remote and preoccupied with the necessity to keep body and soul together, and to deal with the immigration authorities. The patient's experience seems to be of a rather puritanical atmosphere in which a virtue was made of the necessity to ensure "nothing was wasted or ever thrown away". Mother was said to be extraordinarily self-denying, but was known to secretly raid the fridge during the night, when she would binge on left-over food. The patient reports that Mother had little time for her, being much more involved with her younger siblings.

Father rejoined the family after two years or so, but was unable to obtain stable employment. The patient conveys the impression of a father traumatized by his experiences in prison, humiliated by his reduced circumstances, and despised by his wife. He became a contract worker, spending long periods away from home. The patient recalls waiting for his return, looking down the street out of the window, and running down the stairs to greet him. She longed for him to pick her up, but she remembers that he usually turned away.

The patient was moderately academically successful, but, by all accounts, was shy and retiring, spending time on her own in an imaginary world. She managed to obtain sufficient qualifications to train as a physiotherapist, and left home at nineteen for college. On graduation, she obtained employment in her country of origin. Here, she reports running "wild", having numerous simultaneous affairs, but eventually "settling down" with a nurse from her own ethnic group. They returned to the UK, where they married and had two children. The patient feels that she neglected her children as they grew up and is guilty about the damage she feels she has done them. Both children live abroad, where they eke out a hand-to-mouth existence.

At the time of the referral, the patient had recently taken retirement on medical grounds following a serious road accident, and was living with her husband in a run-down estate. After her medical retirement, the patient had obtained casual work in a betting office. In early sessions, she regaled me with stories about this work, which seemed to have taken over her life. She worked long hours and prided herself on her ability to provide an exceptionally fast service to customers. This was particularly gratifying when she had to race the clock to process bets before the start of a big event. She developed an elaborate fantasy about an affair with the manager of the betting office, a man some fifteen years younger than her.

First impulse to end

In the early work with Mrs Z, it was as if she was a perfect patient, arriving on time, never missing sessions, and entertaining me with stories about her deprived but eventful life. Seeing her required little effort on my part and I felt rather special. In some respects, she was the easiest of patients to be with, but she left me with an uncomfortable feeling. It was all rather "too good to be true", but attempts to interpret her compliance as a defence against thoughts and feelings she dare not bring up were brushed aside.

Some twelve months after we began, I had to cancel a forthcoming session immediately before a weekend break. Giving her three weeks notice, I offered her an alternative time. She rejected this out of hand. She was far too busy to rearrange her diary. When we resumed after the extended weekend break in question, she talked of how pleased she was to be back and referred to the "long break". She repeated that she was glad to be back but said that it felt strange that I had not given her a bill. She knew that a bill was not due and she was being "well, rather silly, really. You know what I'm like, but the last break had been followed by a bill."

She then told me that she had been offered some well-paid work as the administrator of a refugee advice service, which would enable her to give up work in the betting shop. The problem was that she would need to change two of her session times so she assumed that she would have to turn the job down. "Such a pity because, as you said (I had not), the betting shop wasn't really appropriate for someone with my education."

I was struck by the synthetic "sweet reasonableness", which I found irritating, but I felt rather thrown and awkward as if I had to be very careful in my response. There seemed to be something tricky and threatening in the air. Eventually, I began to understand something of what was happening. I said that I thought she was letting me know, via her reference to bills, how her pleasure at being back with me was spoiled by the fact that I charged her for her sessions, and having fixed session times meant that, unlike me, she could not come and go as she pleased. I said she was angry about her position in relation to me.

She responded by insisting that she was just being "silly" about the bill. She knew perfectly well she had to pay—this was my *job* after all, and I had to earn money. The same thing applied to the timing of the sessions. She could not just turn up when she wanted to—still, it would be nice if she could take the job. I said that I felt she was letting me know that it would be "nice" if there was no conflict between coming to see me and the other things she wished to do and on which she wished to spend her money. She rejected this, saying there was "no contest. I want to come here. This is the most important thing."

She began the following session in an uncharacteristic way, telling me that she had felt upset and hurt since the previous session, but that she could not understand why this should be. I said that I thought that, in addition to being mindful that she needed to pay me, she felt hurt because I had not simply agreed to her implied request to discuss a change in her session times. Instead, I had made a comment about what this meant to her. Her response was to say that she felt I was, in effect, saying it was time to end. "The trouble is," she said, "you are my life, but that's not right because I am only part of your life—your work life. We're supposed to face things here, so I'd better face things and end it now—we've got to one day." This latter comment was delivered with her characteristic "sweet reasonableness".

Again, I struggled to find a way to respond, but eventually I managed to regain my composure. I linked her idea that I wished to end the analysis to her hurt and anger at my failure to respond as she had wanted. I said that I thought that, in fact, *she* wished to end. However, by making this into my idea, she got rid of the angry feelings about which she was anxious. Also, ending would remove her from the scene of something painful and give me a taste of my own rejecting medicine. Her response at the end of the session was a rather forlorn "I don't know why I tell you these things."

Although I was reasonably satisfied with the *content* of my comments, that is, I thought I had grasped the key elements of what was happening between us, I was struck by how verbalizing this did not seem to have any impact. Rather, my words seemed to disappear into thin air.

Theoretical background: the countertransference

I now turn to consider briefly some of the key themes and issues in recent psychoanalytic theory about countertransference. I hope this will provide a foundation to allow more detailed exploration of the clinical material presented above and a discussion of the development of the work with this patient in relation to the topic of ending.

As is well known, until 1950 the predominant view was that "countertransference was fundamentally pathological, an indication for the analyst's own continuing analysis and self-analysis" (La Farge, 2007, p. 796). Beginning with Heimann's (1950) paper, however, countertransference became recognized as ubiquitous, and the analyst's feelings began to be viewed as having the potential to be utilized to promote growth and development in the patient. There were different views about how the countertransference might be so utilized (Balint, 1950; Fairbairn, 1943; Tower, 1956; Winnicott, 1947). It was Heimann, however, who laid the foundations for the currently influential view that the countertransference is "the patient's creation . . . a part of the patient's personality" (Heimann, 1950, p. 77) and can be used as "an instrument of research into the patient's unconscious" (*ibid.*, p. 74). This heralded a movement away from viewing the analyst as a "dispassionate observer" (Feldman, 1997, p. 227), or a "blank screen" on to which the patient projects. Instead, the analyst was regarded as being actively involved in a process that required him to listen carefully and actively scrutinize his inner responses when with his patient.

The analytic setting permits the process of projection and introjection (which can be said to characterize all human relationships) to be subjected to scrutiny. As La Farge (2007), in her exposition of the classic paper by Racker (1957) suggests, the analyst, when with his patient, will shift back and forth between two kinds of identification, concordant (a sense of being *with* the patient, of the patient's experience resonating with that of the analyst) and complementary (when the material disturbs the analyst in some way so that he feels something *towards* the patient). Such disturbance may arise primarily because of the analyst's own conflicts or because of the quality of the patient's projections. La Farge summarizes, ". . . when the analyst fails in his concordant identification he is . . . captured by the patient's projection instead: that is, he identifies with the internal object that the patient has projected onto him" (2007, p. 801). This limits the analyst's freedom, and, unless he can undertake the psychic work necessary to regain his own identity, there is the danger of the crystallization of a collusive transference–countertransference and the possibility of enactment.

Money-Kyrle (1956) outlines a similar view particularly clearly. He contrasts periods of normal countertransference—"as the patient speaks the analyst will, as it were, become introspectively identified with him and having understood him inside will re-project him and interpret"—with periods of non-understanding. Money-Kyrle proposes that the analyst's "understanding fails whenever the patient corresponds too closely with some aspect of himself which he has not yet learnt to understand" (p. 361).

There is now a high degree of consensus that the analyst's subjective experience is a vital source of information about the patient, but, at the same time, the need for considerable caution is clear. Segal (1997), in her paper "The use and abuse of countertransference", is explicit in her caution: "the countertransference is only a clue; the material still has to be understood. Countertransference is the best of servants but it must remain a servant because it is absolutely the worst of masters" (p. 119). Sandler (1993) endorses this caution. Alluding to the dangers of "wild countertransference analysis", he argues,

> we need to be aware of how silly it is to postulate a one-to-one correspondence between what goes on in the analyst and what is in the mind of the patient and how much work is needed to connect the two. [p. 1103]

Kleinian analysts, in particular, have developed and refined the idea that the countertransference, to the extent that it is the product of the mind of the patient, is the result of projective identification. In his 1997 paper, Feldman extends the contention of Fairbairn that "psychoanalytical treatment resolves itself into a struggle on the part of the patient to press-gang his relationship with the analyst into the closed system of the inner world through the agency of transference" (Fairbairn, 1958, p. 385). Feldman shows how the patient's projection into the analyst of a phantasy object relationship can be seen as an attempt to actualize it or make it real (i.e., diminish the discrepancy between the phantasy of the object relationship and the patient's experience of the analyst). Thus, it is not simply that the object is transformed in the patient's mind, but that an attempt may be made for the phantasy to be enacted with the analyst. He suggests that "the patient's use of projective identification exerts subtle and powerful pressure on the analyst to fulfil the patient's unconscious expectations that are embodied in (these) phantasies" (Feldman, 1997, p. 228).

An example of this might be the "too good to be true" atmosphere in the early work with Mrs Z. I think that in this she was attempting to create a particular way of relating to me and of me to her that fulfilled a particular unconscious phantasy. This, undoubtedly, had an Oedipal dimension. Her "little girl" presentation and my feeling of being "special" might be seen as an example of the typical countertransference in hysteria, as described by Britton (1999).

Feldman suggests three possible outcomes of a projective identification: the analyst may recognize the pressure to which he is being subjected and maintain his analytic composure (equivalent to Money-Kyrle's "normal countertransference"); he may become caught up with the patient's projections and become drawn into an enactment; or, after some time, he may recognize that he has been taken over by the patient's unconscious phantasy.

The received psychoanalytic wisdom is that if the analyst is able to work through his countertransference conflicts and provide an experience that *disconfirms* the patient's archaic unconscious phantasy, the patient will experience relief and psychic development will be promoted. According to this view, in the case of Mrs Z, the interpretation of her projection of the wish to end with me, rather than my ending the work, should have promoted development and change. In fact, this did not happen. Feldman speaks to this dilemma in his suggestion that there can be an overriding pressure to achieve gratification of the unconscious phantasy, and that experience, which might provide disconfirmation and promote development, may not, in fact, do so.

Taking issue with the conventional view about containment (Bion, 1959) and referring to the case of a patient who experienced "an immensely painful and disturbing discrepancy between ... internal representation and the figure she (encountered) in the real world", Feldman (1997, p. 232) says, "I am suggesting this goes beyond and seems to conflict with the need to feel understood and reassured about the capacity of the object to take in and to 'contain' the projections". He continues, "the lack of this identity between the internal and external reality may . . . create an alarming space in which thought and new knowledge and understanding might take place, but which many patients find intolerable" (*ibid.*).

As I think the following discussion of the clinical work with Mrs Z will show, it was the "space" between patient and analyst that she found so alarming, and therefore sought to eradicate. In her discussion of projective identification, Joseph (1987) refers to how "projecting the self and parts of the self onto an object to dominate and control it (avoids) any feelings of being separate" (p. 138). It is not surprising, therefore, that, as happened with Mrs Z,

> an interpretative attempt on the part of the analyst to locate and give back to the patient missing parts of the self must of necessity be resisted . . . since it is felt to threaten the whole balance and lead to more disturbance. [*ibid.*, p.140]

Joseph argues that it is only as the patient moves closer to the depressive position that the space between self and object can be tolerated.

Steiner (1990) spells out what is involved in such a development. He revises Freud's paper "Mourning and melancholia" (Freud, 1917e) and suggests that

> as reality is applied to each of the memories of the lost object, what has to be faced is the painful recognition of what belongs to the

> object and what belongs to the self . . . In the process however, guilt and mental pain have to be experienced and these may be difficult to bear. [Steiner, 1990, p. 88]

Clinical discussion

I would now like to consider the clinical material presented earlier in the light of the foregoing theoretical discussion. I shall suggest that my response to the topic of ending was influenced by a number of factors, some conscious and some unconscious, and that key aspects of the transference–countertransference paradigm were not recognized until later in the work.

In his paper "On communication from patient to analyst: not everything is projective identification", Sandler (1993) proposes that there are "a number of different pathways through which the patient's mental state is communicated to the analyst" (p. 1104). In the first place is "straight forward analytical understanding", which, he suggests, "is not to be underestimated". With my patient, "objective" knowledge obtained via her reports about her history and everyday life, combined with my theoretical knowledge and my psychoanalytic experience, led me to a rough and ready formulation. With the lens of theory and experience, I "scanned" the material she produced and identified particular features as significant. These included her reports of her early history and early attachments (disrupted and fraught), Oedipal conflicts (e.g., waiting to be picked up on father's return, identification with father in his humiliation, the report of mother being contemptuous of father), and her guilt concerning the way she had treated her children, both of whom seemed to have struggled to establish themselves as adults. This led to a preliminary formulation along the lines that her disrupted early life and Oedipal conflicts had contributed to difficulties in establishing mature and satisfying relationships. One implication had been her problems in bringing up her children.

Next, Sandler identifies "recurrent primary identification (but we can call it mirroring or resonance if we like)" (1993, p. 1104). This, he suggests, refers to the analyst's capacity and function and has nothing to do with the patient's conscious or unconscious intention. As I immersed myself in the sessions with the patient, listening to her material and absorbing it, I identified with her. For example, from my own experience I knew something of the longing to be picked up by father but being disappointed. Again from my own experience, it was not hard to understand feeling guilty and how she might feel guilty about letting down her children. To the extent that the analyst makes sense of material, he must be able to get into the patient's shoes and, for a brief moment at least, experience for himself what the patient is reporting.

Third, Sandler distinguishes "the analyst's direct reaction to the patient" (*ibid.*). This includes both conscious and unconscious reactions, but, Sandler suggests, "such reactions do not constitute projective identification unless the patient has the unconscious intention to bring about a specific response in the analyst" (*ibid.*). Included in the general category of my "direct reaction" might be included my sense of being "special" and my irritation at her "sweet reasonableness".

On gathering my thoughts, impressions, and feelings together, a number of these were particularly striking. At the moment she made her comment about ending, I had felt shocked. Where had the topic of ending come from? After all, we had only recently begun. Closely following this was a sense that I had to be careful or she might leave the analysis or have some kind of tantrum. This changed to relief when she said, "you are my life" (I was not being rejected after all) and was quickly followed by sympathy for her predicament of being only part of my life. My feeling then shifted to one of irritation at something that felt disingenuous and aggressive.

These conscious countertransference feelings intermingled with other conscious and unconscious associations to her material, which included thoughts about what happened earlier in the session, previous clinical experience, supervision, and psychoanalytic theory. But also present were many other "personal" associations to this material, including, and especially involving, its unconscious significance. Out of this pool of conscious and unconscious feelings and thoughts came some ideas that eventually crystallized into an interpretation.

My view was that the proposal to end at this time was defensive. Not only were her relationships troubled and unsatisfying and her analysis had only just begun, but, more importantly, there was in the countertransference a sense that I was being ambushed, that caution on my part was needed, and that I felt alternately rejected and wanted. A feeling of sympathy for her was rapidly followed by irritation. None of these countertransference feelings indicated a woman who was ready to end and who was in a position to develop on her own. This led to an interpretative formulation about how she wanted me to fit in with her wish for an exclusive relationship with me, and that my refusal to comply resulted in her feeling hurt. It seemed that the idea of leaving was a response that served both to give me a taste of my own rejecting medicine, and also had the advantage of removing her from the pain of having to face herself and me as separate beings.

While this formulation and the interpretation to which it gave rise may have had some validity, it did little to advance the patient's self-knowledge, and, in fact, fell rather flat. She did not directly associate to the content of the interpretation; it did not lead to a development of the work: rather, she appeared to brush it aside.

What sense might be made of this? I think it is possible to suggest that a particular transference–countertransference paradigm was becoming established. Looking back at this material, and with the benefit of hindsight, a number of her comments are, I think, revealing. For example, she said, "you are my life—this is the most important thing." There was, she said, "no contest" between her job and coming to analysis. She said, with feeling, "I am only *part* of your life—your work life." She went on, "We're supposed to face things, so I'd better face things and end." Her response to my interpretation about the defensive nature of her proposal to leave was a forlorn "I don't know why I tell you these things." These comments and the general emotional atmosphere in the sessions had an impact on me and gave rise to countertransference feelings. I felt invaded with something over-familiar, pulled towards an intimacy that, if denied, meant she would leave. In the countertransference I felt panic, then futility. She was off. Leaving me . . .

Although at the time I was only dimly aware of it, I think her comments and my countertransference indicate that she was seeking to actualize an exclusive bond with me, but this was encountering unwelcome conflict. I am her life, and there is no contest with any other part of her life, even her work. I feel special about this. "You know what I'm like" suggests that we are very close. So close, in fact, that I recoil at her over-familiarity and invasiveness. Then there is her unwelcome realization that I might be the whole of her life but she is only a limited part of mine. "Facing things" means she has to deal with a feeling of terrible rejection and disappointment. She does this via the idea of leaving the scene and giving *me* the experience of rejection.

The lack of correspondence between inner wishes and outer reality does not, however, cause her to stop and think and explore. She turns away. My interpretation is ignored and is responded to with the words, "I don't know why I tell you these things." I think this comment makes perfect sense. Telling me "these things" would make sense only if she wished to explore them with me. If, rather, her intention is to enact a cosy relationship of agreement, "telling" gives the game away and destroys the phantasy.

To summarize: I think some key aspects of a transference–countertransference paradigm can be identified. She attempted to actualize a phantasy of oneness, an undifferentiated bond between us. I struggled to analyse what was going on, but she had a very different agenda. So, when I interpreted the defensive aim of her wish to leave, this had little, if any, impact. It did not promote the development of understanding. I think that, at the time, I understood something of this process, but an important (and perhaps the most important) dimension was hidden from my view. I recognized her struggles with need and dependency, but *not* her lack of interest or capacity to think and explore. Thus, my interpretations fell flat as she clung to her wishes and struggled to actualize these. I, in turn, however clung to my wishes (which, undoubtedly, had personal and unconscious significance) to advance understanding despite the unwelcome reality of her response.

Developments in the external world

Over the next four years, there were considerable changes, and very gradually Mrs Z became less bound to attempts to actualize her phantasy of a close and unending bond between us, and more open to the possibility of the exploration of her anxieties and conflicts.

This allowed the detail of her transference wishes and my (sometimes unwitting) place in these to become more evident.

As far as the external world was concerned, there were a number of developments. She took up the post as an administrator in the refugee advice service. Initially, she found it difficult to frustrate any of the wishes of the refugees, even momentarily, and was quick to take the refugees' side in any complaint against the organization. Gradually, this changed, as her investment shifted from seeking to gratify the refugees' wishes to providing sensitive and appropriate support and practical arrangements to offer them help. There was a striking change in that she began to speak more about the distress of the refugees rather than the failures of the organization.

Early in the analysis it emerged how difficult it was for her to sustain involvement with her family. She tended to withdraw into a rather masochistic posture when with them (perhaps in identification with her mother "working her fingers to the bone") but, very gradually, this began to change. Painful jealously (particularly of the closer and more lively relationship between her husband and the children) emerged from behind the masochistic stance and, once this could be acknowledged and explored, she began to participate in family gatherings a little more actively.

From the beginning of the work, I had been regaled with stories about how her husband was ridiculous and incompetent, and how they led largely separate lives. Eventually, the patient began to shift from her unreservedly contemptuous stance to express some appreciation for his efforts. She gave up her insistence on cooking the meal each evening and allowed him to share this responsibility, even appreciating his help.

Some two years into the analysis, her mother became unable to live independently. The patient dutifully helped with making arrangements for residential care, but it was striking how uninvolved she seemed to be. Soon after the move, her mother died, but this did not appear to have much impact. The patient was, however, disturbed by her lack of any feeling about her mother's death.

A fortuitous coincidence led to the patient being put in touch with the mother of her childhood best friend. The patient developed a close relationship with this woman, whom the patient recognized as a mother substitute, and visited her each week. When the old lady died, the patient was able to feel sad and spoke movingly about her childhood, of which her friend's mother had been a significant part. Mrs Z then began to reflect on the limitations of her friendships. She began to feel uneasy and to puzzle over how she had avoided the efforts of old friends to maintain contact. She took up a rather neglected earlier interest in pottery, through which she met new people and developed some friendships. She was struck, however, by how she found herself putting limitations on these.

Two aspects of these changes seemed significant. First, that she became interested in, and able to reflect upon and explore, what was happening. The modification of her overwhelming need for immediate gratification permitted the emergence of some curiosity. Second, she began to be troubled by what she referred to as a "cold steel barrier", which was understood as being linked to the limitation of the degree of involvement in her relationships. This had been particularly striking when friendships had ended when friends moved away. She then had simply cut off. She also began to notice more subtle manifestations of this coldness in her current relationships. Increasingly, this troubled her and, as deeper exploration became possible, the emergence of the cold steel barrier became evident in both her external and internal worlds.

Second impulse to end the analysis

Significant changes in the patient's external relationships found a parallel in changes in the content and atmosphere of the analytic sessions. Here, there was not only greater curiosity, but a shift from somewhat bland and sometimes irritating compliance ("fitting in") to some apparently genuine feeling, including, at times, some moving sadness. The patient's anger also became more accessible. Increasingly, there were glimpses of a patient who was involved in confronting painful feelings and conflicts within an analytic relationship. However, almost exactly in step with this deepening involvement, there were increasing references to the wish to end the analysis. The changes and developments in her life and relationships, both external and internal, became evidence to justify ending rather than to support continuing and deepening involvement. I was regaled with accounts of how her (newly made) friends told her she must move on from her analysis and involve herself in the real world. She complained of "feeling my age" at work, of needing to face reality and take retirement. Retirement would, however, deprive her of the funds needed to pay for her analysis.

The constant references to the necessity of leaving eventually reached a crescendo. In a series of sessions, the possibility of leaving seemed to be used to try to taunt me. She made claims about her progress that were grossly distorted, spoke of how "its job was done", and she represented the reality of her employment and financial situation in a transparently false way. Despite numerous attempts, it proved somehow impossible to effectively take any of this up without being drawn into a stalemate. This had a sadomasochistic quality. I felt lured into challenging her outrageous statements. But I would then be rebuffed and made to feel hurt and foolish, while she seemed to be excited and triumphant.

At the beginning of the fourth summer term, she had given notice that she would be taking a week off to go on holiday with her family. During the course of our work, this had become an established annual event. When I told her that I needed to change a session due to take place just before this break and, at the same time, gave the dates of my break, matters came to a head. She challenged me, "So you think I'm coming back after the summer do you?", and talked about the possibility of giving notice to end work (and the funds to pay for her analysis) at the end of July. When I interpreted that this was a provocative move designed to shift me into action (to challenge or to agree) rather than to explore, she dismissed this in an off-hand way, saying that I needed to "get real. I can't come here forever." Once again I was pushed away.

Some two weeks later, she arrived for a mid-week session in a sober frame of mind. She began by saying that, as she had been walking up the path to my room, she had wondered what it was like for me to have had her coming for so long. "It must be awful," she said. After some silence, she talked of seeing the household bicycles hidden behind a bush. She could not be sure, of course, but she guessed they must have been deliberately hidden from her. The bicycles had to be hidden, she thought, lest seeing them made her feel jealous and angry. I said I thought she had a sense that these feelings and the intensity of her involvement were too much for me, or at least exerted a very great pressure on me. I said she felt I had tried to hide the bicycles to prevent her seeing them in an attempt to avoid provoking such strong feelings and, thereby, the pressure on me which would result. She said I was right. "But the thing is, it may not be that at all, you may not even have thought that . . . I may have the wrong end of the stick . . . that's even worse in a way." We understood that the idea that the bicycles had not, in fact, been deliberately hidden from her (but had perhaps simply been tidied away, for example), was even worse than her sense that her jealousy and anger would exert a great pressure on me. It was painful for her not to be at the centre of my world. A sober, sad atmosphere enveloped the room, and in the countertransference I felt closer to her.

She went on to talk about a recent session during which my mobile phone (which I had inadvertently left switched on) had buzzed. This she said had made her *furious*. Why hadn't I switched the phone off; why didn't people leave her alone? This was her time, her session. But she said this was a bit disproportionate, very silly. I had only left the phone on after all. It had not even rung properly. I said that I thought she was showing me how she was faced with a dilemma. She could barely stand it if she was not at the centre of my mind; the bicycles behind the bush issue, my not thinking about switching the phone off before *her* session, stirred strong feelings. However, if I became aware of these, she was anxious that I would find the intensity of her response hard to bear.

She agreed, and went on, "But there is even more you see . . ." Referring to the session I had changed prior to her taking a week away for a family holiday, she said, "I know it may not be true, but actually I believe somewhere it is true—it must be true—you changed that session to get back at me for taking the week off." Exploration revealed that she felt we were involved in a ruthless game. Although on the surface all might seem to be well, underneath it was all about a struggle for domination. She believed that I could not stand it when she went off for a week, so I intentionally changed a session to put her in her place. She then, in turn, retaliated via her taunt that she might end the analysis. I must be furious with her for trying to end, unless, of course, I would be pleased—relieved of the burden of her unending presence. The atmosphere was sad and sober, a striking contrast with the excited battles of recent sessions.

The next day she complained of feeling "cold and cut off". She said she had become like this soon after the previous day's session.

She could not understand where the previous day's feelings had gone. It felt as if a cold steel barrier had descended. When she had got home, her husband told her he had made arrangements for a cleaner to come to the house each week, to help her out. This, she told me, made her furious. If he had taken the trouble to talk to her from time to time he would have realized she did not want anyone else "messing up my kitchen". Also, he was "buying me off, he does nothing around the house. If he is not at work he sits in his room with his friends or doing his e-mails. I have to do all the work." Then she stopped. "The thing is," she said, "others see him differently—they say he is kind and generous to a fault sometimes." She spoke of how she had first met him and how he had looked after her, putting up with her infidelities and insecurities. Things had "gone sour"; she cried, "I haven't got it in me to be kind." She spoke of how she resented it when her husband ignored her and took visitors to another part of the house. We understood that (as if in retaliation) she had "cut out" her husband. Any sense of his kindness and generosity had been destroyed. There was a move from hurt to anger, and then the cold steel barrier came down to protect her from the unbearable feeling of having lost his affection. Cutting off protected her, but her coldness and lack of compassion disturbed her and made her feel guilty.

It was not difficult to link her husband's engagement of a cleaner and her feelings about this to my attempts to "mess up *her* kitchen" with my analytic activity, threatening her omnipotence and exposing her to painful feelings of exclusion with my "hidden bicycles" and changed sessions and summer break. She felt these actions of mine were intolerable, and any sense that I was interested and helpful to her was destroyed as the cold steel barrier came down. She agreed that her provocative suggestion that she would leave at the end of the summer term had been designed to turn the tables on me and to rid herself of unbearable feelings. She said that to end in July was a ridiculous idea. She could not manage without her analysis, "but that's a real problem", she said. At this point, there was a sense of real contact between us.

The next day, she complained that, once again, she was feeling cold and cut-off. She was disturbed by this, which was, she said, happening quite a lot now. She said that she had been preoccupied with the forthcoming visit of her family. Overwhelmed by the number of practical tasks, she had begun to feel resentful about their arrival. Driving to the session, she had reflected that all feeling for them seemed to have gone. She just felt nothing.

Exploration revealed that she felt that unless she felt "nothing" she would be faced with unmanageable feelings of hurt and resentment about how she felt excluded, and how jealous she felt that they seemed to get along so well together. She had started to build in her mind a litany of complaints about how badly they treated her and how they took her for granted. She feared that she might explode and destroy the family holiday. "But," she said, "the thing is, I can think about this here but not there." She talked of how sometimes she could tell me a little about how I affected her, even if this was difficult and painful. "I get the full feeling." This "full feeling" contrasted with the coldness of the steel barrier. It was intense (full) and meant that she sometimes hated me, but at other times wanted me above anything else. But she could not feel like this elsewhere. She said that she did not really want to lose the feeling, but we understood that whenever faced with painful conflict she had to "move off", either by putting a physical distance between herself and others or by erecting a defensive coldness.

It felt clear to me that to leave her analysis at this point would allow her habitually to erect such a defensive shield. She was becoming aware that she felt dead when the cold barrier descended and she was beginning to feel better and more alive, with the "full feeling". However, "having the full feeling is difficult and I don't know if I can take it. I need to stay, but I fight against it." Despite this conflict, she resolved to return after the summer break.

On her return, she reported a recurring nightmare. This was striking, as previously she had rarely brought dreams and it had not proved possible to make much productive use of the few fragments that she had reported. Now, she was troubled by a dream and eager to tell me about it.

In the dream

> she is climbing a mountain up a difficult but well-worn track. She comes to a crossroads. On the right is a well-defined but very steep and stony continuation of the first track, leading straight up the mountain. On the left is a less clear, but easy path around the side of the mountain. Initially, she takes the first path, and then she changes her mind, comes back to the crossroads and takes the easier path. All goes well

> until suddenly the path falls away and disintegrates and she falls on to a dangerous precipice from which she cannot escape. She is terrified, and wakes with a start.

She immediately associated to a classic self-help book she had been reading. The author attacked long-term therapy and proposed his own brief therapy. She had discovered, however, that subsequent to writing the book, the author had entered long-term therapy himself. She then went on to tell me about a very difficult weekend she had spent with two people who got along very well with each other. She had felt excluded, and had become angry and withdrawn. Suddenly, she had thought about me and realized that she was withdrawing to protect herself. She reflected that this was something she tended to do both with me and in her other relationships, but that this simply perpetuated the underlying problem. Try as she might, she could not, however, pull herself out of her self-excluding stance. She needed my direct involvement and felt the absence of this during the break.

She was quick to link the dream and her associations to her impulse to leave the analysis. Ending could appear to be the correct and easier path, but, in fact, at this time, it was likely to expose her to danger. All this unfolded in a sober and reflective atmosphere that underpinned a resolve to continue her analysis.

Conclusion

I have argued that it is only when the transference and countertransference is explicated in some detail that it is possible to reach a reliable conclusion about the matter of ending. In the early sessions with Mrs Z, it is possible to understand in broad terms that she sought relief from the recognition of my separateness via *telling* me that she wanted to end. Although she did not leave, neither did she engage in a development of understanding. In fact, my interpretation seemed to have little effect; it was as if we carried on as we were. By the time the question of leaving arose for the second time, there had been some positive developments in her work and relationships. It was, however, the evidence from the consulting room, from the transference and countertransference, which was the most telling and reliable. This exposed the limitations of the developments she had made and the defensive function of the plan to leave the analysis.

Underlying the claims of progress and the representation of ending as "facing reality" was the need to protect herself from the recognition of her need for me and of my separateness. This dilemma infused all her relationships, which were characterized by a combination of superficial compliance and, when involvement became disturbing, by the use of the "cold steel barrier". This alternation between compliance and coldness was a striking feature of the countertransference. In the early sessions, she was an exceptionally "good" patient, but, as the work progressed, her capacity to withdraw and cut me out became increasingly evident.

Eventually, it became possible to uncover a powerful underlying phantasy. The key feature of this seemed to be a defensive merging in which she struggled to control my separateness and independence, while I was seen as doing the same to her. The implication was that she could neither leave (as she threatened to do) nor grieve (i.e., bear the fact of separateness and engage in thinking about the implication of ending).

The later material indicates some development of her capacity to bear separateness. We might speculate that, over a long period, her need to actualize her internal phantasy of control became less pervasive as her anxieties about separateness diminished. If so, the repeated comings and goings in her analysis are likely to have played a key part in this. Whatever the precise reasons for this development, the later material demonstrates a capacity to tolerate (and, at times, even to welcome) the "full feeling" with which separateness was associated.

As the patient said, "I don't know if I can take it." To the extent that she could bear separateness, she became more able to tolerate my function as an analyst and to engage in exploration. Thus, she committed herself to a further period of work in which her depressive anxieties could continue to be confronted.

References

Balint, M. (1950). Changing therapeutical aims and techniques in psychoanalysis. *International Journal of Psychoanalysis, 31*: 117–124.

Bion, W. R. (1959). Attacks on linking. *International Journal of Psychoanalysis, 40*: 308–315 [republished in: *Second Thoughts*. Maresfield Reprints, London: Karnac, 1984].

Britton, R. (1999). Getting in on the act: the hysterical solution. *International Journal of Psychoanalysis, 80*: 1–14.

Fairbairn, W. (1943). The repression and the return of bad objects. In: *Psychoanalytic Studies of the Personality* (pp. 59–81). London: Tavistock, 1952.

Fairbairn, W. (1958). On the nature and aims of psycho-analytic treatment. *International Journal of Psychoanalysis, 39*: 374–385.

Feldman, M. (1997). Projective identification: the analyst's involvement. *International Journal of Psychoanalysis, 78*: 227–241.

Freud, S. (1917e). Mourning and melancholia. *S.E., 14*: 237–260. London: Hogarth Press.

Freud, S. (1937c). Analysis terminable and interminable. *S.E., 23*: 216–253. London: Hogarth.

Heimann, P. (1950). On countertransference. *International Journal of Psychoanalysis, 31*: 81–84.

Joseph, B. (1987). Projective identification: some clinical aspects. In: J. Sandler (Ed.), *Projection, Identification, Projective Identification*. Madison, CT: International [reprinted in: E. Bott Spillius (Ed.), *Melanie Klein Today, Vol. 1, Mainly Theory*, London: Routledge, 1988].

Klein, M. (1950). On the criteria for the termination of a psycho-analysis. *International Journal of Psychoanalysis, 31*: 78–80.

La Farge, L. (2007). Commentary on "The meanings and uses of countertransference" by Heinrich Racker. *Psychoanalytic Quarterly, 76*: 795–815.

Money-Kyrle, R. (1956). Normal countertransference and some of its deviations. *International Journal of Psychoanalysis, 37*: 360–366.

Pedder, J. (1988). Termination reconsidered. *International Journal of Psychoanalysis, 69*: 495–505.

Racker, H. (1957). The meanings and use of countertransference. In: H. Racker (Ed.), *Transference and Countertransference* (pp. 127–173). London: Hogarth, 1968.

Sandler, J. (1993). On communication from patient to analyst: not everything is projective identification. *International Journal of Psychoanalysis*, 74: 1097–1107.

Schacter, J. (1992). Concepts of termination and post-termination patient–analyst contact. *International Journal of Psychoanalysis, 73*: 137–154.

Segal, H. (1997). The uses and abuses of countertransference. In: J. Steiner (Ed.), *Psychoanalysis, Literature and War, Papers 1972–1995* (pp. 111–119). London: Routledge.

Steiner, J. (1990). Pathological organisations as obstacles to mourning: the role of unbearable guilt. *International Journal of Psychoanalysis, 71*: 87–94.

Tower, L. (1956). Countertransference. *Journal of the American Psychoanalytical Association, 4*: 244–255.

Winnicott, D. W. (1947). Hate in the countertransference. *International Journal of Psychoanalysis, 30*: 69–74 [reprinted in: D. Winnicott, *Through Paediatrics to Psychoanalysis*. London: Hogarth, 1949].

CHAPTER NINE

The elusive concept of analytic survival

Ruth Berkowitz

"At least you survived," said a colleague following my presentation at a weekly clinic meeting of a session with an extremely difficult patient. This seemingly ordinary comment stayed in my mind. The notion of analytic survival is one of those terms in common psychoanalytic currency, and it is as though we all know and understand the meaning. Trying to put aside the idea that only I did not know and understand the meaning, I thought on. How has the term been used? How has it been understood? If analytic survival has some importance in our work, in what way does it affect the patient? I considered my own clinical work, and wondered whether the experience of analytic survival was the same with each patient or whether it differed according to the nature and extent of the psychopathology and, if different, how the experience might differ.

The term "survival" is associated mainly with the work of Winnicott and his seminal paper, "The use of an object and relating through identifications" (1971). In this paper, he highlights the importance of destruction, adding that this word is needed "because of the object's liability not to survive, which also means to suffer change in quality in attitude" (p. 109). He asks again

(Winnicott, Shepherd, & Davies, 1989), does the object survive; that is, does it retain its character or does it react? A further question, then, is how, since Winnicott's time, has the understanding of survival altered?

Then there is the phrase "at least". Did this mean survival was fundamental in the analytic exchange, or did it mean that I had done the absolute minimum? These are some of the questions that I will attempt to consider in this paper.

Early indications of the importance of survival

According to Jones (1964), Freud told him more about the ending of Breuer's treatment of Anna "O" than he had written about.

> It would seem that Breuer had developed what we should nowadays call a strong counter-transference to his interesting patient. At all events he was so engrossed that his wife became bored at listening to no other topic, and before long she became jealous. She did not display this openly but became unhappy and morose. It was a long time before Breuer, with his thoughts elsewhere, divined the meaning of her state of mind. It provoked a violent reaction in him, perhaps compounded of love and guilt, and he decided to bring the treatment to an end. He announced this to Anna O., who was by now much better and bade her good-bye. But that evening he was fetched back to find her in a greatly excited state, apparently as ill as ever. The patient, who according to him had appeared to be an asexual being . . . was now in the throes of an hysterical childbirth (pseudocyesis), the local termination of a phantom pregnancy that had been invisibly developing in response to Breuer's ministrations. Though profoundly shocked, he managed to calm her down by hypnotizing her, and then fled the house in a cold sweat. [p. 203]

This recognition of transference and countertransference can be seen as the beginning of psychoanalysis as we know it today. Breuer had clearly not survived the sheer force of the transference and countertransference. Although, as we all know, Freud recommended "neutrality", there are indications in his papers on technique and elsewhere that he was concerned with the impact of the work on the analyst. In his paper "Recommendations to physicians practising psycho-analysis" (1912e), he says that the emotional coldness is advantageous to both analyst and patient. For the doctor, this is a desirable protection for his own emotional life, and for the patient, it is the best way of helping him. Later in this paper he says, ". . . the sacrifice involved in laying oneself open to another person without being driven to illness is amply rewarded" (p. 117). His recognition of the strain of the work is there throughout these papers. In his comments on "Transference-love" (1915a), he writes of a threefold battle that has to be waged: in the analyst's own mind against the forces that seem to drag him down from the analytic level, against opponents, and against his patients. In "Analysis terminable and interminable" (1937c), he notes that the prospects of analytic treatment are influenced not only by factors in the patient, but by the individuality of the analyst, who may make use of defensive mechanisms "so that they themselves remain as they are and are able to withdraw from the critical and corrective influence of analysis" (p. 249). In a letter to Pfister (Meng & Freud, 1963), he wrote that the "transference is indeed a cross" (p. 39).

The recommendation of neutrality has been a source of much discussion within the psychoanalytic community, and there are views that it may not be achievable or desirable. However, the seeds of much that was to follow, both in theory and clinical practice, were sown in those early beginnings.

Some understandings of survival and non-survival

What, perhaps, is typical of most patients who come to analysis, is that in their life experiences, usually very early ones, their objects have not been able to provide them with an experience of survival. There may have been gross breaches of boundaries, such as sexual or physical abuse, or less obvious but, none the less, equally toxic experiences of having to become a narcissistic object for a parent, usually the mother, or of parents not being able to tolerate their development, neither separation nor individuation. Before coming to analysis, these patients usually live out their lives repeating these patterns, recreating scenarios of abuse and, of course, mostly with objects who do not survive.

A male patient, whose mother had indicated implicitly and explicitly that it was his duty to look after her, constantly made comments about whether I was all right and whether he was too much for me. During the analysis, it emerged that all his relationships followed the same pattern: he would become the carer. Exploration of whether or not I could cope with his growing dependence was accompanied by, at times, overwhelming anxiety that I would imminently collapse. Interpretation of these anxieties, in terms of his difficulty in believing that I could bear his dependence without breaking down myself, led to his telling me how, in a previous treatment, the therapist, on hearing the patient's life story, told the patient in a somewhat cosy way that she could understand the patient very well. The therapist then told the patient her life story, and the patient soon left that therapy.

Those who come for psychoanalysis or psychoanalytic therapy have, of necessity, resorted to ways of protecting themselves: through depression, self-sufficiency, compliance, drugs, perversions, or violence, to name a few. They have, in a very general sense, however, reached a point when the old ways are no longer serving them. By coming to analysis, they are seeking out an "other", be it analysis or an analyst. There are, of course, many other motivating factors, but it is the "other" that concerns us here. What this "other" might be remains to be discovered by both analyst and patient. What we do know is that this other will be, in many ways, a re-creation of others from the patient's life experience, with survival or non-survival as an aspect. From the patient's perspective, both consciously and unconsciously, there may be fears and wishes for both the survival and non-survival of the analyst. The patient, therefore, brings to analysis not only his usual ways of relating to others, but his fears and anxieties—sometimes terrors—of these usual ways being undone, as well as his expectations that there will be a repetition of many aspects of his early relationships, including non-survival, this time of the analyst. But here, the interest and emphasis is on the perspective of the analyst, what it may mean, and why it may or may not have something of value for the patient.

What Freud conveyed in his metaphor of the cross was both the idea of a very heavy burden and that this had to be borne. Since then, so much thought and attention, both clinically and theoretically, has been given to the transference and countertransference that we are now aware of the multiple ways in which patients communicate to their analysts—verbally and non-verbally—through projection and projective identification. It is the impact of these communications on the analyst, and his reaction to it, that are at the heart of survival.

How multifarious is this impact: that is, all that the analyst has to go through (Alvarez, 1985)? My own experience echoes that of others. There is the internal resistance of the analyst himself, who is still fearful of the new and unknown, as he is only human (Bolognini, 2004). There may be a reaction of detachment in a narcissistic way (Brenman, 2006), or resistance to a loss of identity (Godbout, 2005). Potentially, there are many fears: of damaging the patient, of excessive demands, of loss of mental balance, of inability to endure catastrophic change (Grinberg, 1997), and of violent projections and recognition of our own psychotic areas (Rosenfeld, 1986).

What is evident is that the idea of "bearing" the impact needs explanation and, perhaps, elaboration. There are repeated references in the literature to "tolerance" and "non-retaliation". Bion's work on containment and reverie are relevant here (1970). Containment has tended mainly to focus on the containment of the other; the reverie, the digestion of indigestible experiences, given back to the other after a suitable sojourn, be it infant or patient. Considered less often is the question of containment of oneself as analyst.

Tolerance is a word that seems so often to be the one of choice, and it has been defined and used in a variety of ways. Carpy (1989) defines tolerance as: "The ability to allow oneself to experience the patient's projections in their full force and yet be able to avoid acting them out in a gross way" (p. 289). Cassoria (2008) writes of the analyst's implicit alpha function to tolerate patiently the obstructive movements and hindrances to recovery without giving up the search for new approaches. Reeves (2007) refers to being received, tolerated, and survived without retaliation by the mother or analyst. Sandler (1992), and Botella and Botella (2005), also use the word "tolerance". Here, however, the field opens up further. Tolerance is not simply the capacity of the analyst not to act out, not to retaliate, not to withdraw, and, importantly, not to enact a supportive or destructive role from the past. Baker (1993) suggests that the analyst's capacity to tolerate and survive attacks obviates "the impasse that would ensue were he to endorse himself as a transference object" (p. 1227). Survival requires, at times, immense internal work on the part of the analyst including, according to some, a degree of moral masochism described by Cassoria (2008) as being similar to the mother's patience and capacity to tolerate suffering without discouragement.

When I agreed to take Mr A, a man in late middle age into analysis, I felt some reluctance in myself, and, at times, some regret at having taken him on. It was an intense emotional struggle for me, and I was aware of strong feelings of dislike, and, at times, repugnance, feelings that could translate in my mind into criticisms of him, of his dirty clothes, of his body, and minding that he "dirtied" my couch. It was some time before I could put my feelings into words in terms of his fears that I would not like him. His story then unfolded. He had felt rejected by his own mother, who found him unappealing. This took time and work on both our parts: on mine, awareness of my feelings and "tolerating" them; on the patient's, growing openness that he felt unlovable, unattractive, and unwanted.

Two ideas seem relevant to the idea of suffering without discouragement. One is the self-analytic element (Bollas, 1990) as an inner experiencing of oneself as an analyst, and the application of mind to such inner experience. The analyst must, therefore, constantly be attending to inner reactions to patients. These may include emotional reactions of anger, irritation, excitement, amusement, boredom, dislike, drowsiness, forms of acting out, such as ending sessions early, or more unconscious reactions, such as his own associations. The work of Zwiebel (2004) elaborates this in great detail, building on his premise that the central analytic task is to survive the relationship with the patient, and, further, that for the analyst to survive that relationship a third position must be developed out of the internal working processes of the analyst, over and over again. In the case of Mr A, I might have, in a simplistic way, responded to my own reactions by accepting them and believing that this was an unappealing person. Being able to question my feelings—rather than being the rejecting mother—was taking up the third position, and, thereby, surviving rather than becoming the transference object.

It is not only countertransference responses that need constant monitoring, but also many personal aspects of the analyst, including the character of the analyst, his internal conflicts, life cycle crises, and age. This includes the professional experiences of the analyst and his analytic training, including the training analysis.

The second idea has to do with another aspect of the internal work, the suffering with the patient, opening up to the patient's experience with a particular kind of receptivity. If we consider the first point, it would seem that the application of the analyst's mind to his own inner experience cannot, and, indeed, for some, should not, be an immaculate one. As to the "cannot be", Varga (2005) suggests that while the countertransference reaction to the transference must continuously be monitored, the major advance in psychoanalysis in recent years has been a better understanding of the inevitability and analytic utility of transference–countertransference enactment in the patient–analyst relationship. While there is agreement about the inevitability of this enactment, not all agree about its value. The "should not" is the valuable thought in the paper by Carpy (1989). He writes of the many ways in which acting out by the analyst might be expressed: through the choice of the area of interpretation, the type of interpretation, the actual words, and tone of voice. (We will consider in the following section in what way this might be mutative for the patient.) Slochower (1991) values the expressions of her own feeling states, saying explicitly in her clinical account that she tried to maintain an extremely firm, slightly irritated stance to the patient's barbs. Baker (2000) agrees that enactments are inevitable, while disagreeing about their therapeutic value.

The inner receptiveness of the analyst is described in various ways, including living the traumatic injured area, putting its vulnerability to the test, and adding carefully to its recovery, bearing pain and suffering (Cassoria, 2008). Cassoria compares this to the masochism of the mother, her suffering along with the baby, bearing the unreality of it, not shattering the unreality of it and detaching herself in a traumatic way. An aspect of receptiveness (Davies, 2007) is surrender to a form of controlled regression, requiring a relinquishing of verbal representations and their logical connections. Godbout (2005) goes further, describing a temporary partaking by the analyst of the experience of the other, which, if deep enough, might shake the analyst's sense of identity. But the analyst must be able to tolerate what might be called depersonalization, allowing himself to be invaded and overwhelmed by the other. The work of Botella and Botella (2005) captures eloquently a receptiveness to the patient's psychic experience, with the analyst's nightmare mirroring the negative hallucination of the patient: "The retrogressive movement of the analyst's thought opens the session to an intelligibility of the relation between two psyches functioning in a regressive state" (p. 49). They call the psychic capacity for such movement "figurability", and its accomplishment, "the work of figurability". They remark that what "figurability" involves is nothing less than a question of psychic survival (*ibid.*).

Mrs B, a single mother who had rarely been able to put any feelings into words, was, in one session, in touch with this impediment. I felt intense strain and pressure to relieve it. She fell into a profound silence, during which I had a vivid image of a mother screaming at her. It was an extraordinary experience for me when she then said she had felt absolutely terrified and terrorized by her mother, who would lose control and rant at her.

Survival of the analyst may, therefore, not only be conveyed by the state of mind of the analyst, but also by a very particular emotional receptiveness.

Destructiveness and destruction

What, we may ask, is being survived in these analytic encounters? In his paper, "The use of an object and relating through identifications", Winnicott (1971) focuses on the destructiveness of the patient and the capacity of the analyst to survive it. There is, as a result, a move from object relating, where the other is mainly a bundle of projections. As the analytic work progresses, the object must, at one and the same time, be destroyed and yet survive, the analyst becoming "real", now to be "used" as a separate object. What is absolutely fundamental in this paper is the understanding of the meaning of destructiveness, which contains within it the thrust of aggression. For Winnicott (1950), aggressiveness is almost synonymous with activity, and part of the primitive expression of love. Importantly, at the very early stages, the infant's aim is not to destroy, his aggressiveness only becoming destructive when there is sufficient ego integration and ego organization for the existence of anger, and, therefore, as Winnicott puts it, fear of the talion. Not retaliating, so central to the notion of survival, is, therefore, all-important in the analytic encounter.

Winnicott points out that there may be confusion in the use of the term aggression when what is meant is spontaneity. This confusion may not be only in the mind of the analyst; there may also be confusion in the experience of patients. For them, spontaneity might, in their early experience, have been received as an attack, so that it fuses with aggression, as Fonagy (Fonagy, Moran, & Target, 1993) says: if the young child's self-expression is repeatedly thwarted or misinterpreted, then his self-expression will become fused with aggression. Therefore, when forceful projections, which can be difficult and painful for the analyst to bear, are interpreted as "sadistic attacks", this can lead to the patient feeling rejected and fearing that the analyst cannot stand being involved with him. That is, the patient experiences the analyst as not surviving (Rosenfeld, 1986).

Ms C, a young single woman, took pride in never expressing emotions such as sadness or anger, which were experienced by her as weakness. However, she would continually say that the analysis was getting her nowhere, what was the point of talking, she was exactly where she had been when she came into analysis. I took this up in terms of her wishing to explore what would happen if she expressed these "negative" feelings towards the analysis and me: would I reject her and say, "Well if you don't feel it is of value, why come?", or would I try to understand her feelings with her. She said that what she did value about the analysis was being able to say these negative things to me, feeling a sense of relief both by saying them and by my response.

We often use the words "testing out" in our accounts of the patient's verbal or non-verbal "attacks", which implies that the patient is on the lookout for the survival or non-survival of the analyst, doing what Cassoria (2008) describes as the patient unconsciously scrutinizing the analyst and assessing his containing capacity. What can be overlooked in the interpretation of the aggression as an attack is the search on the patient's part for both the non-surviving and the surviving object, that there is both aggression (spontaneity included) and love. Moreover, what is being called aggression may contain within it the resistance. As we know, Freud viewed the transference as resistance. This, according to Sandler (1992), has a self-preservative aspect, and he cautions against neglecting this aspect of resistance, which is a self-protective measure against a loss of safety and familiarity with old ways, however painful. The exploratory nature of the "testing out", the resistance, and the fact that the patient has come for analysis, speaks of the complexity of responding to such communications from the patient.

A young man in a lifelong enmeshed relationship with his widowed mother had made desperate bids to escape, not only from the mother's dependence on him, but also his dependence on his mother. He cancelled session after session, always returning contrite, anxious about my response. I might have taken this up as an attack on the analysis and me, and, in some ways, it *perhaps* was. However, I took it up in terms of his wish to explore the impact upon me of being rejected by him. Would I in turn reject him? Or would I try to understand his need to absent himself from the analysis? This interpretation needed reiteration, and I needed to contain my own irritation and, at times, feelings of rejection. Slowly, we could understand his hatred of his feelings of dependence and the power of the regressive pull to self-sufficiency, as well as his wish that I should remain sitting in my chair in the usual way, a constant and reliable figure.

Avoidance by missing sessions suggests that the patient is afraid and, if so, what is it that he is afraid of when he expresses himself in this way? Green (2008) offers a perspective by asking what people are afraid of when they are under the influence of id impulses: "They are afraid of destroying the object, disappearing themselves or destroying their own working-through processes—that means there is a breakdown as a subject" (p. 1037). This brings us back to the central theme of this chapter, the survival of the analyst as object. There may be in all patients a sense of the frailty of the object, that under the threat of the patient's self-expression, whether it is seen as spontaneity, aggression, or even love, the object will collapse. Following Green, could it then be said that non-survival of the object presages the non-survival of the subject and of the relationship?

What of the analyst's fear of collapse? From the very beginning of any treatment, there may well be a threat to the analyst *qua* analyst, a figure who, perhaps in his own mind as well as that of the patient, is on the side of change. The patient's resistance and need to protect himself by his familiar, well-worn ways opposes the analyst's core identity, and this may lead to feelings of helplessness or uselessness on the part of the analyst, which may or may not be a countertransference response. The notion of change, however, is not confined to the patient. Every analysis makes considerable internal demands on the analyst to respond to this particular patient, who has his own particular thoughts, feelings, and beliefs, his idiosyncratic responses to analysis, his unconscious ways of expressing himself, whether it is through dreams or non-verbal communications. How far can this be truly experienced, moving from tolerance, through moral masochism, to the surrender of self as described by Botella and Botella (2005)? Offering oneself as an analyst for use has a deep, devastating, and dangerous meaning. To be used by others meaningfully, we have to be ready to be destroyed by them (Erlich, 2003). Perhaps it was this that Bion in part recognized when he spoke of relinquishing memory and desire, that to be an analyst one has to give up preconceptions and be receptive to change oneself. However, while there may be change within the analyst, there is a fundamental requirement to survive, to retain his character, his analytic attitude.

When we think about the form of surrender that is required of analysts, the destruction of their identity could be experienced as a considerably high risk. The true source of resistance to the erosion of identity boundaries in analysis ought to be looked for in the analyst's fear of feeling traces of helplessness within himself (Godbout, 2005). Thus, both analyst and patient may come to the analytic encounter with fears about the survival of the analyst.

What might be mutative about survival?

Thus far, I have been considering survival as an aspect of analysis. Several questions arise from this. First, in what way might the survival of the analyst be mutative? Second, is the survival of the analyst only positive? Finally, do we need to consider the survival of the analyst in relation to the nature of the patient's psychopathology?

"The internalization of the analyst's tolerant attitude to the contents of the patient's unconscious is vital" (Sandler, 1992). However, both survival and internalization are elusive concepts. While we may not know the precise nature of these processes, there may be room for speculation about what may be "taken in" by the patient. There are those who hold the view that "the tolerating figure, or the function of this figure can be introjected and momentarily identified with" (Joseph, 1992, p. 238). There may be the effect of the analyst's greater tolerance on the patient's superego, allowing ideas formerly repressed to be verbalized and communicated (Rycroft, 1986). Loewald (1960) and Baker (1993) emphasize the new discovery of objects:

> The essence of such new object relationships is the opportunity they offer for the rediscovery of the early paths of the development of object relations, leading to a new way of relating to objects as well as of being and relating to oneself. [Loewald, 1960, p. 225]

It is the function that is taken in, not the good object (Godbout, 2005). How, though, might the patient internalize either the tolerance of the analyst or the new object relationship?

It might be valid to postulate that, since the survival of the object is fundamental to the survival of the patient, the patient begins his analytic work in a state of acute sensitivity, albeit unconscious, to the analyst's state of mind. Fonagy (Fonagy, Moran, & Target, 1993) outlines the process whereby this capacity develops, beginning with the invitation to conceive of the analyst's mind through transference and countertransference interpretations. The patient observes and momentarily identifies with his analyst (the transference object), and is then able to explore his own mind. Here, Fonagy brings in an important aspect of "tolerance" and survival: that all this occurs in the context of a friendly and comfortable relationship. Racker (1968) has described this as reliving childhood under better conditions, and suggests that the analyst's continuous empathy, tolerance, and interpretations that reduce tension and anxiety, are all reacted to as manifestations of affection: not the need for love, but the capacity for loving. A further dimension, already mentioned, is added by

Zwiebel (2004), which may be implicit, and sometimes explicit, in the work of other writers in this field. This is the capacity to develop what he calls a *third position*. A third position is an intersubjective concept, and refers neither solely to the subjectivity of the patient nor of the analyst; it is also not a static position. It is a position that evolves, is continually in a state of flux, and is constantly transformed by the understandings of both patient and analyst. For Zwiebel, survival can only be sustained if there is an expansion of the analytic position into this third position. What is most crucial in his thinking is that while there may be what he calls derailments (non-survival), if the analyst can reflect on these the third position can be restored.

Mr C, a middle-aged patient, could not speak unless I was completely inert. A deep breath or a movement of my arm conveyed a loss of interest in him, a turning of attention to myself. This enraged him. It was as though only one of us could be alive at any one time. Either I killed him off with my aliveness, or he killed me off with his insistence on my inertia. Talking to him about this enabled me to convey that I could have a relationship with myself (the third position) *and* with him. There were ongoing derailments because I sighed and moved from time to time. What mattered was that I could understand my impact on him, his impact on me, and talk to him about it.

Tuch's (2007) view is that providing the patient with the opportunity to witness the analyst's capacity to consider how he is being viewed, as an experience with which to identify, may not be enough to prompt reflective thought in the patient. His view is that the patient needs the analyst to survive the patient's view of him, which may not be shared by the analyst; indeed, may be quite contrary to the analyst's view of himself. What Tuch conveys is that the analyst has a mind that can appreciate the relativity of perspectives.

Mr X took an instant dislike to me, and in his mind I was an exact replica of his mother: cold and critical. Due to this, there was, in the early stages of the treatment, an ongoing attack on me. It was forceful and unrelenting. I was not, for some time, able to find the right words to respond to this attack, as it seemed superficial simply to take up his aggression or fear that I was like his mother. As there was never any thought that he would like to find another analyst, it felt as though there may have been something more positive which brought him to treatment. I eventually said, "I think you are letting me know how unlikeable I am." I felt surprised by the directness and clarity of my tone. He asked almost immediately for more frequent sessions. What seemed to matter to this patient was that I could bear his view of me that I was an unlikeable person. Perhaps it was my capacity to entertain a different perspective of myself that contributed to the patient's response. My interpretation spoke of his view of me that I did not contradict, or convey, through either my tone of voice or choice of words, could be a source of pain for me.

We return now to the question of the acting out of the analyst, understood here as conveying perhaps that he has feelings of a more reactive and less benign kind. In his work with the patient K, Cassoria (2008) describes how he showed himself to the patient to be a person who gets nervous, and that his (the analyst's) patience was not as omnipotent as it appeared to be: "When he realized that his analyst could take care of himself and not be destroyed he was more at ease with the violence of his destructiveness" (p. 170). Partial acting out, according to Carpy (1989), allows the patient to see that strong feelings are being induced in the analyst, and to observe how the analyst deals with these—that he is struggling to tolerate them. It is Carpy's belief that if the analysis is to be effective, it is necessary to convey that he is managing sufficiently to maintain his analytic stance without grossly acting out. This may link with Winnicott's (1971) thoughts on movement towards object use and the finding of an external world, which survives the patient's destructiveness, indicating a degree of change in the analyst while retaining his character.

The analyst's response to his own enactments, to what might be described as his "failure to survive", is as important as survival. Bion (1970) talks of unfortunate decisions and unfortunate interpretations in analysis, saying it would be terrible if they were never made: "In analysis it is recovery from the unfortunate decision, the use of the mistaken decision that we have to accustom ourselves to deal with" (p. 50). Both Balint (1969) and Rosenfeld (1986) recognized the importance of taking seriously the patient's observations of the analyst's mistakes. The paper by Balint is one that is rarely quoted, but one to which I referred (Berkowitz, 1999) when considering the traumatic as opposed to the therapeutic effects of failure to acknowledge such mistakes. To be able to see oneself as failing, bear ourselves as failing mothers, is important, say Baraitser and Noack (2007). Once again, there is the notion that for the patient it is important that analysts can bear—survive—their own mistakes and fallibility, thus, not projecting these feelings into/on to their patients as their former objects might have done

Analytic survival, it seems, as the theories and thoughts of various analysts are considered, is regarded as very important, although its dynamic mechanism may not be fully understood.

For Loewald (1960), the mutative effect is to open up pathways of development that were formerly arrested. For others, it may be the development of a capacity to reflect. Whatever the ensuing process, there seems to be some agreement that it rests on the greater tolerance of the patient towards his internal objects, derived from the experience of being tolerated by the analyst, especially when the patient perceives that this is a process in the analyst with which he, the analyst, has to struggle.

Could it be said that there are different forms of analytic survival? Could survival of the analyst be experienced by some, or perhaps even by many, patients as a sense of loss? In relation to resistance, the survival of the analyst is a new and different experience, opening up the possibility of giving up familiar ways, or, in Loewald's (1980) terms, the old object relationship for a new one. He gives this further thought, outlining the impact of new organization, which impedes the return to an earlier organizational level. There could be the sense of loss of the familiar, however painful, impoverishing, or uncomfortable it might have been. He emphasizes that we need to pay attention to the importance of the connections between remembering, working through, and the work of mourning.

I have outlined some ideas that speak of the importance of the analyst's survival in terms of his capacity to reflect on his own psychic functioning, as well as that of the patient. Winnicott (1971) would seem to imply that the move from object relating to object use, one from relative merger to separateness, is achieved through the destruction and survival of the object. As Phillips (2007) points out, the most difficult aspect of human development is the changeover from object relating to object use. Why may this be so? Davies (2007), while stressing the importance of analytic survival, draws attention to the possibility that the patient may be alerted to the terrifying possibility of the separateness of the other by the analyst's capacity to think about and verbalize his own emotional experience. Importantly, while recognizing that it may be mutative for the patient to observe how the analyst deals with his own emotions, she suggests that the notion that the analyst has an independent mind may make the patient feel more isolated, and even envious of the analyst's superior psychic capacities.

In a similar way, Tuch (2007) considers that the threat to the patient that he is being thought about—reverie—may be that the analyst cannot tolerate the full force of the "patient's being", thus leaving the patient feeling abandoned. Might it then be possible to consider that "survival" might need to be conveyed to patients in the ways that are most appropriate to them? For those who are the most damaged, to convey a sense of separateness through the verbal expression of transference interpretations, or the communication, even non-verbally, of the sense of another mind, might be overwhelming. Survival of the analyst for such patients is the analyst's surrender of a separate identity, enduring, suffering what it is like to be them. But the surrender is never total, because it is the analyst who must slowly give definition to the patient's experience as it comes into view. With less damaged patients, the mind of the analyst can come into use through language, using modes of communication suited to more complex stages of organization (Loewald, 1960).

It may be, however, that with certain patients with more severe psychopathology (borderline, narcissistic, and perverse patients), analytic survival may signify something different. Baker (2000) suggests that some patients who are severely damaged may only be able to experience their analyst as tormentors. Bollas (1987) writes of those patients who convert the analyst into a negative object who is his double, carrying his projections and identifications. An object who is differentiated is lost or a non-object. It is with these patients that the struggle to survive is hardest, described by Alvarez (1985) as frenzied efforts on the part of the analyst. For Brenman (2006), the most challenging of the narcissistic problems is the feeling of meaninglessness and futility of analysis induced in the analyst; yet, it seems right to struggle and contain. A similar sense of futility may be experienced with some patients with perversions. The rigidity of the perversion may appear in the transference, in the form of each session being characterized by a similar rigid repetitiveness. Under the domination of their internal objects, analytic survival may pose a threat to their fragile internal world.

Mr Z, a man in his early thirties, presented with a perversion that had been part of his psychic structure since adolescence. He was seductive, charming, and false. As the therapy unfolded, the repetitiveness of his material, as though mimicking the perversion, became increasingly striking. Equally striking was his response to transference interpretations. His fear that I might actually *become* the transference object was evident, but was nothing compared to his *wish* that I would be that object. His fears that his internal objects would destroy him if he gave them up overrode his wish for something that would relieve him of his suffering. Survival, in his treatment, has had several aspects. It has meant bearing the tedium of being subjected, session after session, to repetitive themes. I have felt hopeless as the status quo has been reinstated again and again. And I have felt like part of the furniture, because he has never felt anything for another human being except a longing for appreciation. Yet, Mr Z, over seven years, feels he has made progress. He feels better about himself, his friends notice changes, he is resuming a previously successful career, is sought out by friends, and acts out very rarely. His therapy is vitally important to him. It is perhaps in a case like this that the implicit nature of the communication of analytic survival is most evident. Analytic survival that makes demands on his capacity to alter his relationship to his internal objects may threaten his psychic structure.

As to the mutative value of survival of the analyst to patients with varying degrees of pathology, it would seem that the more damaged the patient, the greater are the demands on the analyst, not only for self-analysis, but also for suspension and surrender of self to the experience of the patient. Could it then be said that the more severe the patient's psychopathology, the greater are the threats to, and the demands on, the analyst for survival?

This brings up the importance of the analytic setting in this whole question of survival. There is not only the analyst and the patient, there is the analytic setting, whose keeper is the analyst, and perhaps this should not be neglected in this discussion. The analytic setting, with the attention to keeping the environment unchanged, from day to day, even from year to year, the regularity of the sessions, their frequency and length, the rituals that commonly become established within an analysis, all offer an aspect of "survival" of the analyst. This, too, is a communication, albeit implicit, that the structure, with its constancy and continuity, is not destroyed. The setting for some patients may well be one reflection of the analyst's state of mind, and may represent the survival of the analyst (or the analysis) with less demand made on the requirement for psychic change through the use of language, especially transference interpretations. Technically, the survival of the setting may form the bedrock for the survival of the analyst.

Conclusion

The patient has a need for a mature object (Loewald, 1960), and a quiet, thoughtful state of mind (Rosenfeld, 1986). Are these counsels of perfection? Perhaps what I have been trying to consider in this paper is that, while these ideals may at times be achievable, either with certain patients or by certain analysts with certain patients, the reality is that an aspect of our work is constant attention to the deviations, those situations in which the analyst is, to a greater or lesser extent, not surviving. The use of the word "surviving" conveys more than the word "survive". It conveys the sense that survival itself is always in a state of flux.

This has been a brief overview of the concept of survival. Few papers have had the word in their title, yet it has been cited as an important factor in analytic work. As far as I am aware, no index of a book or journal has contained this word. In casual discussions with colleagues about this omission, it has raised neither eyebrows nor questions. It has felt as though it is dumb: not stupid, but voiceless.

Is it because survival is both an implicit and a ubiquitous transference interpretation in the analysis? I have tried to allude to survival implicit in verbal transference interpretations and in non-verbal communications, but it permeates much else. The rituals of analysis contribute to survival by keeping time and timing constant; the setting, too, is kept constant. As with other deviations, any alterations in these aspects are considered within the analysis, and attempts are made to think about the effect of such changes on the patient, to think of them as deviations, not decay or erosion leading to collapse. Someone knows about them, attends to them, and keeps the structure intact. These ideas, to some extent, meet Winnicott's definition of survival described above. But to survive also means to continue, to go on, another implicit communication to patients.

When Anna O's strong feelings towards Breuer emerged, he could only react by terminating the treatment, so he did not "survive". But he did not have the benefit of his own analysis, nor of the creative understanding that Freud brought to the experience that Breuer described to him, nor all that has subsequently followed. None the less, psychoanalysis owes him a huge debt.

Is it grandiose to infer or to imply that "survival" may define the analytic attitude? It is a communication, usually implicit to our patients via many experiences, most importantly through the ongoing intention and capacity to attend to and recognize all those small and large deviations or divergences from our analytic character or analytic setting.

"At least", then, may have two meanings, and maybe more. One is that "survival" is fundamental in psychoanalysis, and that my colleague's comment was to convey that, perhaps, with all the difficulties of that particular treatment, there had been that "at least". If the analyst survives, the patient and the analysis survive. But this may give an indication of the other meaning of "survival". That it is not all there is to psychoanalysis, that there is far, far more, but without it the patient may not be able to begin the process of living, which we can assume has, for some, been arrested, and, for others, never contemplated. It is striking that the authors quoted in this paper have come from widely differing theoretical backgrounds: Independent, Kleinian, Contemporary Freudian, and Ego Psychology, and yet this quality of "analytic survival" has been relevant to all. Where they might and do differ is in their understanding of the process of living, and of how, through long, often laborious, sometimes creative work, this can come about.

References

Alvarez, A. (1985). The problem of neutrality: some reflections on the psychoanalytic attitude in the treatment of borderline and psychotic children. *Journal of Child Psychotherapy, 11*: 87–103.

Baker, R. (1993). The patient's discovery of the psychoanalyst as a new object. *International Journal of Psychoanalysis, 74*: 1223–1233.

Baker, R. (2000). Finding the neutral position: patient and analyst perspectives. *Journal of the American Psychoanalytic Association, 48*: 129–154.

Balint, M. (1969). Trauma and object relationship. *International Journal of Psycho-Analysis, 50*: 429–435.

Baraitser, L., & Noack, A. (2007). Mother courage: reflections on maternal resilience. *British Journal of Psychotherapy, 23*: 171–188.

Berkowitz, R. (1999). The potential for trauma in the transference and countertransference. In: S. Johnson & S. Ruszcsynski (Eds.), *Psychoanalytic Psychotherapy in the Independent Tradition* (pp. 111–132). London: Karnac.

Bion, W. R. (1970). *Attention and Interpretation*. London: Tavistock.

Bollas, C. (1987). *The Shadow of the Object: Psychoanalysis of the Unthought Known*. London: Free Association Books.

Bollas, C. (1990). Regression in the countertransference. In: L. Bryce Boyer & P. Giovacchini (Eds.), *Master Clinicians on Treating the Regressed Patient* (pp. 339–352). Northvale, NJ: Jason Aronson.

Bolognini, S. (2004). Intrapsychic–interpsychic. *International Journal of Psychoanalysis, 85*: 337–357.

Botella, C., & Botella, S. (2005). *The Work of Psychic Figurability*. Hove: Bruner-Routledge.

Brenman, E. (2006). *Recovery of the Lost Good Object*. London: Routledge.

Carpy, D. (1989). Tolerating the countertransference: a mutative process. *International Journal of Psychoanalysis, 70*: 287–294.

Cassoria, R. M. S. (2008). The analyst's implicit alpha-function, trauma and enactment in the analysis of borderline patients. *International Journal of Psychoanalysis, 89*: 161–180.

Davies, R. (2007). Regression, curiosity, and the discovery of the object. In: R. Perelberg (Ed.), *Time and Memory* (pp. 85–102). London: Karnac.

Erlich, S. H. (2003). Working at the frontier and the use of the analyst: reflections on analytic survival. *International Journal of Psychoanalysis, 84*: 235–247.

Fonagy, P., Moran, G., & Target, M. (1993). Aggression and the psychological self. *International Journal of Psychoanalysis, 74*: 471–485.

Freud, S. (1912e). Recommendations to physicians practising psychoanalysis. *S.E., 12*: 111–120. London: Hogarth.

Freud, S. (1915a). Observations on transference-love. *S.E., 12*: 159–171. London: Hogarth.

Freud, S. (1937c). Analysis terminable and interminable. *S.E., 23*: 216–253. London: Hogarth.

Godbout, C. (2005). The "economic problem" of interpretation. *Canadian Journal of Psychoanalysis, 13*: 77–93.

Green, A. (2008). Freud's concept of temporality: differences with current ideas. *International Journal of Psychoanalysis, 89*: 1029–1039.

Grinberg, L. (1997). Is the transference feared by the psychoanalyst? *International Journal of Psychoanalysis, 78*: 1–14.

Jones, E. (1964). *The Life and Work of Sigmund Freud*. Harmondsworth: Penguin.

Joseph, B. (1992). Psychic change: some perspectives. *International Journal of Psychoanalysis, 73*: 237–243.

Loewald, H. (1960). On the therapeutic action of psychoanalysis. In: *Papers on Psychoanalysis*. New Haven, CT: Yale University Press, 1980.

Loewald, H. (1980). Some considerations on repetition and repetition compulsion. In: *Papers on Psychoanalysis*. New Haven, CT: Yale University Press.

Meng, H., & Freud, E. (Eds.) (1963). *The Letters of Sigmund Freud and Oskar Pfister*. London: The Hogarth Press.

Phillips, A. (2007). *Winnicott*. London: Penguin.

Racker, H. (1968). *Transference and Countertransference*. London: Maresfield Library.

Reeves, C. (2007). The mantle of Freud: was the use of an object Winnicott's *Todestrieb? British Journal of Psychotherapy, 23*: 365–382.

Rosenfeld, H. (1986). *Impasse and Interpretation*. London: Routledge.

Rycroft, C. (1986). An enquiry into the function of words in the psychoanalytical situation. In: G. Kohon (Ed.), *The British School of Psychoanalysis: The Independent Tradition* (pp. 237–252). London: Free Association Books.

Sandler, J. (1992). Reflections on developments in the theory of psychoanalytic technique. *International Journal of Psychoanalysis, 73*: 189–198.

Slochower, J. (1991). Variations in the analytic holding environment. *International Journal of Psychoanalysis, 72*: 709–718.

Tuch, R. H. (2007). Thinking with and about, patients too scared to think: can non-interpretive maneuvers stimulate reflective thought? *International Journal of Psychoanalysis, 88*: 91–111.

Varga, M. P. (2005). Analysis of transference as transformation of enactment. *Psychoanalytic Review, 92*: 659–674.

Winnicott, C., Shepherd, R., & Davies, M. (1989). *D. W. Winnicott: Psychoanalytic Explorations*. London: Karnac.

Winnicott, D. W. (1950). Aggression in relation to emotional development. In: *Through Paediatrics to Psycho-Analysis*. London: Hogarth Press, 1975.

Winnicott, D. W. (1971). The use of an object and relating through identifications. In: *Playing and Reality*. Harmondsworth: Penguin.

Zwiebel, R. (2004). The third position: reflections about the internal *analytic* working process. *Psychoanalytic Quarterly, 73*: 215–265.

INDEX

For Product Safety Concerns and Information please contact our EU representative GPSR@taylorandfrancis.com Taylor & Francis Verlag GmbH, Kaufingerstraße 24, 80331 München, Germany

Batch number: 10726011

Printed by Printforce, the Netherlands